DEVELOPMENT CENTRE STUDIES

# PLANNING FOR GROWING POPULATIONS

edited by
Robert CASSEN and Margaret WOLFSON

with an Introduction
by
Göran OHLIN

DEVELOPMENT CENTRE
OF THE ORGANISATION
FOR ECONOMIC CO-OPERATION AND DEVELOPMENT

The Organisation for Economic Co-operation and Development (OECD) was set up under a Convention signed in Paris on 14th December 1960, which provides that the OECD shall promote policies designed:
— to achieve the highest sustainable economic growth and employment and a rising standard of living in Member countries, while maintaining financial stability, and thus to contribute to the development of the world economy;
— to contribute to sound economic expansion in Member as well as non-member countries in the process of economic development;
— to contribute to the expansion of world trade on a multilateral, non-discriminatory basis in accordance with international obligations.
The Members of OECD are Australia, Austria, Belgium, Canada, Denmark, Finland, France, the Federal Republic of Germany, Greece, Iceland, Ireland, Italy, Japan, Luxembourg, the Netherlands, New Zealand, Norway, Portugal, Spain, Sweden, Switzerland, Turkey, the United Kingdom and the United States.

*The Development Centre of the Organisation for Economic Co-operation and Development was established by decision of the OECD Council on 23rd October 1962.*

*The purpose of the Centre is to bring together the knowledge and experience available in Member countries of both economic development and the formulation and execution of general policies of economic aid; to adapt such knowledge and experience to the actual needs of countries or regions in the process of development and to put the results at the disposal of the countries by appropriate means.*

*The Centre has a special and autonomous position within the OECD which enables it to enjoy scientific independence in the execution of its task. Nevertheless, the Centre can draw upon the experience and knowledge available in the OECD in the development field.*

THE OPINION EXPRESSED AND ARGUMENTS EMPLOYED IN THIS PUBLICATION ARE THE RESPONSIBILITY OF THE AUTHORS AND DO NOT NECESSARILY REPRESENT THOSE OF THE OECD

\*
\*  \*

© OECD, 1978
Queries concerning permissions or translation rights should be addressed to:
Director of Information, OECD
2, rue André-Pascal, 75775 PARIS CEDEX 16, France.

## CONTENTS

Foreword .................................................. 9

### Chapter 1

**INTRODUCTION: SOME IMPLICATIONS OF RAPID POPULATION GROWTH FOR SOCIAL AND ECONOMIC PLANNING**
by Göran Ohlin

| | | |
|---|---|---|
| I. | Minimizing the Costs of Population Growth ........... | 11 |
| II. | Planning for Basic Needs ........................... | 13 |
| III. | The Demographic Background ....................... | 15 |
| IV. | Food Supplies and Nutrition ........................ | 15 |
| V. | Education ......................................... | 17 |
| VI. | Health ............................................ | 18 |
| VII. | Housing ........................................... | 21 |
| VIII. | Employment ....................................... | 22 |
| IX. | General Observations .............................. | 24 |

### Chapter 2

**RAPID POPULATION GROWTH IN DEVELOPING COUNTRIES**
by Julien Condé

| | | |
|---|---|---|
| I. | Introduction ...................................... | 26 |
| II. | Characteristics of Rapidly-Growing Populations ...... | 27 |
| | - Age and Sex Structure ........................... | 27 |
| | - Migration Movements ............................. | 28 |
| | - Social and Economic Characteristics ............. | 31 |
| III. | World and Regional Population Prospects ........... | 33 |
| | - For the World as a Whole ........................ | 33 |

- Regional Differences .............................. 34
- Assumptions for Birth and Death Rates ............ 35
- Demographic Consequences of Population Projects .. 37

IV. Future Population Growth .......................... 44

Chapter 3

PLANNING FOOD SUPPLIES FOR AN
EXPANDING POPULATION
by Jacqueline Mondot-Bernard

I. Introduction ....................................... 49

II. Food Requirements ................................. 49
- Definition of Food Requirements .................. 49
- Difficulties Arising over Basic Data .............. 54
- Incidence of Malnutrition on Requirements ......... 57

III. The Food Problem: Analysis of Data ................ 60
- Available Food Supplies at National Level ......... 60
- Food Supply and Distribution ..................... 61
- Nutrition Level and Income ....................... 63
- Nutrition Level, Food Habits and State of Knowledge. 65

IV. Analysis of Action Programmes .................... 66
- India's Experience .............................. 66
- Lessons to be Learned from Nutrition Action
  Programmes ..................................... 70
- Concluding Remarks on Action Programmes ....... 73

V. Conclusion - A Newer Approach to Food and Nutrition
Planning as Part of Rural Development Planning ...... 74
- Some Examples ................................. 74
- Food and Nutrition Planning ..................... 76

Chapter 4

HEALTH
by Robert Cassen

I. Introduction ....................................... 79

II. Health Services ................................... 80

III. Primary Care ..................................... 81

IV. Facilities ........................................ 91

V. Vertical Campaigns ............................... 93

| | | |
|---|---|---|
| VI. | Water Supply and Sanitation | 95 |
| VII. | Health Planning | 98 |
| VIII. | Obstacles | 101 |

### Chapter 5

### HOUSING AND SETTLEMENT
### by Patrick Crooke

| | | |
|---|---|---|
| I. | Settlement, Housing and the Urbanization Process | 103 |
| | – Customary Rural Practices | 104 |
| | – Transitional Rural Practices | 105 |
| | – Transitional Urban Market Practices | 106 |
| | – Urban Newcomers and their Housing | 108 |
| II. | Governmental Aims and Actions | 110 |
| | – Present-day Problems and Shortcomings | 110 |
| | – Present-day Innovations and Trends | 114 |
| III. | Towards Productive Public-Sector Performance | 117 |
| | – Present and Future Programmes and Projects | 117 |
| |     Slum Rehabilitation Programmes | 118 |
| |     Improvement Programmes in Unauthorized Areas | 120 |
| |     Site and Service Programmes | 123 |
| | – Longer-term Changes and Reforms | 125 |
| |     Settlement Land | 126 |
| |     Settlement and Housing Finance | 127 |
| |     Housing Technology | 128 |
| | – Summary | 129 |

### Chapter 6

### DEMOGRAPHIC CONSTRAINTS AND EDUCATION POLICIES
### by Jacques Hallak
### and Ta Ngọc Châu

| | | |
|---|---|---|
| I. | Introduction | 132 |
| II. | The Traditional Approach | 134 |
| | – The Financial Constraint | 134 |
| | – A "Qualitative" Imbalance | 136 |
| | – Educational "Stagflation" | 139 |
| III. | The Radical Approach | 142 |

## Chapter 7

### POLICIES FOR EDUCATIONAL REFORM
### by Christopher Colclough

| | | |
|---|---|---|
| I. | Introduction | 146 |
| II. | Quantitative and Qualitative Reforms | 148 |
| III. | Costs and Equity | 155 |
| IV. | The Integration of Social, Economic and Educational Reforms | 160 |
| V. | Conclusion | 166 |

## Chapter 8

### EMPLOYMENT PROBLEMS
### by Denyse Harari

| | | |
|---|---|---|
| I. | The Roots of the Problem | 169 |
| | - The Social Meaning of Employment | 169 |
| | - New Attitudes Towards Employment Planning | 169 |
| | - Urbanization - Surge in LDC's | 172 |
| | - Dualism and Segmentation in Developing Countries | 172 |
| II. | The Socio-Economic Context | 174 |
| | - The Traditional Structures | 174 |
| | - The Modern Structures | 176 |
| | - The Price of Change | 177 |
| | - The Informal Sector | 180 |
| III. | The Magnitude of Employment Problems | 184 |
| | - The Numerical Aspect | 184 |
| | - Difficulties of Measurement and Conceptualisation | 185 |
| IV. | The Several Dimensions of Employment Problems | 188 |
| V. | Policies and Strategies | 194 |
| | - Present Trends in Employment Policy | 196 |
| | - The ILO Basic Needs Programme | 197 |
| | - Redistribution with Growth Study | 197 |

## Chapter 9

### EMPLOYMENT POLICIES
### by Frances Stewart

| | | |
|---|---|---|
| I. | Background Analysis | 198 |
| | - Technological Dualism | 199 |

|      |                                                          |     |
|------|----------------------------------------------------------|-----|
|      | - The Rate of Growth of Population                       | 201 |
|      | - Sectoral Imbalance                                     | 201 |
|      | - The System of Prices                                   | 202 |
|      | - The Payments System                                    | 203 |
| II.  | Approaches and Strategies                                | 204 |
| III. | Policies                                                 | 207 |
|      | - Policies Directed at Raising the Level of Investment   | 208 |
|      | - International Trade Strategy                           | 210 |
|      | - Technological Policy                                   | 212 |
|      | - Income and Asset Redistribution                        | 215 |
|      | - Sectoral Balance                                       | 217 |
|      | - The Agricultural Sector                                | 217 |
|      | - Prices and Project Selection                           | 218 |
|      | - Government Expenditure and Public Works                | 219 |
|      | - Education and Training                                 | 219 |
|      | - Payments System Reform                                 | 221 |
| IV.  | Conclusions                                              | 221 |

## LIST OF TABLES AND GRAPHS

Table:

| | | |
|---|---|---:|
| I. | Summary Table .................................. | 36 |
| IIA. | Structure of the World Population by Age and Category, 1970 ........................................ | 38 |
| IIB. | Population Distribution by Major Age Groups and Regions in 1970, 1985 and 2000 .................... | 39 |
| III. | The World's Population by Major Areas and Regions, 1970 and according to Low, Medium and High Variant of Population Projection for 1980, 1990 and 2000 ..... | 40 |
| IV. | The Future of Population Growth ................... | 46 |
| V. | Comparison between World Energy Requirements and Available Supplies 1961 and 1970 .................... | 60 |
| VI. | Medical Practitioners in Tanzania: Independence to 1973 ........................................ | 87 |
| VII. | Classification of Infective Diseases in relation to Water Supplies ...................................... | 97 |
| VIII. | Aggregate Indicators of Relative Levels of Economic and Educational Development for 123 Countries, 1960 and 1970 ..................................... | 147 |
| IX. | Classification of the Various Socio-Economic Structures of Production in the Developing Countries .. | 175 |
| X. | Participation Rates ............................. | 186 |
| XI. | Annual % Growth Rate in GDP Constant Prices and Employment ....................................... | 205 |

Graph:

| | | |
|---|---|---:|
| 1. | Future World Population Growth by the More Developed and Less Developed Regions, 1970-2125 ... | 41 |
| 2. | Calorie and Protein Coverage in India ............. | 62 |

# FOREWORD

The idea for this book grew out of a conversation between Professor Göran Ohlin and Margaret Wolfson, the Head of the Social Development and Demography Programme at the OECD Development Centre. They were discussing the contribution that research could make in the complex and baffling field of population and, in particular, the significant gaps in the current state of knowledge.

Professor Ohlin pointed out that at the present time an enormous amount of research activity was being directed to the problem of population limitation - the determinants of fertility, the technology of fertility control, the conditions, economic and social, likely to be conducive to fertility reduction, etc. - all with the goal of reducing the size of the population of the future. Very little attention, however, was being given to the condition of the population of here and now.

In developing countries, vast masses of the population lack the basic goods and services that are indispensable for a decent human existence, not because of the indifference of their governments, but because resources are inadequate and their utilization tends traditionally to favour the stronger elements of society rather than the most deprived. With the population explosion that has characterized the developing world in the 1950s and 1960s, the ranks of the hungry and deprived have grown inexorably. The problem of providing them with even the bare necessities of life is accordingly getting greater all the time. It is to this problem, said Professor Ohlin, that we need urgently to address ourselves.

The implications of the problem seemed obvious - if the traditional methods of government provision (the "public works approach") have proved unable to do the job, then other approaches need to be explored. Indeed, other approaches are already being explored - in different sectors of human need, in different countries, under different conditions, and for different purposes. Some have proved successful, others not, some may have been single-shot initiatives, others offered potential for adaptation on a larger scale. Much more work needs to be done to examine these alternative approaches, to analyse the lessons to be drawn from them, and to make the possibilities that they offer more widely known.

The Chapters on the main areas of human need have been contributed by 9 different authors, some outside specialists, some members of the

Development Centre research staff. The whole has been edited by Robert Cassen, and Professor Ohlin has contributed an Overview.

Robert Cassen, who had already been working along similar lines, was asked to help in organising the volume, and different authors were found to contribute chapters on the main areas of human need. Most of them were outside specialists, some were members of the Development Centre research staff. The papers were discussed at joint meetings and then edited by Mr. Cassen.

Since this work was begun, the concept of "basic human needs", first given international recognition in the Declaration of Principles and Programme of Action adopted by the ILO World Employment Conference in 1976, has been given wide discussion. These principles were endorsed by the General Assembly of the United Nations in December 1976. The concept of basic needs was further given prominence in the Declaration on Relations with Developing Countries adopted by the OECD Council meeting at Ministerial Level in June 1977 and by the communiqué adopted by the 16th Annual High Level Meeting of the Organisation's Development Assistance Committee in October 1977.

This increasing concern on the part of the international community is accompanied by an important research effort. This book, it is hoped, will make a useful contribution to the current search for new approaches. It does not purport to provide any firm answers. It is a documentary review which examines some of the approaches that have been tried, or are being planned, or which might be considered for meeting basic needs in the most important areas of daily life. Each developing country will need to make its own selection of which of these various possibilities might be worthwhile in its particular set of political, economic, social and cultural circumstances, and then determine what are the structural, administrative and financial implications of putting them into effect. This book does not attempt to answer these questions. It will have served its purpose, however, if it prompts planners in developing countries and the aid community to begin asking them.

Louis Sabourin
President
OECD Development Centre

Paris, June 1978

# 1

## INTRODUCTION: SOME IMPLICATIONS OF RAPID POPULATION GROWTH FOR SOCIAL AND ECONOMIC PLANNING

by

Göran Ohlin

### I. MINIMIZING THE COSTS OF POPULATION GROWTH

It is now widely accepted that rapid population growth in developing countries is likely to entail heavy costs, although the gravity of the issue is assessed very differently by different observers in different parts of the world, partly because population densities, resource endowments, and attitudes vary considerably. In the views of some, the population explosion jeopardizes the hope of substantial economic and social progress, and the public interest therefore dictates forceful government programmes, possibly even coercive ones, to bring down rates of fertility. On the other hand, in sparsely settled countries a larger population is often assumed to be capable of reaping economies of scale and enhancing national power and security. It is increasingly conceded that even in such circumstances, sudden declines in mortality create strains on population groups without access to the knowledge or means of family planning, and that the need for large "demographic investments" will impinge on other development expenditures.

When the conclusion is that government policy should aim at restraining fertility and population growth, it is in full awareness that such results will be slow in coming. Even on optimistic views about the prospects for fertility decline in the developing countries, whether spontaneous or assisted by energetic government policy, populations will clearly continue to increase very fast over the coming decades. This is partly due to the fact that fertility itself will only decline gradually, and partly to the "demographic inertia" described in Julien Condé's paper - the acceleration of growth since the 1950's has made for a very young age distribution which will for some time keep crude birth rates high in spite of declining fertility.

What this means is that the problems associated with rapid population growth cannot be avoided by policies to reduce fertility. Although such policies may make a great difference in the long run, most developing countries will have to live with high rates of population growth for some decades and must expect to see their populations approximately double within a generation or so.

It is somewhat surprising that the considerable literature devoted to the undesirable implications of growth has been so preoccupied with the conclusion that fertility should be restrained that very little specific attention has been devoted to the task of coping with the massive growth that is certain to come.

The purpose of the papers in this book is to raise some of the problems faced by planners responsible for accommodating such growing populations. It is true that population projections are not free from uncertainty, in part because population trends will be affected by the success or failure in many other areas, but compared to most other trends entering into the planners' assessment of the future, the uncertainty attached to population forecasts two or three decades ahead is of a smaller order of magnitude, partly due to the great momentum of growth in the early phase of the demographic transition.

In any thinking about the state of a developing country in the year 2000 or thereabouts, a population projection is a natural point of departure. What will the country be like at the not very distant date when the population has doubled?

A great number of important options have to be considered immediately, but it is also true that whatever is done and however successful or unsuccessful the development strategy, population growth alone is going to entail momentous change. If past trends are continued, the urban population may have grown by a factor of 4 or 8 when total population has doubled. What will the urban network look like, and how will primary cities, already bursting at the seams, provide basic services and uphold public health standards? Ecological change of great magnitude must be expected, and deforestation, salination, and water shortages anticipated. The structure of agriculture will be subject to continued pressure towards sub-division and pauperization unless new lands can be opened up. The system of transportation must be assessed, not just in terms of present needs but in terms of those proximate future needs. Energy supplies and infrastructure of all kinds require long-term forward planning. Patterns of industry and commerce, notably foreign trade, will be transformed.

Although many of those changes cannot be foreseen with any precision, a skeleton plan with a genuinely long term thrust is a useful, perhaps even indispensable, way of raising some of the issues implied by continued population growth. It would, for one thing, serve to offset the myopic bias inevitable in five-year planning. Over a five-year period, populations may increase by some 10-15%, which is not inconsiderable but easily swamped by the margins of uncertainty affecting many short term targets. It is the sustained increase with compound interest that makes demographic pressure such a relentless force, and this is easily overlooked when the time horizon is only a few years ahead.

At least some of the coolness with which economists and economic planners, in developing countries as well as in developed ones, have received the alarm signals from ecologists and other scientists concerned with resource scarcities and environmental deterioration is probably due to this difference in time perspective. In part, it also seems rooted in the economists' greater belief in technological change and in adjustment processes involving the substitution of more abundant resources for scarce ones. Long-term planning offers the opportunity for realistic appraisals of the prospects within a time-frame that is not irrelevant for investments with long lead times and life spans of many decades.

The conclusion must be that it would be advisable, in countries that have not already embarked on this course, to complement present planning with an attempt to leapfrog a decade or two and seek to visualize the dim outlines of an acceptable future state of affairs in which a considerably larger population is fed and employed and its needs catered to.

## II. PLANNING FOR BASIC NEEDS

The present book, however, is no handbook in long-term planning. Its aims are much more modest. It focuses on some of the issues arising in areas of self-evident importance - nutrition, health, education, housing, and employment. This study was initiated in 1975, and since then these topics have come to be referred to as areas of "basic needs". In all of them, governments and public authorities have far-reaching responsibilities. In health and education, these are discharged through large public services absorbing a considerable part of the public revenue. Food supplies and their distribution are affected by agricultural policy. Settlement and housing policies are closely regulated by public authorities. Employment raises some of the thorniest issues of development strategy.

In one important respect, the results of the inquiry differ significantly from what was expected when it was initiated. When the authors collaborating in this book were invited to prepare their papers, it was thought that rapid population growth would be seen to make a very distinct difference to the task of meeting the needs in the different sectors.

This premiss can hardly be said to have been borne out. Although in some cases - notably that of urban housing - population growth overshadows other determinants of the needs, in general it emerges as a factor which compounds the task of meeting fundamental social needs but nevertheless is not the dominant concern. In health and education, for instance, present needs are so inadequately met that problems of appropriate objectives and organisation take precedence over those of quantitative increases dictated by population growth. Even in the absence of population growth the besetting concerns in those fields would be very similar.

The conclusions to which the authors independently arrive fall into a remarkably consistent pattern, but because the demographic dimension is so inextricably tied up with others, they tend to focus on the general opportunities for doing better with available resources.

This is not to say that population growth is of no consequence. On the contrary, it casts its shadow over all the analysis and serves to underline the need for major institutional reform, emphasizing in particular the magnitude of the tasks which lie ahead.

The particular interest of the fields that were chosen for study is not only their recognized importance to the welfare of the population. It also seems likely that fertility decline will be promoted by the success with which those basic needs are met, and that it is retarded by failure. The possibility of designing policies in the social field in such a way as to promote fertility reduction has been examined by others with fairly inconclusive results.[1] Nevertheless it is widely believed that success in making these social and economic benefits more widely available would assist the decline of fertility.[2] That is not the issue here, but the standards and the objectives of such policies will be seen to be extremely important, especially when they are unrealistic and self-defeating.

It should be added that it is somewhat artificial to consider the various basic needs sectors in isolation one from the other. In many ways they are closely linked, as in the case of education, nutrition, and health. Progress in one field is likely to yield improvements in another. Efforts in only one of them may be thwarted by neglect of the others. Although the evidence of such links is not easily quantified, it is clear that malnourished children are poor students, that nutrition and basic health improvements depend on instruction and education, etc. In some cases, the basic services required to promote the wellbeing of the population could often to some advantage be supplied by an integrated corps of development workers rather than by parallel networks. Most importantly, the direct concern with basic human needs embodies a view of development which differs rather sharply from one with primary emphasis on economic growth.

---

1. Ridker, Ronald, ed., Population and Development: The Search for Selective Intervention, Washington, D.C., 1976.

2. For a review of some of the evidence, see e.g. Robert H. Cassen, "Population and Development: A Survey", World Development, Vol. 4:10-11, October-November, 1976.

## III. THE DEMOGRAPHIC BACKGROUND

None of the papers deals with a specific country, and given the level of generality of the analysis there is little reason to stress the differences with regard to the demographic prospects in different countries. In Chapter 2, Julien Condé reviews the essential features as illustrated by the UN projections. Although population projections have a poor track record, it remains fairly likely that most, if not all, developing countries will see their populations double in 25-35 years.

This entails a persistently young age distribution and a high dependency burden although the latter declines somewhat as birth rates drop. The rate of growth of the population at working age, on the other hand, will lag behind that of the overall population. The growth of urban populations is expected to remain as high as 6-8%.

The UN projections are based on an implicit assumption that growth of this magnitude will not be obstructed by disasters such as major food shortages that would halt mortality decline or even send death rates up. But the decline in mortality has slowed down and there have been occasional instances of increased mortality in various parts of the world in recent years. This may well be a temporary phenomenon and it is much too early to be sure, but it seems entirely possible that the mortality projections will turn out to have been too optimistic. However, for the purposes of this book a sweeping picture is all that is required and a possible modification of the expected fall in mortality will not affect the certainty of massive and sustained growth in the coming decades.

## IV. FOOD SUPPLIES AND NUTRITION

Food supplies were at the heart of the early concerns about population growth and lack of food is still a very real concern. The gravest aspect of the poverty of some parts of the Third World is the prevalence of undernourishment and its attendant toll in mortality, morbidity, and lethargy.

As Jacqueline Mondot shows in Chapter 3, it is extremely difficult to determine food "requirements" and equally hard to assess actual food intake in developing countries. Statements about the number of underfed or ill-fed people in the world have little meaning. It is probable that on any criterion the absolute number of under-fed people in the world has increased, but it is impossible to say whether their proportion in total populations has changed in recent years or not. We know the proportion is large, though not how large.

Undernutrition is mainly a consequence of poverty and a lack of effective demand. Increasing food production is not a remedy unless it involves greater productivity or is accompanied by redistribution measures. But in countries with a preponderantly rural population, agricultural development will necessarily be a main avenue to higher income levels as well as an enlarged local food supply.

There is where the impact of population growth is most evident. If average per capita food deficits are estimated at 25% in 1977, and if the population is increasing at 3% per annum, then it might be argued that for this deficit to be eliminated by 1990, food supplies would have to be increased by close to 100% by that time, or 3 times as much as if the population were stationary.

Such exercises with compound interest may be striking but they are quite mechanical and should be taken with a grain of salt. The necessary rate of growth of per capita food supplies is the same in the two cases, and what is really at issue is whether and why such aspects as land scarcity, erosion, capital shortage, tenure problems, water shortage, or the nature of available technology would set limits to the greater absolute increase. In some circumstances - for instance, where populations now live in conditions of sparse settlement - one may even expect certain economies of scale.

However, when nutritionists have shown that even available supplies would in principle suffice to remedy many serious nutritional deficiencies, it is only natural to search for ways to raise nutritional standards promptly, without waiting for the long-run improvements which economic growth and increasing agricultural productivity will bring in a more remote future. A strong case can even be made for a nutrition-oriented food policy on the grounds that growth itself may in early stages not solve nutritional problems but even affect nutritional standards negatively. A general disruption of traditional food habits results in greater dependence on industrial food products, a decline in breast-feeding, and a shift away from protein-rich pulses towards food grains which have become cheaper, relatively speaking, as high-yielding grain varieties have been successfully introduced.

Direct interventions - involving, for instance, enrichment of commercially - distributed foods, and distribution of supplementary foods to pregnant mothers, infants and children - have proved more difficult, and more expensive, than first expected. It must be admitted that such policies are still in an experimental stage and so far not too successful. Attempts to create a price structure that would promote a balanced diet seem attractive. Few countries may be willing to go as far as Sri Lanka in subsidizing basic foods at heavy cost, but food prices are everywhere subject to numerous interventions, and a first and reasonable task is to examine the price structure for accidental and haphazard damage to nutrition. Unlike more specific intervention, such measures would rely on individual initiative and self-interest.

Jacqueline Mondot also points to the interesting experience of Kerala where the nutritional situation is more satisfactory than in most other parts of India although the average income level is lower. A more favourable distribution of incomes and assets may be a major explanation, but it also seems that Kerala's long-standing achievements in the field of education, perhaps especially of girls, account for the impressively low mortalities having enabled mothers to care for themselves and their infants in a resourceful manner. There is similar evidence from other countries suggesting that simple programmes combining nutrition, health education and primary health care by local health workers can reduce infant and child mortality quite rapidly.

The significance of population growth in this context is exaggerated if the potential contribution of a growing labour force is ignored. But unless growing dependence on external food supplies is warranted by strong comparative advantages in manufacturing or minerals, local food supplies have to be increased at such rates that in most countries a major rural transformation is required. Infrastructure requirements for production, storage, and distribution will have to be met, or at any rate planned by governments, and the need for long-term programmes of the kind mentioned earlier seems evident.

## V. EDUCATION

In the field of education, present deficiencies are glaring in most parts of the developing world. Countries that embarked on national independence with a colonial legacy of low literacy and limited educational resources and were then exposed to the youthful age distributions associated with rapid population growth were obviously not well placed for a rapid realization of ambitious targets of universal literacy and major increases of secondary and higher education.

In fact, expenditures on education have risen sharply in most developing countries and their share in governments budgets and GNP has increased, and enrolment has also increased enormously. Educational planning, as Gavin Jones has observed, has often become an exercise in applied demography, and complex models have been used to trace the changing requirements for teachers and facilities on different assumptions about population growth and enrolment rates.[3] In a number of countries the contribution of population growth to the increase in recurrent costs of primary education over a 20-year period has been found to be of the order of 50-70%; if capital costs were added the share should be even higher. It is only too likely, in view of the scarcity of development resources available, that rapid expansion will be at the expense of quality upgrading or even result in lower standards.

Much of the current dissatisfaction with the educational systems in developing countries is in fact not focused primarily on the quantitative inadequacy of the resources but on their uses. These systems are

---

3. Gavin W. Jones, "Educational Planning and Population Growth", in Warren G. Robinson, ed., Population and Development Planning, New York: The Population Council, 1975.

indicted on charges of profound inequality, favouring urban populations over rural, rich over poor. Worse yet is the common charge of irrelevance or even harmfulness. In countries with evident shortages of skills on all levels, the drop-out rates and the failure of school leavers to find employment is an indication of something seriously wrong.

The crisis of confidence in traditional systems of education on which Jacques Hallak and Ta Ngoc Châu dwell in their Chapter is in those circumstances very understandable. Colclough's demonstration of the high cost and disappointing performance of tertiary education also draws attention to a major structural problem which would be very real even in the absence of any population growth.

The educational system will feel the impact of declining fertility fairly soon after it begins, but even so the number of children of school age will continue to increase quite fast. Given the budgetary constraints on educational expenditure, this growth in potential demand often makes it starkly clear that whatever the other merits of fundamental reform, traditional approaches to education simply cannot cope. The proposals for new approaches are many and various. Some would involve the use of more capital equipment, including educational television satellites and other sophisticated hardware, but most experiments aim at greater community involvement, more attention to relevant educational needs, and lower cost. However, both the Chapters on Education, from their different standpoints, describe the limitations of any such programmes in the absence of political initiatives.

## VI. HEALTH

Even with a great array of statistics it is not easy to sum up the state of health in any country in the world. Health may seem like a very simple concept, but on closer scrutiny it does not lend itself to easy quantification.

The cutting edge, as it were, is provided by mortality which is fairly well documented and has long been considered a measure of morbidity as well. One may certainly imagine situations in which crippling diseases impair the health of a population without raising mortality, and the definition of health can be a source of great philosophical complexity. In practice, however, the measures of mortality are likely to be accepted as a proxy for an index of health, if only because there is little alternative. This does not mean that disease and malnutrition which do not result in early death are ignored. The hypothesis is, however, that there will be a broad correlation between disease and mortality.

The estimates of life expectancy at birth in developing countries have showed steady and remarkable increases in the post-war period.

In the late 1960's, the average for the developing regions as a whole was about 50 years, which may be compared with an average of 56 for the developed regions of the world no longer ago than the late 1930's. Judging by this pervasive decline in mortality, which occurred in all parts of the Third World, health conditions have improved greatly, sometimes even in regions or periods which have not been characterized by much noticeable economic advance.

The causes of this improvement are not entirely clear, but the provision of local health services is not likely to have made much of a contribution. The control of major epidemic diseases by public health measures has probably been a significant factor, along with some improvements in sanitation and nutrition, but the networks of primary health facilities remains grossly inadequate in most countries.

The decline in mortality has slowed down or ceased in many places in the 1970's, which has served to focus new attention on this sector. The economic implications of trying to extend health services along earlier lines, with population continuing to grow rapidly, are in themselves serious, and if the service level is to be raised, a major increase in the share of GNP devoted to health expenditures will be necessary. A case study of Thailand concluded that with a trebling of the service ratio outside of Bangkok in the period 1970-2000, the share of GNP going to the health sector would rise by 64% even if fertility was approximately halved; on the assumption of much slower fertility decline, with the population in 2000 about 20% higher than in the first case, the increase would be 96%.[4]

The implications of such figures are in reality that the inequalities that are already one of the most serious flaws of most health systems would be accentuated. Some groups would continue to be well served, but growing numbers might well be beyond reach of the health services. However, the examples of some countries and experimental projects confirm that it is possible to do better with relatively simple means, and it is to such reorientation of health planning that Robert Cassen's Chapter is mostly devoted.

There are several dimensions to the proposals for turning available resources in the health field to better use. One is the theme of participation, motivation, and mobilization of the public's own interest in raising health standards. Another is the attempt to reduce capital intensity, which deserves brief comment.

Medical services in rich countries absorb huge investments both in equipment and in human capital. Great efforts are being made to substitute equipment for labour, and the progress of medical science is closely linked to the development of new and sometimes extremely expensive devices, and to lengthy training of staff.

Even very much less capital-intensive approaches to the problem of health and education can be crippling to any attempt to maintain,

---

4. Robinson, op. cit.

let alone raise, the standards of services in poorer countries. If the constraints on public finance make it impossible to raise the share of health in public expenditure significantly, and the latter grows only in step with GNP, heavy investment expenditure will cut deeply into the possible expansion of current expenditure and set strict limits to the rate at which services can be expanded.

A simple calculation may illustrate the problem:

Suppose that a certain health system operates in such a way that, with no expansion at all, it requires recurrent expenditures of 100 million. Investments in physical and human capital, to maintain buildings and equipment and to train replacements for staff attrition, amount to 10% of the total capital which is supposed to be 400 million. The total cost of maintaining the present level of services is thus 140 million.

If population increases at a rate of 3% and the modest target is to raise the output of services at the same rate, this first of all involves raising current expenditures to 103 million. In addition, new investments in buildings, equipment, and training would add 3% of 400 million to the 40 million required for maintenance, so capital expenditure would amount to 52 million. The total would be 155 million, which is 11% more than the 140 million of the previous year.

This is not all. Medical staff as well as those participating in the construction of new health centres and other purveyors of capital goods are likely to demand increases in their real income at least commensurate to those of the population at large. If GNP is increasing at 5%, per capita incomes increase 2% a year which raises the rate of increase in real costs to 13%, which is a far cry from the stipulated 3% population increase and totally out of line with a 5% increase in GNP and the constraints on sectoral allocations in the government budget.

The calculation can be reversed to suggest what such constraints imply for the feasible rate of increase of output of services. If the resources available grow only at 5%, and the capital labour coefficient and the maintenance and training requirements are those earlier assumed, then service output can only increase by 0.8% a year, which is so much less than the postulated 3% of population increase as to point to a catastrophic deterioration of the situation.[5] Instead of an improvement it means a steady deterioration of the per capita supply of health services.

The previous exercise is very crude but it captures one part of the dilemma facing countries which try to adopt patterns of social service modelled on those of richer countries. The physical and human capital required is likely to be so expensive as to make the effort self-defeating.

---

5. With the rate of increase in output as r, the equation is:
$400 (0.1 + r) + 100 (1 + r) = 140 \times 1.05/1.02$.

It is probably no exaggeration to say that much of the Third World is littered with monuments to the failure of realizing the simple and basic dimensions of this problem. Well-intentioned providers of aid and prestige-seeking politicians have erected impressive modern hospitals which drain the more basic services of resources. When they are left unused or underused because recurrent costs are too high, this may often be the wisest course in spite of the waste involved.

Whatever approaches are taken to the task of reducing the costs of health services, the acid test is whether they will be compatible with the foreseeable expansion of the population in different parts of the country. The Chapter suggests a range of measures to enhance the capacity of the health services, including redesign of the network of referral services and of medical education.

## VII. HOUSING

In the field of city planning and housing the impact of population growth manifests itself most bluntly, in part because the growth rates of urban population are so much higher than those of the population at large. This is not to say that the problems are simple and quantitative. Public policies and regulations in the field of urban housing usually add up to a tangled web of more or less grandiose schemes of urban planning, administrative standards and legal restraints, which all too often clash violently with economic and financial realities.

The failure of urban housing authorities in developing countries to cope with the flood of settlers is such that by now the larger share of the population often lives outside the regime of rules and regulations supposed to secure satisfactory housing standards. Although the task of providing urban accommodation - whether by public building or private, subsidized or market-based - may seem very different from that of ministering to needs in health or education, the picture drawn by Patrick Crooke in this book suggests that unrealistically high standards bring the same pernicious consequences. Official housing standards are liable to hurt rather than help, if they reflect the notions of the elite or are borrowed from abroad, without awareness of the multiple needs of the poor and the new urban migrants.

Institutional change on the scale required in the cities of the Third World could not be expected to be painless or simple. But the crisis in urban housing has also given rise to imaginative experimentation. The actual needs of the population have increasingly come to be recognized. Legalization, rehabilitation and improvement of housing which has sprung up outside the framework of public regulations has replaced indiscriminate razing or official neglect. People are allowed or even encouraged to finance and organise low-cost and self-help housing in accordance with their needs and their means. Even so, one recent study claims that up to two-thirds of the families in Ahmedabad, Bogota, Hong Kong, Madras, Mexico City, and Nairobi could not afford the cheapest housing that was being built.[6]

Sheer failure to anticipate population growth has apparently been a major source of the weakness of urban housing policies. Urban migration has been essentially uncontrolled - in sharp contrast with the situation in most European pre-industrial cities - and the overloading of existing cities has often been the inadvertent result of policies discriminating against rural sectors and a failure to promote new urban nuclei.

Cities seem to offer both economies and diseconomies of scale, and their function as a network for the organisation of internal commerce is not simple or easily analysed. Plans for the shape of an urban sector which in only a few decades is likely to be several times as large as now must be flexible enough to accommodate to unpredictable changes in the structure of the economy, but faced with the gigantic investment costs in urban infrastructure in cities with many million inhabitants, countries would obviously be wise to consider alternatives and to do it before it is too late.

## VIII. EMPLOYMENT

It is often asserted that unemployment is both intolerably high and increasing in developing countries, and a common view is that this is due to the fact that the labour force is growing faster than the number of jobs.

In fact, relatively little can be said with any precision about unemployment in developing countries where the definition of a job is much more diffuse than in industrialized countries. Where many people work on their own, in the household or in the "informal sector", where there is no compensation to be had by registering as unemployed if one cannot find a job, and where most people are too poor to wait long for a suitable job, the concepts of a labour force consisting of those who wish to work, and of the "unemployment" of those who fail to find work, lose their accuracy - which, for that matter, is not very great even in richer countries.

The employment problem in developing countries is therefore often described as one of underemployment rather than unemployment. Very high estimates of underemployment are frequently cited, but as Denyse Harari demonstrates, the complexity of the situation is such that underemployment and related terms, such as "disguised unemployment", have been made to carry a variety of different meanings, and there have been few satisfactory attempts to measure it.

---

6. Grimes, Orville, Jr., Housing for Low Income Urban Families, Baltimore: The Johns Hopkins University Press, 1976.

The employment problem is in any case quite different from that of meeting other basic needs - indeed employment is often the most important means to meet those needs.  Occasionally, public sector jobs are created primarily to provide employment and with little concern for the usefulness of the work.  But whether or not there is work for all is a more complex issue.  Where formal labour markets prevail, the situation may be analysed in terms of the supply and demand for labour, although it must then be remembered that jobs are as heterogeneous as the individuals who are to fill them.  Where self-employment or the informal sector prevails, employment is limited by inadequate access to resources - land and other assets, education, etc.

    Rapid growth of the labour force need not in itself pose any employment problem if the demand for labour is equally dynamic and if there is an ample supply of land, as for instance in North America in the 19th century.  In many developing countries it nevertheless seems true that there is a problem of absorption in which the difficulties of institutional change are of major importance.  In growing villages, holdings are fragmented, and even if new land is available, it may be at uneconomic distances, and the founding of new village units may be impeded by legal and administrative barriers.

    In the modern sector, expansion is held back by capital shortage. Much attention has been given to the danger of "inappropriate technology", which absorbs a large share of capital formation without creating many new jobs, but it is rarely appreciated how vast the discrepancy is between available savings and the capital requirements of modern technology.  In a country with a net savings ratio of 15% and a per capita income of $200, capital formation would amount to $30 per capita.  If the labour force is half of the population and grows at 2.5%, p.a., and if the entire amount of new capital could be used to absorb the increment in the labour force, there would thus be $2,400 per man for plant, equipment, infrastructure, etc.  While this is the order of magnitude of investment per man in the textile industry, heavy industry absorbs far more - $10,000-50,000 - and refineries or plants for metal processing many times that.  If 10% of the increase in the labour force, or one-quarter of 1% of the total labour force, were to be given employment in capital-intensive plants requiring $24,000 per man, this would in principle absorb the entire domestic capital formation in one year, draining the rest of the economy of any new capital.

    The example is extreme, but so is the gap between capital supplies per man in rich and poor countries, and it would be reasonable to conclude that few things can be more important in raising the capacity for labour absorption in developing countries than to watch capital use and search for technologies that economize on capital.

    Employment policy in developing countries thus merges with general development strategy, as Frances Stewart shows in her survey of possible approaches to the employment problem.  Modern sector growth is patently incapable of absorbing a rapidly expanding labour force, but the various suggestions to redistribute opportunities, incomes, and assets in favour of poor, rural, and small-scale sectors involve very fundamental social change. Governments resting on a precarious political base or wedded to the status quo will not venture in such directions unless forced to, e.g. by intolerably high unemployment and mass poverty.

The growth of population contributes to the pressure for such reforms. In no other context are the political implications of population growth more evident, although the response should not be expected to be uniform. As Frances Stewart makes very clear, many different strategies to promote employment in Third World countries are being proposed and positive experience is still limited.

## IX. GENERAL OBSERVATIONS

As noted in the introduction, the impact of population growth on the task of basic needs cannot usually be disentangled from a range of fundamental questions about what is to be provided, how and for whom it is to be done. The problems raised by the expansion of the population are inseparable from large development issues which come to the fore when attention is focussed on the failure of economic growth to meet the basic needs of large population groups.

In all the sectors surveyed, the solution of a number of other problems thus came to be seen as a prerequisite for any satisfactory absorption of the large additions to population that the future will bring.

### 1. Over-ambitious standards and inequality

When the costs of setting high standards cannot be met, the consequence is not a uniform provision of sub-standard services, but a high degree of concentration of available resources in favour of privileged areas and groups, reflecting a general dualism in the distribution of incomes and assets and also consolidating it.

### 2. Capital and cost

Related to the question of standards but also to the pervasive influence of the practices of richer countries is the problem of capital intensity. Capital costs include the cost of long training of educational and medical staff, as well as the cost of housing to middle-class standards, or the cost of advanced industrial equipment. High recurrent costs may also be burdensome, but capital costs are of special significance to the needs for expansion occasioned by population growth. To the proportionate increase in recurrent costs must be added the wholly disproportionate cost of new investment. Naturally enough, the search for new solutions which would hold out some promise of being able to improve living conditions in basic respects is oriented towards low-cost approaches requiring less costly equipment and less ambitious training, without necessarily being less effective in meeting the actual needs of the population.

3. Participation

Great hopes are also attached to greater community involvement, both as a means to ensure that resources are used to meet genuine and felt needs and as a way of mobilizing what is felt to be a major and often untapped resource. To bend the bureaucratic machinery towards the stimulation of individual initiative and community action is not easy, and it may require the use of a great variety of existing as well as new forms of social organisation, such as villages, political parties, churches, co-operatives, armed forces, etc. The search for alternatives to "trickle-down" strategies of development is going on all over the Third World, and its importance is obviously far-reaching. It is not only an attempt to revitalize and stimulate production and consumption but amounts to a redefinition of development in terms of human fulfilment.

The impact of rapid population growth in the past has contributed to the failure to meet basic needs, which lies behind this search for a new orientation, and the prospect of continued population growth well into the next century only underscores how indispensable new approaches are. The lessons of experience which this book has tried to gather together is that much can be done even with limited resources if social planning is oriented towards less imitative and more relevant solutions.

# 2

## RAPID POPULATION GROWTH IN DEVELOPING COUNTRIES *

by

Julien Condé

### I. INTRODUCTION

In recent years, people all over the world have become increasingly aware of population problems. Famines, wars, epidemics and natural catastrophes in various parts of the world have revived the disputes about the evils or blessings of large populations and demographic growth which divided philosophers, economists and other thinkers right up to the 18th century.

In the 1950's and 60's, a large number of countries which had hitherto been under colonial rule acceded to nationhood. In order to make up for their backwardness in economic development, the countries then known as "underdeveloped" evolved global and sectoral strategies which were described in economic and social development plans.

The poor results obtained with the initial development plans prompted planners, economists and other government officials to seek out the deep-seated causes of under-development and of the failures recorded. These causes were recognized as being manifold, complex and interdependent. Whatever the approach adopted the population factor was no longer regarded as being an exogenous variable of growth or economic development but indeed as a fundamental parameter which it was possible and essential to control. These considerations formed the basis for the preparation of policies for the purpose of curbing population growth rates which were considered to be too high and incompatible with the desired economic growth rates - and hence with a rise in living standards - of the populations of the developing countries.

In the 1960's, a wealth of demographic, economic and social literature was devoted to the causes and effects of what was known as the population explosion, whose main features were a high birth rate, a fast declining death rate and a high population growth rate. All the writers were agreed that the population explosion could be said to have occurred immediately after the second world war.

---
\* Original text in French.

This paper does not set out to study the causes and effects of this population explosion but to examine the characteristics and future prospects of the populations responsible for the explosion.

The world's population grows as a result of the excess of births over deaths. Populations do not all contribute to this growth to the same extent. Some of them have very low growth rates, as is the case in the industrialized countries of Europe, North America, Oceania and Japan, where birth and death levels are not very high and tend to cancel each other out.

By contrast, other populations have a very high growth rate because of their high fertility and constantly declining death rate. Even though the birth rate in recent years has tended to fall in some countries and the decline in the death rate to slow down in others, the gap between the two is still broad enough to make possible a very high rate of increase.

Thus, out of the 80 million people by which the world's population increases every year, nearly 70 million are to be found in the second category, which includes the populations of the so-called Third World countries of Africa, Central and South America and Asia. These are the populations designated as fast-growing in this study. Although these populations have a number of features in common, it has to be borne in mind that there are sometimes very significant differences within the group in population variables, the levels of those variables, and the purely demographic characteristics of the populations concerned.

## II. CHARACTERISTICS OF RAPIDLY GROWING POPULATIONS

Age and Sex Structure

A certain population profile emerges from the pattern of birth and death rates: the greater the number of births in relation to deaths, the younger the population. The socio-economic consequences of the age structure are very important: a population of young or of elderly people implies a specific distribution of the community's resources, particularly in terms of education or retirement benefits.

The age structure also depends on the history of the population being studied. The combined losses due, say, to wars, epidemics or natural catastrophes give rise to a "depleted cohorts" effect in the age pyramid and this has repercussions on all the generations deriving from the numerically deficient cohorts involved. Populations which increase at a rate of more than 1.5% over a given period have a "young" structure because of the high proportion of people under 15 years of age. The higher the growth rate, the greater the extent to which that proportion increases. There is accordingly a close relationship between a population's natural rate of increase and its age structure. In countries with high population growth, the problems listed below are intimately bound up with the age structure.

a) In instances where fertility is high, there is a correspondingly high proportion of young children in the 0 to 4-year age group. The nutrition, health, hygiene and general welfare of these young children ties up a sizeable amount of a number of scarce resources - although children can be satisfactorily fed and cared for in Asia, Africa or Latin America at a much lower cost than in the developed countries. However, in view of the larger number of children in this age group, the developing countries are often unable to ensure that this category of the population can be supplied with the minimum requirements and this accounts for the group's very high death rate.

b) In the developing countries, the relative number of children of school age (5 to 14 years) is much higher than it is in the industrialized countries. The cost of schooling and education is also much higher. It is difficult and indeed very often impossible to provide instruction for all the children in this age group in the developing countries largely on account of the considerable numbers involved.

c) A larger number of young adults come on to the labour market in the developing regions but the scarcely developed economies of the countries involved are not in a position to absorb these new entrants every year, some of whom go to swell the already high number of unemployed.

d) Adults in the 15 to 64-year age group, who represent the potential working population, have to bear the burden of a larger proportion of unemployed young people and old people (0 to 14 years and 65 years and over) in the less developed countries. It should be recalled that the size of the working population depends both on the size and the age and sex structure of the population and on the activity rates by age for the two sexes. Countries with a fast population growth have a relatively low proportion of economically active people and a very high dependency ratio. In addition, the global rate of participation in economic activity depends on the activity rates by age or age groups of the potential working population. If that population is relatively small, the global participation rate will also be small and will accordingly contribute to one of the causes of under-development.

e) A population's growth potential depends on the size of the successive generations attaining the reproductive stage. This dynamic potential, in which women represent the most important aspect, depends essentially on the age pyramid and hence on the age and sex structure.

Migration Movements

High population growth gives rise to problems that are not only bound up with the age structure but also with the movement of individual persons both inside and outside a country's boundaries. The causes of migrations are not merely of a demographic nature but may be economic or social in origin.

The most commonly cited causes underlying population movements are as follows:

Economic factors:
- the differential between rural and urban incomes;
- job-seeking;
- the search for fertile land;
- the financial pull exerted by regions growing cash crops;
- enforced idleness during part of the year;
- the search for water points for both men and animals;
- the changeover to a money economy;
- the relative poverty of rural areas.

Socio-cultural factors:
- the pull of urban life;
- the desire to escape from family constraints;
- the search for a more favourable environment in terms of education and health;
- the aura of prestige surrounding city-dwellers.

Other factors:
- political factors (civil wars, lawlessness, tyranny);
- natural catastrophes (earthquakes, drought, etc.).

Migrations are fostered by differences in development levels between regions of the same country or between two countries in the same geographical sub-region. In West Africa, for instance, most of the migratory flows from the countries of the sub-retion are in the direction of Ivory Coast, while in that country itself they are from north to south. The same is true of movements from the countries of North Africa to Europe.

In developing regions, demographic growth has been so vast that the rural population has continued to increase (at a rate of 1.6% a year) while at the same time contributing to very rapid urban growth (4.4% a year) as a result of the flight from the countryside. The disparities are much more pronounced between developing regions than between industrialized regions. Africa is the least urbanized continent (some 20% of the population is urban compared with almost 60% in Latin America and 28% in Asia) and is currently experiencing the highest urban growth rate (slightly more than 5% a year as against 4.5% in Latin America and 4% in Asia).

One of the most striking phenomena of our time is the accelerated urbanization of the developing countries which has come about through the transfer of the unemployment and poverty of over-populated rural areas to the urban environment. In the industrialized countries, urbanization was a forerunner of the rise in living standards at the same time as being one of its consequences. In the developing countries, there is a disparity between the number of people leaving the countryside and the limited job-creation capacity of towns. In some cases, towns develop without any semblance of order in a process of elephantine growth in which there are no real functional links between urban nuclei and between urban and rural environments.

This type of urban growth, which the present-day industrialized countries never experienced and which is taking place at a faster pace than is warranted by economic development, is giving rise to considerable difficulties. Moreover, the wretched conditions existing in towns are such that there is heavy pressure to make social investments that are not directly productive. At about the end of the 1960's, it was estimated that some nine million people were living in shanty towns or slums in Latin America.[1]

International and domestic migrations triggered off by the imbalances stemming from population growth and economic and social development create problems for the developing countries and all kinds of measures are needed to solve them. This is especially so since migrations to the towns and to other countries do not relieve the pressure on rural areas, where the population continues to increase at a rate of more than 1% a year, as a result of which the land problem is constantly being exacerbated in some countries. In the rural areas of the industrialized countries, on the other hand, the population has for many a decade tended to drain away to the towns. It is true that vast expanses of land are available in the developing countries, but these are largely arid and some of them could only be made fit for cultivation at the cost of substantial investment, particularly in irrigation works, and thus the rigours of the law of diminishing returns are brought into play. Excessive population growth can relentlessly bring in its train a reduction in agricultural productivity, owing to the fragmentation of holdings or the increase in the number of agricultural day-labourers. In Mexico, for example, where the land reform that has been in force for more than forty years has to some extent made it possible to prevail on the population to stay on in rural areas by altering the relationship between people and land, this policy is now being jeopardized because of the growth in population. Calculations have shown that 250,000 plots of land have still to be distributed but that the number of people joining the ranks of the labour force in rural areas amounts to that figure in a single year and will exceed 320,000 in 1980. This accounts for the growing political tensions in the Mexican countryside. The situation is scarcely any brighter in urban areas since the peasants who forsake their villages descend on the shanty towns.

---

1. Léon Tabah: <u>Problèmes démographiques des pays en voie de développement</u>, 1970-71, Centre de Formation des Experts de la Coopération Technique Internationale, Fondation Nationale des Sciences Politiques, 27-30, rue Saint-Guillaume, Paris, 7ème.

Social and Economic Characteristics

Demographers do not confine themselves to determining the variables of population movements but also study the socio-economic trends affecting the population, including such features as marital status, education and the degree of literacy in the social sphere, and occupations and earnings in the economic field.

a) Marital status

People are classified according to their marital status under the four headings of married, divorced, widowed and single. If information on the marital status is available, it is possible to ascertain the proportion of the population contributing to fertility since married people are the main agents of procreation in most countries.

The study of nuptiality in Africa shows that the marriage rate is one of the factors involved in high fertility. In this respect, the African continent displays a number of unique features: women marry when they are very young and have only just reached puberty, and first marriages take place at the very early age of 13 to 16 years. The married state is virtually universal and only about 1% of women never marry. Marital mobility is very common. Frequent and early marriage is bound to foster high fertility, which is made necessary by the very high infant and child mortality rate and ensures both the collective survival of the group (family, clan or tribe) and its economic viability. Marriage also plays an extremely important sociological role, since it enables a whole system of alliances to be established between clans and more generally speaking ensures the stable working of the social and economic structure.

In Central America (including the Caribbean) and Latin America, high fertility prevails despite the marriage pattern (nuptiality). There is a high proportion of consensual unions which, because of their instability, are generally less fertile than legal marriages.

The marriage rate in Asia is marked by the influence of three main religions, i.e. Buddhism, Islam and Hinduism. People subject to Buddhist influences, such as the Chinese, have always married late and, in recent decades, the relatively late marrying age has become even later. This deferment of marriage is reflected in the reduction in the proportion of married women among young women in the 20-24 year age group.

In India, people marry fairly early, unions are stable and marriage universal. In countries where Islam predominates, marriage is widespread and takes place at a relatively early age, although marital mobility seems to be quite common.

It is obviously rather rash to make such a generalization about Asia, which has more than half the world's population, since we have to contend with the fact that the data for the individual countries vary in quality or are even non-existent, and that a wide variety of cultures are involved.

b) Instruction and education

Data on the level of education are unsuited to international comparisons owing to the differences existing between educational systems and the subjects taught. On the other hand, notwithstanding the differences in definitions, the percentage of people who can read and write or who are illiterate in the different countries and regions can provide information on the level of education of the population. These rates vary to a considerable extent depending on whether they relate to industrialized or developing countries. In the countries in the first category, almost 98% of the population are literate while this figure ranges between 70 and 25% in countries with fast-growing populations.

c) The economically active population

According to the United Nations,[2] the economically active population covers all persons of either sex who furnish the supply of labour for the production of economic goods and services, while the not economically active population comprises people who are not engaged in any economic activity during census or survey periods. In addition to this classification, which at first sight appears simple but in fact often prevents international comparisons from being made owing to the lack of uniformity of the definitions, other items of information are collected on the economic characteristics of the population, such as economic activity, occupation, sector of activity, post occupied, and so on. Regions with a high proportion of young people, in other words the developing regions, have an economically active population which is smaller in relative terms than that in developed regions. On the other hand, the non-active population is larger. The distribution of the active population between the different sectors of economic activity, i.e. occupations, depends much more on the level of economic development. It is not surprising, therefore, that there should be disparity between the industrialized and developing regions in this regard.

For instance, if we merely take the world's agricultural population,[3] we are struck by the contrast between the two regions: the agricultural population has declined in the industrialized regions and has increased in the less developed regions. The reduction in the first-mentioned regions is due to population transfers from agriculture

---

2. Principles and Recommendations for the 1970 Population Censuses, paragraph 292 (1969 English Edition).

3. According to the United Nations definition, the agricultural population consists of people actively engaged in agriculture and their dependents. This concept is more restricted than that of the rural population.

to industry and services and is related to advances in agricultural productivity. The increase in the developing regions stems from the lack of outlets other than agriculture, due to the lack of capital, skilled manpower and so on.

Any economic and social development plan which sets out to promote education, industry, agriculture, health, housing and job creation is compelled to take account of the structure of the population for which it has been drawn up, i.e. the structure by age and sex and according to all the economic and social characteristics involved. Similarly, any planning exercise, which is by nature concerned with the future, ought normally to take account of trends in those structural features. These trends can be predicted by means of prior population forecasts, which can provide information about the structural features.

## III. WORLD AND REGIONAL POPULATION PROSPECTS

The United Nations estimates[4] for the population of the world and its main areas and regions are quite accurate and are currently the best set of statistics available. The figures represent aggregates obtained from population estimates and projections by sex and age for the population of every country and territory in the world. Different assumptions have been made for population growth rates.

For the World as a Whole

Four assumptions are made and are designated as "medium", "low", "high" and "constant fertility". The last-mentioned assumption does not seem to be realistic but it is useful for illustrating the demographic effects of a fertility rate standing at the same level as it did in 1970. In view of the age structure, if the fertility rate remains constant, the rate of population increase in the developing countries will rise from 2.4% to 3% between 1995 and 2000. At the end of the century, therefore, these countries will have a population of 5,798 million people compared with 1,402 million people in the developed countries, making a total world population of 7,200 million people. The other assumptions show the effect of an expected fall in the fertility rate on the population.

   i)   The "medium" assumption

This assumption presupposes a population growth rate of 2% per year until 1985. This rate should then fall until it reaches 1.7% a year

---

   4.   United Nations, World and Regional Population Prospects, and Single-Year Population Estimates and Projections for Major Areas, Population Division. ESA/P/WP/56, 6th October, 1975.

by the year 2000. The world population will then amount to 6,407 million people and will have thus grown by 77% between 1970 and 2000. This is chiefly due to the growth in the population of the developing countries, which will increase by 99% as against 26% in the developed countries.

There will be a slow but steady decline in the population growth rate in the developed countries. It is estimated that the quinquennial growth rate will amount to 4% until 1990, after which it will drop to 3%. Their population will accordingly increase from 1,084 million to 1,368 million people.

On the other hand, the growth rate in the developing countries will rise by 13% every five years until 1985 and then will decrease by 11% between 1995 and 2000. Their population will accordingly increase from 2,537 million to 5,039 million people.

At the end of the century, owing to the difference in growth rates, the prospective population of the developing regions will be more than three and a half times as high as that of the developed regions (3.7 to 1), whereas the ratio in 1970 was only 2.3 to 1.), whereas the ratio in 1970 was only 2.3 to 1.

ii) The "low" assumption

This assumption entails a moderate growth rate falling from 2.3% a year to 1.7% a year in the year 2000. At that rate, the world population will amount to 5,999 million people, 4,685 million of whom will be in the developing countries.

iii) The "high" assumption

This assumption presupposes that the population will grow at a rate of about 2.5 to 2.6% a year until 1990, and will then fall by 2.4% per year until the end of the century. The world population will then amount to 6,803 people, 5,367 million of whom will be in the developing countries.

Regional Differences

It is quite clear that growth rates will not be the same throughout the world and that they will grow in magnitude in some regions to the detriment of others. Examples of some of these differences are given below.

i) South Asia:

It has a population of 1,111 million in 1970, and accounts for almost one third of the present-day world population. If the "medium" assumption is confirmed, there will be 2,384 million inhabitants in South Asia in the year 2000, representing some 37% of the world population. According to the "high" assumption, the population will rise to 2,529 million or 40% of the world population. It may be noted that according to the "constant fertility" assumption, the population would be 14% higher than under the "medium" assumption.

    ii) East Asia:

Although the estimated growth rate is moderate (1.6 to 1% a year), there will be a significant absolute increase in population from 926 million to 1,373 million.

    iii) Latin America:

In this region, according to the "medium" assumption, the population would rise from 284 million to 625 million. According to the "constant fertility" assumption, it would increase by a further 16%.

    iv) Africa:

The population would increase 2.4 times and would rise from 352 million to 834 million.

Table I sets out details of the population prospects according to the three assumptions made (i.e. the low, medium and high variants).

## Assumptions for Birth and Death Rates

As already stated, population growth rates depend on both the birth rate and the death rate.

As far as the developed countries are concerned, there is no reason to expect any radical changes in the fertility and death rates except as a result of wars or significant changes in economic and population policies.

On the other hand, major changes are expected to occur in the developing countries. It is hoped that the fertility rate will start to fall at the end of the 1970's and that the overall level will be reduced by 30% in twenty-five years. There will obviously be considerable variations from one country to another. It is also hoped that the death rate will fall from 14 to 8 or 9% and accordingly that the life expectancy at birth will have risen by ten years before the end of the century.

    A.   Trends in the fertility rate

In the developed countries, birth rates may fall slightly - from 17.2 to 15.7% - between 1970 and 2000. The gross reproduction rates will change very little. However, the birth rate in the developing countries may fall significantly between the beginning and end of the projection period, i.e.:

- from 38 to 29% according to the "medium" assumption;
- from 38 to 26% according to the "low" assumption;
- from 38 to 32% according to the "high" assumption.

Table I. SUMMARY TABLE

| ASSUMPTIONS | TREND IN RATES OF POPULATION INCREASE | "EXPECTED" POPULATION IN YEAR 2000 | | |
|---|---|---|---|---|
| | | WORLD | INDUSTRIALIZED COUNTRIES | DEVELOPING COUNTRIES |
| "Medium" | 2% per year until 1985 then declining to 1.7%............ | 6,407 | 1,368 | 5,039 |
| "High" | 2.5% until 1990 then declining to 2.4%............ | 6,803 | 1,436 | 5,367 |
| "Low" | Moderate rate decreasing from 2.3 to 1.7%............ | 5,999 | 1,314 | 4,685 |
| "Constant fertility" | | 7,200 | 1,402 | 5,798 |

Regional differences will occur in the net reproduction rates and the developed countries will move closer to the exact replacement rate leading to population stabilisation.

B. Trends in the death rate

All the assumptions made in the projections for the developing countries predict a significant reduction in the death rate. This would result in a death rate situated between 9.3% in the case of the "low" assumption and 7.9% in the case of the "high" assumption. This figure is impressive compared with the estimated figure of 14.2% for the period from 1970 to 1975. If the "medium" assumption is confirmed, the crude death rates in the developed and developing countries will be identical by about 1990, owing to the younger age structure of the developing countries. The increase in the death rate (from 9.2 to 9.9 per thousand) in the more developed regions is entirely due to the continued ageing of the population. In the developed regions, the life expectancy in the less-developed countries, which was estimated at 54 years in the period from 1970 to 1975, may increase by more than 10 years before the end of the century. The gap of almost 20 years between life expectancies in the developed and developing countries may accordingly be reduced by half. All regions will share in this significant decline in the death rate.

According to the "medium" assumption, the increased life expectancy of the population will be 8.7 years in Latin America, 8.3 years in East Asia, 11.7 years in South Asia and 12.2 years in Africa. The lower the death rate over the period from 1970 to 1975, the greater the increase in life expectancy will be.

## Demographic Consequences of Population Prospects

If the "medium" assumption is confirmed, what will the demographic situation be in the year 2000? We shall single out three essential points:

1. The ageing of the world population, especially in the developed countries (see Tables IIA and B). The proportion of young people will decline in favour of adults and old people. This will give rise to the well known problems we have already mentioned.
2. The growing importance of South Asia and Africa (see Table III).
3. The widening gap between the populations of the developed and developing countries (Graph I), when the population of the latter will account for almost 79% of the total world population.

The assumptions made in these projections are essentially based on assumptions for future fertility trends. However, of all the factors entering into demographic projections, the fertility rate is the most important and yet the most unpredictable.

Table IIA. STRUCTURE OF THE WORLD POPULATION BY AGE AND CATEGORY, 1970

| REGION | AGE GROUP 0-4 | 5-14 | UNDER 15 | 15-24 | 25-44 | 45-64 | 15-64 | 65 AND OVER |
|---|---|---|---|---|---|---|---|---|
| **Category 1** | | | | | | | | |
| Eastern Europe | 8.0 | 16.6 | 24.6 | 16.9 | 27.2 | 20.8 | 64.9 | 10.4 |
| Western Europe | 8.0 | 16.1 | 24.1 | 14.7 | 26.6 | 21.7 | 63.0 | 12.8 |
| Northern Europe | 8.1 | 16.1 | 24.2 | 15.2 | 24.2 | 23.8 | 63.2 | 12.7 |
| Southern Europe | 9.0 | 17.4 | 26.4 | 15.6 | 27.4 | 20.7 | 63.7 | 9.8 |
| North America | 8.4 | 20.0 | 28.4 | 17.9 | 23.8 | 20.3 | 62.0 | 9.7 |
| USSR | 8.4 | 20.2 | 28.6 | 16.7 | 28.8 | 18.0 | 63.5 | 7.8 |
| Japan | 8.5 | 15.5 | 24.0 | 19.0 | 31.8 | 18.1 | 68.9 | 7.0 |
| Australia and New Zealand | 9.7 | 19.7 | 29.4 | 17.5 | 24.9 | 19.9 | 62.3 | 8.4 |
| **Category 2** | | | | | | | | |
| Temperate South America | 11.0 | 20.7 | 31.7 | 17.5 | 26.3 | 17.9 | 61.7 | 6.6 |
| China | 12.2 | 22.2 | 34.4 | 19.5 | 25.1 | 15.6 | 60.2 | 5.4 |
| Other countries of East Asia | 14.0 | 27.5 | 41.5 | 19.3 | 23.6 | 12.2 | 55.1 | 3.4 |
| Caribbean | 15.8 | 26.0 | 41.8 | 18.2 | 22.4 | 13.0 | 53.6 | 4.7 |
| South Africa | 16.3 | 23.9 | 40.2 | 18.5 | 24.6 | 12.9 | 56.0 | 3.7 |
| South-East Asia | 17.0 | 26.1 | 43.1 | 18.1 | 24.0 | 11.5 | 53.6 | 3.0 |
| North Africa | 17.6 | 26.8 | 44.4 | 18.8 | 22.7 | 11.0 | 58.3 | 3.1 |
| **Category 3** | | | | | | | | |
| Micronesia and Polynesia | 16.0 | 26.9 | 42.9 | 20.6 | 23.0 | 10.6 | 54.2 | 2.8 |
| Melanesia | 16.8 | 25.6 | 42.4 | 18.2 | 24.3 | 12.0 | 54.5 | 3.0 |
| Tropical South America | 16.9 | 27.1 | 44.0 | 19.2 | 22.7 | 11.1 | 53.0 | 3.0 |
| South-West Asia | 17.0 | 26.1 | 43.1 | 18.5 | 23.1 | 11.6 | 53.2 | 3.7 |
| South Asia (central region) | 17.0 | 25.4 | 42.4 | 18.6 | 24.2 | 11.7 | 54.5 | 3.0 |
| Central Africa | 17.2 | 25.7 | 42.9 | 18.2 | 24.7 | 11.4 | 54.3 | 2.8 |
| Central America | 18.1 | 28.3 | 46.4 | 18.8 | 21.3 | 10.1 | 50.2 | 3.4 |
| West Africa | 18.2 | 26.5 | 44.7 | 18.6 | 23.8 | 10.4 | 52.8 | 2.5 |
| East Africa | 18.2 | 27.0 | 45.2 | 17.6 | 23.4 | 10.6 | 51.6 | 3.2 |

SOURCE: Calculated from the United Nations Demographic Yearbook, 1974.

Table IIB. POPULATION DISTRIBUTION BY MAJOR AGE GROUPS AND REGIONS IN 1970, 1985 AND 2000

(Medium assumption)

|  | 1970 | 1985 | 2000 |  | 1970 | 1985 | 2000 |
|---|---|---|---|---|---|---|---|
| **World** |  |  |  | **East Asia** |  |  |  |
| Total | 100.0 | 100.0 | 100.0 | Total | 100.0 | 100.0 | 100.0 |
| 0–4 | 13.5 | 13.3 | 11.8 | 0–4 | 11.9 | 10.3 | 8.5 |
| 5–14 | 22.9 | 22.4 | 21.6 | 5–14 | 21.7 | 20.2 | 16.5 |
| 15–64 | 58.1 | 58.6 | 60.4 | 15–64 | 60.9 | 63.1 | 67.1 |
| 65+ | 5.5 | 5.7 | 6.2 | 65+ | 5.4 | 6.4 | 7.9 |
| **More Developed Regions** |  |  |  | **South Asia** |  |  |  |
| Total | 100.0 | 100.0 | 100.0 | Total | 100.0 | 100.0 | 100.0 |
| 0–4 | 8.5 | 8.4 | 7.6 | 0–4 | 17.0 | 16.3 | 13.7 |
| 5–14 | 18.2 | 15.5 | 15.2 | 5–14 | 25.7 | 26.4 | 25.0 |
| 15–64 | 63.7 | 65.3 | 64.8 | 15–64 | 54.2 | 54.1 | 57.7 |
| 65+ | 9.6 | 10.8 | 12.3 | 65+ | 3.1 | 3.2 | 3.7 |
| **Less Developed Regions** |  |  |  | **Europe** |  |  |  |
| Total | 100.0 | 100.0 | 100.0 | Total | 100.0 | 100.0 | 100.0 |
| 0–4 | 15.6 | 14.9 | 13.0 | 0–4 | 8.3 | 7.8 | 7.4 |
| 5–14 | 24.9 | 24.7 | 23.3 | 5–14 | 16.6 | 14.7 | 14.7 |
| 15–64 | 55.7 | 56.3 | 59.2 | 15–64 | 63.7 | 65.4 | 64.4 |
| 65+ | 3.8 | 4.0 | 4.5 | 65+ | 11.4 | 12.1 | 13.5 |
| **Africa** |  |  |  | **Oceania** |  |  |  |
| Total | 100.0 | 100.0 | 100.0 | Total | 100.0 | 100.0 | 100.0 |
| 0–4 | 17.7 | 18.1 | 16.8 | 0–4 | 11.1 | 11.5 | 10.4 |
| 5–14 | 26.7 | 26.7 | 27.0 | 5–14 | 21.0 | 20.2 | 19.4 |
| 15–64 | 52.7 | 52.3 | 52.9 | 15–64 | 60.6 | 60.6 | 62.4 |
| 65+ | 3.0 | 2.9 | 3.2 | 65+ | 7.3 | 7.7 | 7.8 |
| **Latin America** |  |  |  | **USSR** |  |  |  |
| Total | 100.0 | 100.0 | 100.0 | Total | 100.0 | 100.0 | 100.0 |
| 0–4 | 16.3 | 15.4 | 13.5 | 0–4 | 8.4 | 9.3 | 8.2 |
| 5–14 | 26.5 | 25.3 | 24.0 | 5–14 | 20.2 | 15.9 | 16.4 |
| 15–64 | 53.5 | 55.2 | 58.0 | 15–64 | 63.6 | 65.2 | 63.4 |
| 65+ | 3.7 | 4.0 | 4.5 | 65+ | 7.8 | 9.6 | 12.0 |
| **Northern America** |  |  |  |  |  |  |  |
| Total | 100.0 | 100.0 | 100.0 |  |  |  |  |
| 0–4 | 8.4 | 8.8 | 7.3 |  |  |  |  |
| 5–14 | 20.0 | 15.3 | 15.4 |  |  |  |  |
| 15–64 | 61.9 | 65.0 | 66.4 |  |  |  |  |
| 65+ | 9.7 | 10.8 | 10.8 |  |  |  |  |

SOURCE: United Nations, op. cit.

Table III. THE WORLD'S POPULATION BY MAJOR AREAS AND REGIONS, 1970, AND ACCORDING TO LOW, MEDIUM AND HIGH VARIANT OF POPULATION PROJECTIONS FOR 1980

(In millions)

| AREA AND REGION | 1970 | LOW VARIANT | | | MEDIUM VARIANT | | | HIGH VARIANT | | |
|---|---|---|---|---|---|---|---|---|---|---|
| | | 1980 | 1990 | 2000 | 1980 | 1990 | 2000 | 1980 | 1990 | 2000 |
| World | 3,621 | 4,351 | 5,174 | 5,999 | 4,401 | 5,346 | 6,407 | 4,441 | 5,508 | 6,803 |
| More Developed Regions | 1,084 | 1,175 | 1,253 | 1,314 | 1,183 | 1,282 | 1,368 | 1,195 | 1,319 | 1,436 |
| Less Developed Regions | 2,537 | 3,176 | 3,920 | 4,685 | 3,218 | 4,064 | 5,039 | 3,247 | 4,190 | 5,367 |
| Africa | 352 | 460 | 605 | 768 | 462 | 622 | 834 | 464 | 634 | 878 |
| Eastern Africa | 100 | 132 | 176 | 225 | 132 | 180 | 246 | 132 | 183 | 258 |
| Middle Africa | 40 | 51 | 66 | 84 | 51 | 67 | 89 | 51 | 68 | 93 |
| Northern Africa | 86 | 113 | 149 | 188 | 114 | 154 | 202 | 115 | 158 | 216 |
| Southern Africa | 24 | 32 | 41 | 51 | 32 | 42 | 56 | 32 | 43 | 59 |
| Western Africa | 101 | 132 | 174 | 221 | 133 | 179 | 241 | 133 | 181 | 252 |
| Latin America | 284 | 370 | 470 | 573 | 374 | 489 | 625 | 377 | 506 | 676 |
| Caribbean | 26 | 31 | 38 | 45 | 32 | 40 | 49 | 32 | 41 | 52 |
| Middle America | 67 | 92 | 123 | 160 | 93 | 128 | 173 | 94 | 133 | 187 |
| Temperate South America | 36 | 42 | 46 | 51 | 42 | 48 | 53 | 42 | 48 | 54 |
| Tropical South America | 155 | 205 | 262 | 318 | 207 | 274 | 351 | 210 | 285 | 383 |
| Northern America | 226 | 246 | 266 | 279 | 249 | 275 | 296 | 256 | 296 | 334 |
| East Asia | 926 | 1,056 | 1,167 | 1,269 | 1,087 | 1,235 | 1,373 | 1,103 | 1,288 | 1,463 |
| China | 772 | 878 | 971 | 1,056 | 907 | 1,033 | 1,152 | 923 | 1,083 | 1,236 |
| Japan | 104 | 117 | 125 | 131 | 118 | 126 | 133 | 118 | 127 | 134 |
| Other East Asia | 50 | 61 | 72 | 82 | 62 | 75 | 88 | 63 | 78 | 93 |
| South Asia | 1,111 | 1,443 | 1,843 | 2,248 | 1,449 | 1,885 | 2,384 | 1,456 | 1,929 | 2,529 |
| Eastern South Asia | 285 | 372 | 475 | 577 | 374 | 490 | 617 | 376 | 505 | 659 |
| Middle South Asia | 749 | 967 | 1,232 | 1,502 | 971 | 1,255 | 1,584 | 975 | 1,281 | 1,677 |
| Western South Asia | 77 | 103 | 136 | 169 | 104 | 140 | 183 | 105 | 143 | 193 |
| Europe | 459 | 485 | 504 | 519 | 488 | 515 | 540 | 491 | 527 | 562 |
| Eastern Europe | 103 | 109 | 114 | 117 | 110 | 116 | 122 | 110 | 119 | 127 |
| Northern Europe | 80 | 83 | 86 | 89 | 84 | 88 | 91 | 85 | 91 | 98 |
| Southern Europe | 128 | 136 | 143 | 149 | 137 | 147 | 156 | 138 | 149 | 161 |
| Western Europe | 148 | 156 | 161 | 164 | 157 | 165 | 171 | 158 | 168 | 176 |
| Oceania | 19 | 23 | 27 | 30 | 24 | 28 | 33 | 24 | 29 | 35 |
| Australia and New Zealand | 15 | 18 | 20 | 22 | 18 | 22 | 25 | 19 | 22 | 26 |
| Melanesia | 3 | 4 | 5 | 6 | 4 | 5 | 6 | 4 | 5 | 7 |
| Micronesia and Polynesia | 1 | 2 | 2 | 2 | 2 | 2 | 3 | 2 | 2 | 3 |
| USSR | 243 | 268 | 292 | 311 | 269 | 297 | 321 | 269 | 299 | 325 |

SOURCE United Nations, World Population Prospects as Assessed in 1973 (preliminary results), E/conf. 60/CBP.31.

## Graph 1

### FUTURE WORLD POPULATION GROWTH BY THE MORE DEVELOPED AND LESS DEVELOPED REGIONS, 1970-2125
(Medium Variant)

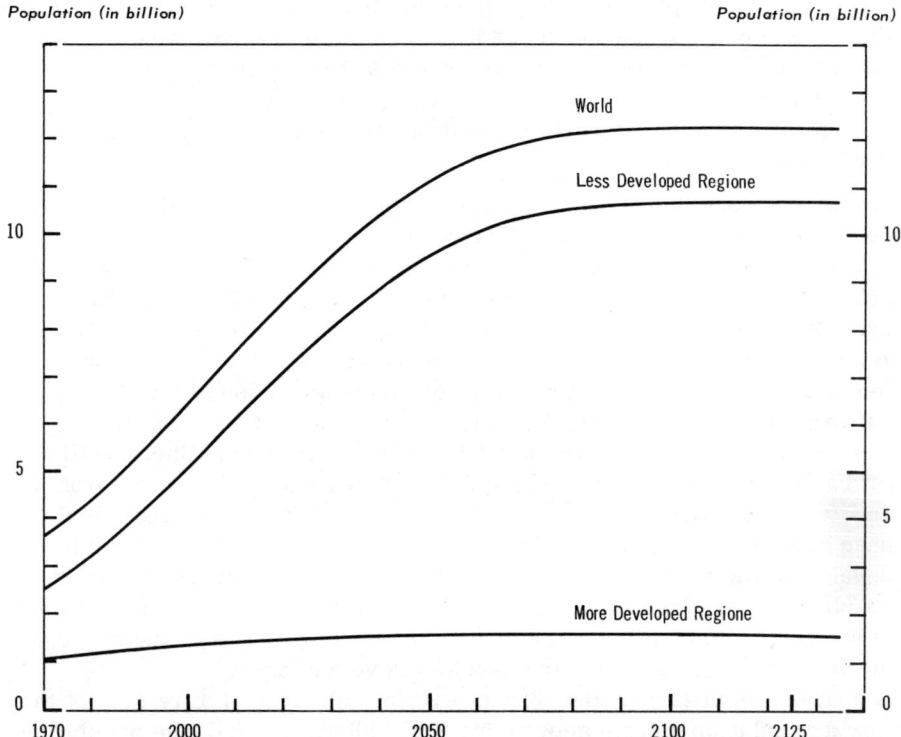

With respect to the developed countries, the projections do not point to any significant variation in fertility and death rates up to the end of the century. It could be argued that these countries should contemplate reversing their policies and current thinking in regard to fertility.

In the developing countries, on the other hand, the projections are based on the assumption that the decline in fertility will become more widespread over the next thirty years. The time at which the impact of this phenomenon will be felt will depend on the pace of economic and social development, on cultural factors and on national population policies.

However, these countries may be caught up in a vicious circle in as much as the economic development which would bring about a decline in fertility may prove impossible because the population is growing too quickly as a result of too high a fertility rate. The question is whether economic development will make sufficient progress in the next thirty years to cause a change in attitudes to fertility for, in the long run, the adoption of family planning is governed by the success of the development process. It might be asked, therefore, whether the "constant fertility" assumption is completely unrealistic in such an eventuality.

In point of fact, if world population trends are examined closely, it will be seen that:

a) No population has ever been subject to exponential growth over a relatively long period (50 years).[5]

b) The populations whose development has been most adversely affected are those which are now growing at the fastest pace. They are like trees which have been pruned and then sprout up again with renewed strength until they reach a certain size. This is currently the situation in Africa and Latin America, where population trends suffered distortions in past centuries. When a certain level of equilibrium is reached, the populations of these two continents will probably grow at reasonable rates, like trees which have been pruned and, after growing at a prodigious speed, reach the stage they would have reached in any case had they not been pruned and then go on to develop in the same way as unpruned trees. If the pruning has been too drastic, the trees may be stunted or they may die. This is true of certain human societies which have disappeared or are in the process of disappearing, or which are developing very slowly.

There is still considerable uncertainty about the future size of the world population and its geographical distribution. Will the population in 2075 be 80 billion or 12.2 billion or will it be only 5.6 billion? All these figures are based on assumptions for the variables of the dynamic process involved.

Whatever the methods used to draw up population projections, there is an element of uncertainty about the results they give. All population forecasts are based on assumptions that are justified by past trends for demographic variables, by the economic situation, by the likely impact of various economic and social factors on future trends or by comparison with trends recorded in circumstances that are considered to be identical in countries where statistics are satisfactory. The choice of assumptions is therefore fundamental and has to take account of certain variants which do not appear to be beyond the bounds

---

5. Assuming a population growth rate of 1% a year a couple, that is to say one man and one woman, in the year one would have become 685 million people by the year 1975; and 50 couples in the year one would have become 68 1/2 billion people.

of the possible. As a general rule, it is useful to draw up projections of each type starting from several separate sets of assumptions so as to obtain some idea of the reliability of the results and the likely order of magnitude of future figures. However, the publication of the results can only show three or four sets of figures which will be used to bracket a range of possible assumptions.

Population projections should accordingly be regarded as orders of magnitude. The rules governing population trends are not precisely known and are subject to many contingencies. Attitudes of individuals and couples to procreation are guided by considerations which sometimes obey criteria that can be discerned and quantified but often remain undetected and unquantifiable. It is almost impossible to foresee epidemics or natural calamities which boost the death rate or economic disasters which trigger off population movements.

Countries with the best possible facilities for gathering statistics have difficulty in predicting even medium-term trends for their population and this is even more true of countries where data are defective or no figures are available at all.

The example of India illustrates the uncertainty involved in population projections. Several projections have been made in India in recent years by both individual researchers and international institutes and organisations. A comparison of six of these projections shows to what extent the assumptions influence the results obtained, since the size of the total population in year 2001 varies between 846 million and 1,249 million.[6] This significant difference over a relatively short period is essentially due to considerations as to the level of the prospective decline in fertility and death rates.

In addition to the difficulty involved in justifying and substantiating the assumptions, the basic data themselves are often unreliable. The adjustment of data gives rise to problems which involve difficult decisions, e.g., adjusting the overall size of the population, the age pyramid or the fertility or death rate curves. The discrepancies between the figures given for India by the six authors can partly be explained by the techniques they used to refine the rough data.

In view of the degree of inaccuracy involved in establishing projections, there is scarcely any point in extending them any further into the future than is strictly necessary to draw up development plans and lay down official policy on relevant issues. The most suitable period varies with the purpose of the projection and the use for which it is intended. Population projections covering a period of 20 or 25 years are usually adequate for essential economic and social development planning purposes. Since they are based on assumptions relating to the future, they have to be corrected every so often in the light of the specific data available. It is only on that understanding that they can be a useful tool for people in charge of economic and social planning.

---

6. Population and Development Review. Vol. 2, No. 1, March 1976. "New Population Projections for India", Robert Cassen and Tim Dyson.

## IV. FUTURE POPULATION GROWTH

The World Population Conference which was held in Bucharest in August 1974 was an important turning-point in demographic policy-making. At that Conference, population problems were recognized as being endogenous factors in economic and social development rather than exogenous factors, as in the past. The interdependence existing between demographic situations and economic and social development was acknowledged. However, no solutions were proposed for translating that interdependence into practical measures.

The following Chapters of this book will examine some of the problems of growing populations. In order to gain a better understanding of the effects which population and development have on each other, it would be interesting to survey some of the demographic phenomena which may promote or inhibit the development of the various social sectors in the short, medium or long term.

The present state of a population is only the reflection of that same population's past and of the interplay of fertility, mortality and migratory flows. Fast-growing populations have specific problems which all come under the heading of what is known as demographic inertia.

From the purely demographic standpoint, one of the most crucial problems which the developing countries have to contend with in the long run is the phenomenon of demographic inertia. The growth potential of a population depends on the size of the generations which successively reach the fertility stage. This dynamic potential is encountered to a much greater extent among the young populations of the developing regions than in the industrialized regions. The population potential which is accumulated in the age structures is the product of high fertility both in the past and in the present. For young populations, the dynamic effect of the age structure implies a growth process which would continue for almost a century even if there were a significant decline in fertility.

This is one important rationale of the present book. Others have calculated the possible benefits arising from reductions in population growth rates.[7] The emphasis here is rather on the fact that, whatever one may think of the desirability of slowing the growth of population, very substantial growth lies ahead for developing countries on almost any assumptions. One way of appreciating the magnitudes involved is to examine the growth of population, assuming that fertility at some given point reaches the level which, in the long run, guarantees eventual zero growth of population. This is a number of children per couple somewhat in excess of 2 - how much depends on mortality. The figure varies for different countries, mostly within the range 2.1-2.3. When fertility is at that level, the Net Reproduction Rate (NRR) is said to

---

7. See, e.g., W.C. Robinson, ed., Population and Development Planning, Population Council, New York, 1975.

equal unity: fertility is such that once the age-distribution reaches its long-term stable proportions, females in the population will exactly reproduce their numbers in each generation. The key point is, however, that the existing age distribution with its preponderance of people at, or soon to enter, child-bearing age, implies substantial growth for several decades after fertility reaches the level where NRR = 1. Typically, a population with this characteristic age distribution, if it numbers, say, 60 million today, will grow to at least 80 million (and possibly much more) over some 8 decades if fertility reached NRR = 1 immediately. Naturally the longer the period before this fertility level is reached, the higher the ultimate figure to which the population will grow.

Some illustrative calculations were provided by Frejka.[8] As can be seen from Table IV, the projections for Ghana show a growth of 68% over 80 years from 1970-2050 even with NRR = 1 at the start of the period. The population grows by 176% over the same period if NRR = 1 is reached 30 years later, and by 455% if NRR = 1 is only reached in the last decade of the period. In the Morocco figures cited, the proportionate differences are even greater between the three projections owing to more adverse initial conditions.

Fertility is falling in the developing countries, but in most of them it is far from the NRR = 1 level, and will probably continue to be so at least for the next twenty years. Clearly, very substantial population growth lies ahead, and that of the developing world as a whole will at least double before it stops growing. The rate of decline of mortality seems to have fallen off in many places, either because mortality has already reached quite low levels, or because difficulties are being experienced in combatting the obstacles to further decline. But these tendencies, while dampening somewhat the high current growth rates, will not reduce them greatly. The one thing that could prevent these very high forecast population totals would be a decline of fertility below replacement levels. This has already occurred, or is on the verge of occurring in several of the developed countries, but it is at present a remote prospect in the developing world.

---

8.   T. Frejka, The Future of Population Growth: Alternative Paths to Equilibrium, Wiley, New York, 1973.

Table IV. THE FUTURE OF POPULATION GROWTH

Alternative Paths to Equilibrium, Tomas Frejka

Indices of population size (1970 = 100), Ghana and Morocco, Projections 1, 3 and 5, Standard set, 1970–2050

|  | GHANA | | | MOROCCO | | |
|---|---|---|---|---|---|---|
|  | PROJECTION (a) (NRR = 1.0) IN 1970–1975 | PROJECTION (b) (NRR = 1.0) IN 2000–2005 | PROJECTION (c) (NRR = 1.0) IN 2040–2045 | PROJECTION (a) (NRR = 1.0) IN 1970–1975 | PROJECTION (b) (NRR = 1.0) IN 2000–2005 | PROJECTION (c) (NRR = 1.0) IN 2040–2045 |
| 1970 | 100 | 100 | 100 | 100 | 100 | 100 |
| 2000 | 136 | 187 | 225 | 141 | 211 | 262 |
| 2050 | 168 | 276 | 555 | 175 | 328 | 735 |
|  | Projection (a) (TNR = 1.0 for the period 1970–1975 | Projection (b) (TNR = 1.0 for the period 2000–2005 | Projection (c) (TNR = 1.0 for the period 2040–2045 | Projection (a) (TNR = 1.0 for the period 1970–1975 | Projection (b) (TNR = 1.0 for the period 2000–2005 | Projection (c) (TNR = 1.0 for the period 2040–2045 |

REFERENCES

1. "La population du Monde: Situation en 1974 - Un Guide du Citoyen Conscient", Bulletin de Démographie et de Planning Familial, July 1974, No. 15, Population Council, New York.

2. Léon Tabah, Problèmes démographiques des pays en voie de développement, Fondation Nationale des Sciences Politiques, 27-30, rue Saint-Guillaume, Paris 75007.

3. Jean Bourgeois Pichat et Si-Ahmad Taleb, "Un taux d'accroissement nul pour les pays en voie de développement en l'an 2000; Rêve ou réalité ?", Population, 1970, No. 5, INED, Paris.

4. Cairo Demographic Centre, How to bring the Tunisian Population to Stationary State - "Hypothetical Situation", Cairo, November-December. General Diploma in Demography, 1974.

5. La croissance de la population mondiale urbaine et rurale, 1920-2000, United Nations ST/SDA/Séries A44, New York, 1970.

6. Population in History, Edited by D. V. Glass and D. E. C. Eversley, London, Edward Arnold (Publishers) Ltd.

7. Rapid Population Growth: Consequences and Policy Implications, Published by the National Academy of Science by the Johns Hopkins Press, Baltimore and London.

8. Population Dynamics, Ralph Thomlinson, Random House, New York.

9. "La situation démographique dans le monde en 1970". Etudes démographiques, No. 49, New York, 1972.

10. "La population du monde et la Conférence de Bucarest", Yves Charbit, Notes et Etudes documentaires, Nos. 4218-4219-4220, la documentation française, Paris, 1975.

11. United Nations Demographic Year Book, 1970 and 1973.

12. La transition démographique appliquée à l'Afrique tropicale, Julien Condé, OECD Development Centre, 1971.

13. Quelques aspects démographiques des ressources humaines en Afrique, Julien Condé, OECD Development Centre, 1973.

# 3

## PLANNING FOOD SUPPLIES FOR AN EXPANDING POPULATION[1]

by

Jacqueline Mondot-Bernard[*]

### I. INTRODUCTION

The right of every individual to have sufficient food to preserve him from hunger, under-nourishment and malnutrition is recognized, but is nevertheless far from being satisfied. Hunger and under-nourishment assail large sections of the population in the developing countries of Africa and Asia. This persistence of hunger and under-nourishment raises a number of problems.

The purpose of this Chapter, then, is to look into the causes of this situation in order to offer some reflections and suggestions on possible approaches which might enable developing countries to arrive at a situation whereby the whole population, including the poorest, could satisfy their nutritional needs; this is an especially disturbing problem because, given demographic laws, the world's population is increasing rapidly, while other basic resources necessary for food production such as water, cultivable land, etc., are finite under the present state of technology and approach.

### II. FOOD REQUIREMENTS

Definition of food requirements

Food intake can only be assessed in relation to requirements. Requirements are of various kinds: energy, protein, vitamin and mineral. These requirements must be determined to assess the individual intake needed, and also to calculate whether the population's present food level is adequate.

---

1. The author is grateful to Mr. Robert Cassen for his comments on the original version of this paper.

[*] Original text in French.

Nutritional standards are defined in terms of physical needs in relation to growth, body maintenance and activity. It should be stressed that while the physiological requirement for any of these purposes can be quite accurately measured, nutritional standards usually incorporate subjective elements. They attempt to specify desirable nutritional levels, and therefore embody views as to what physical attainments (especially those concerning activity) are deemed at least minimally appropriate. These together with other characteristics, as well as changes in objective measurements have led to a variety of standards being proposed at different places and times.

Different nutritional standards have been proposed in France, in the United Kingdom, in the United States, by the FAO and the WHO, to mention only a few examples. These differences arise partly from the fact that the basic figures used do not have the same meaning. The British and FAO standards refer to the requirements of an average individual in good health, and are designed to maintain him in a proper state of nutrition. The National Research Council (United States) used an optimum requirement: everybody in the United States (in good health) requires a proper level of nutrition to be able to resist the normal aggressive factors in the environment (sickness, etc.). This, therefore, is theoretically higher than the average requirement. France takes account of present consumption levels and thus refers to a sociological rather than a physiological concept. The "standard" so defined is that considered "acceptable" for French people, having regard to their food habits.

1. Energy requirements

The FAO and the WHO have endeavoured to work out a method for assessing energy requirements[1] which would be applicable throughout the world. These Organisations have therefore considered a "reference" man and woman living in a temperate country (and consequently in an industrial society). The latest report of the FAO/WHO Committee on energy and protein requirements (1973)[2] gives a more precise definition of physical activities[3] for the "reference" man and the "reference" woman. Requirements are determined for each sex in relation to body weight and age, the final formula taking the level of activity into account. The corrective for climate used up to then was discarded. The Committee merely recommends that when the climate hampers physical activity, the latter should be determined accordingly.

---

1. Calorie requirements, FAO nutritional studies, No. 15, FAO, 1957.

2. Energy and protein requirements, FAO Nutrition Meetings, Report Series No. 52, Rome 1973.

3. Four levels of activity: light, moderate, very active, exceptional. Energy and Protein Requirements, op. cit., p. 30-31.

It is thus possible to calculate the energy requirements for a given individual (his characteristics such as age, sex, weight and level of activity being determined), and even for a population, although account must be taken of the interaction between the different nutrients.

## 2. Protein requirements

Assessment of protein needs is much more critical. Protein standards have been established on a physiological basis, which means essentially the minimum level to ensure nitrogen balance under laboratory conditions. They take account of weight, age, sex and also of the quality of the proteins. A safe level of protein intake has been defined.[4] For adults, the levels recommended by FAO are lower than those previously given.[5] For children from birth to the age of six, they are higher than those previously given but still lower than those recommended by the US Food and Nutritional Board (1973) for children over two. The US National Research Council has also reduced its standard;[6] at present it recommends 0.80 g of protein per kg of weight for an adult man.

The FAO/WHO Report of 1973 (op. cit., p. 68, para. 6.4.4) emphasizes that "all estimates of protein requirements are valid only when energy requirements are fully met. When the total energy intake is inadequate, some dietary protein is used for energy and is not available to satisfy protein needs".

Calories have, of course, a decisive influence on the utilization of protein, but this is a very complex subject. Protein balance is attainable with calorie levels much below requirements on condition that they exceed 1,000 k-calories or, better still, 1,500.[7]

---

4. Safe level of protein intake: quantity needed to cover physiological requirements and maintain the health of nearly all the people in a specified group. This health level equals the average physiological level of an adult in good health, plus 30% to take account of individual variations in needs, op. cit., p. 69, para. 6.5.

5. FAO/WHO

| | |
|---|---|
| 1965 Adult (man or woman): | 0.71 g/protein/kg/day |
| 1973 Adult man | : 0.61 g/protein/kg/day |
| 1973 Adult woman | : 0.52 g/protein/kg/day |

(The figure indicated for 1965 is also the figure for the safe level of protein intake, column III, and refers in both cases to egg protein).

6. National Research Council, 1968

The NRC in the United States recommended 1 g of protein/kg body weight per day, 50% being protein of animal origin.

1973 Adult man (23 years and over): 56 g/protein per day

Adult woman ("    "    ") : 56 g/protein per day

(i.e. for an adult man weighing 70 kg: 0.80 g of protein per kg).

7. Bour, H., "Les protéines en alimentation et diététique humaine" in Revue de pathologie comparée et de médecine expérimentale, 73rd year, Vol. 10, special No., December 1975.

Tremolières, J., Nutrition, Physiologie, Comportement alimentaire, Paris/Brussels, Montreal, Dunod, 1973. FAO, Report No. 52, p. 19, para. 4.2, op. cit.

The concept of satisfactory protein coverage is based on the quality of the amino acid mixture in the diet compared with the proportions of essential amino acids in the "ideal" reference mixture. A diet which is unbalanced in amino acids is worse than any balanced diet, even one low in nitrogen. The limiting factor of insufficiency or excess of a particular amino acid leads to nitrogen wastage and energy breakdown of unused amino acids.

The latest FAO/WHO[8] recommendations on protein requirements have given rise to some controversy. Considering the recommendations made for "energy intakes" and for the "safe level of protein intake", it seems that diets containing only 6 to 7% of calories of protein origin would be satisfactory (except for young children, pregnant women and nursing mothers, and provided that energy needs are satisfied).

One member of the Committee, Dr. R. Passmore, made a point of his reservations being included in the document. There is no evidence, he said, that "such a low protein derived energy intake is compatible with a healthy vigorous life"...[9] This reservation was supported by Professor Dupin.[10] On the other hand, members of the Committee of the Agricultural Research Council and of the Medical Research Council in the United Kingdom[11] consider that the normal development of young children indirectly supports this recommendation, because mother's milk provides only 8% of energy of protein origin. Without claiming that it is impossible, they doubt whether adults can have a higher protein requirement than growing children.[12]

In its latest recommendations, a special joint FAO/WHO Committee considers that,[13] "to sum up, for individuals or population groups exercising 'moderate activity', as understood in the 1973 Report, a protein concentration of 5 to 5.5% of energy would suffice to meet the requirements of almost all individuals who met their energy needs". It would be desirable to have the value of their protein/calorie ratio of 5 to 5.5%, which the latest FAO/WHO Committee considered sufficient for a grown man, confirmed by clinical observation. Calloway,[14] through

---

8. FAO, Report No. 52, op. cit., p. 63.
9. Ibid., p. 63 and p. 77 (footnote).
10. Dupin, Henri, "Les besoins nutritionnels et les apports recommendés pour la satisfaction de ces besoins", in L'Alimentation et la Vie, Vol. 62, No. 2, 1974, annex IV, p. 116.
11. Agricultural Research Council, Medical Research Council, Food and Nutrition, Research, Report of the ARC/MRC Committee, 1974, p. 110.
12. Report of the ARC/MRC, op. cit., p. 110. "It would be strange, although not perhaps impossible, if the adult required relatively more protein than the growing child".
13. "Energy and Protein Requirements, Recommendations by a joint FAO/WHO informal gathering of experts", in Food and Nutrition, Rome, FAO, 1975, No. 2, p. 17.
14. Calloway, D.C., "The Influence of Energy Intake on Nitrogen Balance in Men with Marginal Intakes of Protein and Energy" in Journal of Nutrition, 1976.

direct experiments with adults, showed that 5% of energy in the form of egg protein is not sufficient to ensure a balance, but that 7% of energy in that form is enough. The FAO/WHO Committee considered that the levels they recommended should be corrected, not only in the light of the quality of the mixture of proteins considered, but in the light of their digestibility, which is in inverse proportion to the vegetable polysaccharide content of the diet; diets rich in whole seed cereals or pulses (also whole seed) thus do not allow such a full use of protein.

In many developing countries diets are based on cereals, and the poorest people have few other sources of protein, if any. In other words, the same foods supply both energy and proteins. Because it is common for food intake on the whole to become insufficient (e.g. in inter-crop periods), to recommend diets without a wider margin of safety might well be imprudent. It must be accepted that calorie and protein insufficiency will be linked, even if the inadequate calorie intake seems to cause the protein deficiency. But in their Report, the members of the FAO/WHO Committee were quite cautious,[15] and considered that it was not possible to translate the prediction of individual protein requirements into meaningful guidelines for population needs.[16]

3. Lipid requirements

In general, the FAO/WHO recommendations do not emphasize the lipid requirements. The quantity of lipids in the diet need not represent 30% of the calorie intake, as in most of the developed countries; it should, however, represent at least 10%, and if possible 20% of the total k-calories. These lipids provide k-calories and liposoluble vitamins, and care should be taken to see that they also provide essential fatty acids, particularly linoleic acid (sometimes classified among the vitamins: vitamin F).

Special emphasis must be laid on the lipid requirements, because certain diets in developing countries are very poor in them; enrichment of diets with lipids would make it possible to cover the need for essential fatty acids, and above all to improve the calorie position in some cases:

Percentage of total calories in lipid form

e.g.[17]  Burundi: lipid k-calories: 3%
Niger Office: " " 7%
Cameroun Batouri
Savanna Zone: " " 6%

---

15. FAO, Report No. 52, op. cit., p. 77.

16. It should be noted that the FAO/WHO solution could lead to a "waste" of energy if the protein-proportion in the diet was relatively low so that the individual would need more than the recommended calorie intake in order to satisfy protein needs.

17. J. Mondot-Bernard, <u>Attempted Analysis of the Food Situation in Africa</u>, OECD Development Centre, May 1974, p. 19.

Conclusion

Obviously, for a given population, the determination of requirements will differ according to the standards of reference used. Extrapolations based on a "reference" man and woman are unreliable: it is for each society to define its standards.

While recognizing that the basic data are somewhat imprecise, and emphasizing the necessity for a more accurate assessment of requirements according to the individual concerned, not solely relating to a "reference" man with Western type food habits, it must be admitted that the satisfaction of requirements as defined by the FAO/WHO standards already represents an improvement, setting up a first objective to be reached. The necessity of ensuring a balanced diet must also be emphasized. The various nutrients are all important, and certain ratios between them must be respected.

As far as protein is concerned, not only must there be a balance between the various essential amino acids; there must also be a certain balance between essential and non-essential amino acids. Here again, there is no unanimity on the basic data. Some consider that, in general, the non-essential amino acids have little effect,[18] others that a satisfactory ratio between these two types of amino acids makes for some saving in protein utilization.[19]

Satisfaction of calorie requirements must remain a priority objective, so as to supply the necessary energy and promote the proper use of protein; since the quality of protein in turn plays some part in economizing on its use, it is also important to maintain the balance of amino acids in the diets (if necessary by using supplementary foods).

Difficulties arising over basic data

Difficulties arise in every field covered by the basic data: population, agricultural production, food consumption, heath and nutrition levels. Such data are non-existent or inadequate in many countries; furthermore, the data for any one country are not always consistent, owing to differences in methodology.

Caution is necessary in using the statistics, but to reject them would mean rejecting all analysis. Let us look in more detail at the data concerning assessment of food intake and nutritional level.

1. Food consumption

   a) Food consumption surveys

Food consumption surveys (i.e. sample measurements of actual food intakes) permit relatively accurate estimates of consumption.

---
18. Report of the ARC/MRC, op. cit., p. 113.
19. Kofrany, quoted by H. Bour "Les protéines en alimentation diététique humaine", op. cit.

They are few and far between, usually out-of-date, and for many countries non-existent. Too often they give average figures of little or no value. When the variance is calculated, it indicates considerable dispersion around the average. For example, studies in Cameroon, Madagascar and Burundi showed large proportions (about half) of the population consuming less than the average daily energy intake. Without knowing more about the dispersion, however, it is difficult to interpret such information. (The inequality in protein cover may differ from that in energy cover and call for special attention. In Burundi, for example, the average protein cover was 120%, but 35% of the food groups surveyed did not satisfy their requirements.)[20]

While food consumption surveys may provide accurate data for the families and periods covered, they are expensive to conduct, and can only with the deployment of very large resources give adequate data on a national sampling basis, on variations in intake among individuals or households in various categories and at various points in time. (Because of seasonal fluctuations, the latter are obviously most important.)

b) Food balance-sheet

This method permits an assessment of the per capita food supply in a region or country. Agricultural and commercial statistics (production, trade, export, import) are taken into account. Losses as well as food fed to livestock are deducted. The available energy sources may be under-estimated, as home consumption is imperfectly known. Furthermore, this balance-sheet establishes an average which is of no interest nutritionally. Apart from cases of famine, if often shows virtually satisfactory coverage, quite concealing the under-nourishment due to very unequal distribution of the available supplies.

Protein supplies are usually over-estimated because of imperfect knowledge of herd management. Here too uneven distribution may play a greater role for protein than for energy foods.

c) Household expenditure surveys

In some countries food consumption is estimated from household expenditure data. If sufficiently detailed information is gathered on expenditure on individual food items, it can be converted into consumption estimates. There are, of course, numerous problems with such estimates: apart from the usual ones of accuracy of recall, these include consumption in kind, all the difficulties of estimating nutrient intake from data on food purchased, and the distribution of intake within the household. Even where the age, sex and other relevant characteristics of household members are known, one will not know how the food is distributed within the household; a household may on average be in

---

20. J. Mondot-Bernard, op. cit.

deficit or surplus relative to requirements, but contain some individuals whose requirements are satisfied and others whose are not.

2.   Food composition tables

The absence of food composition tables giving the composition of local foods was an obstacle when the first food surveys were being made, and led to inconsistent data. Today, the FAO food composition tables, prepared from a very large quantity of data, may be used. Caution must be exercised in expressing the results for vitamins and even for minerals; vitamins sustain losses in storage and preparation - peeling, soaking and finally cooking. The study carried out on this subject by S. Le Berre in Cameroun is illuminating.[21] Mineral losses may be considerable through soaking after chopping. The present study does not cover data on vitamins or minerals, but it seems unreliable to express levels of satisfaction of vitamin requirements on the basis of raw food quantities, taking no account of losses in cooking or traditional methods of extraction.

3.   Health and nutritional diseases

Many countries are medically under-equipped. Medical statistics, when they exist, record diseases and causes of death, and are not, therefore, representative. Except in the case of notifiable diseases such as smallpox and cholera, the number of cases recorded in a hospital or medical centre seems to fall short of the real figure.

Systematic studies will be a source of reliable data. Clinical surveys on nutritional diseases indicating, in addition, the state of health of the population, will permit weighting and proper evaluation of specific diets. The majority of consumption surveys, however old, include a summary clinical survey, which is much more systematic in recent surveys (examples, Rwanda and Zambia). In the absence of other data, the level of infant and child mortality may give some indication of the presence of malnutrition since high mortality in the 0-4 age group is almost always the result of the combination of malnutrition and infection.

a)   Clinical signs

The presence of clinical signs of malnutrition may be used as a type of measurement. Indications vary in severity from acute states such as kwashiorkor or marasmus to milder skin or hair conditions. The most acute states are rarely observed in more than a tiny percentage of cases, in part because a child suffering from them is unlikely

---

21.   Orstom, Le Berre, S., Carence saisonnière en vitamine C chez les habitants du nord Cameroun et dosage vitamine C, banane plantain, tubercules après cuisson.

to survive for very long. An assessment that x per cent of children in
a given age group exhibit clinical signs of malnutrition is thus a broad
indication covering a wide variety of conditions. It must also be noted
that diagnosis can vary significantly from one clinician to another.

b) Anthropometric measures

A number of measures are used which are relatively inexpensive
to collect for large samples of a population. They include height or
weight for age, and height/weight or height/arm circumference ratios.
The main problems in their use are the definition of standards, and the
interpretation of departures from those standards. It has been common
to use the so-called 'Harvard standards' for height or weight for age,
and to describe particular percentage shortfalls from those standards
as indicating 'mild', 'moderate' or 'severe' malnutrition. But while
gross deficiences by such measures clearly indicate undernutrition, for
most countries there is a need to establish appropriate standards in
terms of their own conditions. In particular, the health consequences
of shortfalls from the standards require additional research almost
everywhere. Most studies of the effects of malnutrition have been based
on clinical observation of the acutely malnourished. Relatively little is
known about the effects of moderate departures from norms of this kind.[22]

A widely used method for infants and young children (especially
in Africa) is the growth chart, which depicts a band within which a child's
growth should lie; if regularly maintained, such a chart can give the
mother a reliable warning of incipient problems. This method, however,
requires interaction between clinics and parents, and thus a certain level
of health service development before it can be used as a form of nutritional
surveillance on a national basis.[23]

Incidence of malnutrition on requirements

1.  Interdependence of the variables: health; nutrition

Cross-effects between the two variables, health and nutrition,
are of two kinds: under-nourishment or deficient nutrition reduces the
resistance of the organism, which becomes more easily infected, but
conversely a poor state of health (parasitism, fever, malaria) influences
the nutritional state (particularly anaemia). Requirements vary with
physiological condition; marked changes are caused by serious disorders
(fevers, traumas, surgical operations ...). As regards chronic com-
plaints (parasitosis, malaria), further research is needed to ascertain

---

22.  For an exception, see Sommer and Lowenstein, American Journal of Clinical Nutrition (28), 1975.

23.  See D. Morley, Paediatric Priorities for Developing Countries, London, 1973.

the changes in requirements. This again demonstrates the importance of clinical investigations, to enable specific intakes to be properly assessed.

2. Nutrition-infection relationship; infant mortality

Scrimshaw[24] points out the need for further study of the effects of specific infectious diseases on the nutritional state, although it has already been demonstrated that most infections adversely affect it. Even slight infections increase the urinary nitrogen losses. Infection and fever reduce appetite and food tolerance; the serious diarrhoeas which often occur in sick children (intestinal infections) reduce nitrogen absorption. Children's ailments such as diarrhoea, measles and bronchitis thus greatly favour the onset of kwashiorkor and marasmus in infants whose food intake is already low in protein and sometimes in calories. Furthermore, the higher need for protein during convalescence is not satisfied.

Infection also affects vitamin and mineral metabolism. Let us take a few examples which are frequent among young children. Intestinal parasitosis causes anaemia through loss of iron (intestinal and sometimes urinary haemorrhages); repeated infections can impair iron metabolism and the formation or red corpuscles. Acute diarrhoea disturbs calcium and phosphorus metabolism.

Similarly, protein deficiencies have an aggravating effect on infectious diseases.[25] The child in a developing country whose diet is deficient in protein during the weaning period is often a victim of this aggravation, which causes a high mortality rate from certain sicknesses (diarrhoea, measles ...). Serious underfeeding is also synergetic with most infections. At a period of food scarcity or famine, illness and death is more common among children (for example: famine in the Sahel).

Vitamin A deficiency reduces resistance to infection and severe deficiency may cause blindness. Little data exists on this deficiency among young African children; certain types of diet which do not include milk, and are mainly based on pap made from tubers or cereals, tend to be poor in Vitamin A. In India the problem is of serious proportions.

Three factors are involved in infectious diseases: the pathogenic agent, the host and the environment. There are multiple interactions between these three factors. On the one hand, infection affects nutrition; on the other hand, nutritional deficiency clearly reduces the invalid's resistance to infection and its consequences.

---

24. N.S. Scrimshaw, C.E. Taylor and J.E. Gordon, <u>Interactions of Nutrition and Infection</u>, Geneva, World Health Organisation, 1971.

25. Ibid.

Conclusion

The collection of basic data must be improved. These data are generally lacking for the African Continent and most particularly in those countries and regions which are the poorest and the most affected by malnutrition. This scarcity of data is unfortunately just one more consequence of under-development and its attendant lack of personnel, roads, transportation and other facilities for data collection.

As a priority, it is necessary to identify the individual areas affected by undernourishment and malnutrition, and the causes of these, in order to be able to provide relief to those who are suffering. To do this, it is preferable to work from proven and easy-to-use indicators. In most countries more research is needed to identify the most cost-effective indicators.

## III. THE FOOD PROBLEM: ANALYSIS OF DATA

Food consumption

Available food supplies at national level

Although the data must be interpreted with the same reservations as stated previously concerning the difficulties of estimating food consumption, Table V emphasizes the disparity between developed and developing countries. It brings out the virtual non-existence of food surpluses at world level in 1970. These averages do not take account of country-to-country disparities, and still less of national disparities between rich and poor, town and country-dwellers, etc.

One of the best nutritional indicators is mortality in the 1-4 age group; in all developing countries, it is in fact infants 12 to 36 months old who are most severely affected by malnutrition. Studies by the Pan American Health Organisation[26] have shown that in Argentina, Bolivia and El Salvador mortality rates in children under five are almost twice as high in rural areas as in urban areas. The rural areas studied are near medical centres and it may be supposed that the mortality rates are even higher in backward villages. Studies carried out by the ORSTOM (French Organisation for Overseas Scientific Research)[27] in the French-speaking countries of the African continent and Madagascar lead to the same conclusion. Factors other than nutrition are also involved in 0 to 4 age group mortality. Improved medical coverage in the towns (including treatment of acute malnutrition) has a clear effect on

---

26. Ruth R. Puffer and Carlos V. Serrano, Patterns of Mortality in Childhood, p. 61.

27. Dr. P. Cantrelle, La mortalité différentielle urbain-rurale, to be published by ORSTOM.

## Table V. COMPARISON BETWEEN WORLD ENERGY REQUIREMENTS AND AVAILABLE SUPPLIES, 1961 AND "1970"

| | ENERGY REQUIREMENTS KG CALORIES PER HEAD PER DAY[1] | AVERAGE CALORIE AVAILABILITY[1] | | % COVERAGE |
|---|---|---|---|---|
| | | 1961 | AVERAGE 1969-71 | AVERAGE 1969-71 |
| North America ....... | 2,642 | 3,110 | 3,320 | +26 |
| Western Europe ..... | 2,565 | 3,020 | 3,130 | +22 |
| Oceania ........... | 2,656 | 3,210 | 3,260 | +23 |
| Others .............. | 2,363 | 2,420 | 2,550 | + 8 |
| Total for developed market-economy countries .......... | 2,555 | 2,950 | 3,090 | |
| Africa .............. | 2,335 | 2,120 | 2,190 | - 7 |
| Latin America ...... | 2,383 | 2,410 | 2,530 | + 8 |
| The Near East ...... | 2,456 | 2,200 | 2,500 | + 1 |
| Asia and the Far East. | 2,223 | 2,050 | 2,080 | - 7 |
| Total for developing market-economy countries .......... | 2,284 | 2,130 | 2,210 | |
| Asian countries with centrally planned economies .......... | 2,355 | 2,020 | 2,170 | - 8 |
| USSR and Eastern Europe ............. | 2,570 | 2,990 | 3,260 | +27 |
| World .............. | 2,385 | 2,380 | 2,480 | + 4 |

1. Most recent assessment of requirements, FAO standards.

SOURCE: Assessment of the World Food Situation Present and Future, United Nations, World Food Conference, Rome, November 1974.

this mortality. But the fact that child mortality rates are distinctly higher in rural than in urban areas proves that, at present, the rural population in developing countries suffers more from undernourishment and malnutrition than the urban population.

At national level the calorie coverage is insufficient, or barely sufficient, as illustrated by the following two examples. In India even for the average there is clearly an overall deficit, according to the FAO norm: and in Kenya the average coverage of 2,245 k-cal. is just sufficient, but calorie intake is only satisfied in 50% of the families.[28]

Food supply and distribution

As is obvious, what matters for the extent of nutritional deficiency is not only the overall supply position but its distribution, by region, by individuals, and over time. If countries are in overall deficit, there is bound to be extensive undernutrition; but as already noted, this is also frequently the case for countries in surplus. At any level of analysis, the important condition is the presence of locally available surpluses of appropriate foods; aggregate figures of per capita availability can always conceal, even at sub-regional levels, production surpluses which are not available for local purchase but are siphoned off into export or urban markets. The equality of land distribution may affect such availability: the more unequal are land-holdings, the more likely it may be that food surpluses are sold beyond the reach of nearby persons in need. It is not difficult to document the existence of local communities in average deficit, even in areas where food supplies are adequate overall.[29]

Undoubtedly the greatest difficulty in estimating the extent of undernutrition arises from the fact that most data is only in average form, without details of distribution. Since individuals differ in nutritional needs depending on age, sex, stature and activity - and even for individuals identical in these respects there may be differences in nutritional needs - it is only when one can match requirement with intake person by person that one has any accurate measure of the numbers in deficit in a given population or sample. It is rare in developing countries to have information on this basis, and as a result most published estimates of population proportions malnourished are very rough approximations, which may depart from the 'true' proportion by very large margins.

---

28. Bohdal M., Gibbs N.E. and Simmons V.K., Nutrition survey and campaign against malnutrition in Kenya, 1964-1968. Report to the Ministry of Health of Kenya on the WHO/FAO/UNICEF assisted project. WHO.

29. S. Schofield, Village Nutrition Studies: An Annotated Bibliography, Village Studies Programme, Institute of Development Studies (Sussex), 1975.

Graph 2. CALORIE AND PROTEIN COVERAGE IN INDIA

|      | Kcal. | PROTEIN/G |
|------|-------|-----------|
| 1961 | 2,093 | 53.9 |
| 1962 | 2,064 | 52.1 |
| 1963 | 1,982 | 50.7 |
| 1964 | 2,013 | 50.5 |
| 1965 | 2,123 | 53.3 |
| 1966 | 1,850 | 46.0 |
| 1967 | 1,809 | 45.2 |
| 1968 | 2,005 | 51.1 |
| 1969 | 1,984 | 49.1 |
| 1970 | 2,038 | 50.9 |
| 1971 | 2,085 | 51.4 |
| 1972 | 2,053 | 50.3 |
| 1973 | 1,886 | 47.0 |
| 1974 | 1,976 | 48.0 |

SOURCE: FAO 1976.

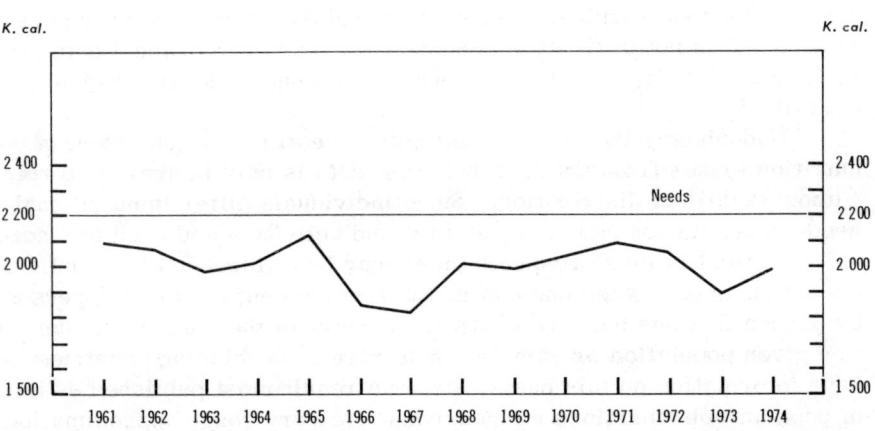

Much investigation has concentrated on particularly vulnerable groups: pregnant women, nursing mothers, infants, young children and adolescents.[30] Significant energy, protein, iron and vitamin deficiencies are commonly observed in these groups. Nutritional

---

30. FAO, Bibliography of Food Consumption Surveys, 1973; Schofield, op. cit.

stress may also arise due to fluctuations in food availability over time - year to year harvest changes, or seasonal variations.[31] It is thus important that the true causes and character of nutritional deficiency be carefully determined if policy is to succeed in remedying it.

Nutrition level and income

The few data available[32] for Brazil, Bangladesh, India, Madagascar, Pakistan and Tunisia show that calorie intake decreases with income. In India, it was estimated that in 1971[33] Indians would have to spend 26 rupees per head per month in a small town, and 47 rupees in a large town, to feed themselves satisfactorily. According to estimates by the Indian Government, 30 to 40% of the population do not have incomes allowing them to reach this essential minimum.[34] Holder estimates the cost of this minimum at 99 per rupees per month in 1974 in Calcutta; the figure falls to 60 rupees if cereal consumption is kept down to 285 g (the authorized allocation) instead of 475 g, and pulses are substituted for meat and fish.[35] In Kenya, too, incomes are very unevenly distributed; workers in the rural sector are the least well-paid, and the smaller the farm, the less they earn.[36] The considerable mobility of rural manpower means that everybody who needs to work can find work. Thus, the smallholders do not live solely on a subsistence basis; they can earn money, which is the only means whereby the poorest can raise their standard of living;[37] the calorie level is also related to income.[38] Children in Mukui, a poor area, are much more widely affected by protein-calorie malnutrition than children in the Gitonbani region, which is a rich area.[39] The same observation has been made for children in Hyderabad (India) and in Lagos.

---

31. In Kenya, Bohdal et al., op. cit., found a protein deficit occurring before harvest in 40% of families, although the diet normally included a high intake of protein from pulses.

32. United Nations World Food Conference, Assessment of the World Food Situation Present and Future, p. 60, 61, 62.

33. Source: India 1971-1972, Government Handbook.

34. Called the "poverty line".

35. Halder, K. "Planning of a Balanced Diet - Practical Considerations", Journal of the Indian Medical Association, Vol. 62, No. 7, April 1974.

36. ILO, Geneva, 1975, Employment, Incomes and Equality: A Strategy for increasing Productive Employment in Kenya, pp. 39 and 40, Tables 5, 6 and 7.

37. ILO, op. cit., p. 40.

38. Keller, W. et al., Some Observations Regarding Economy, Diet and Nutritional Status of Kikuyu Farmers in Kenya, "Different variables were correlated, it was found that the calorie adequacy of the diet was positively correlated with total cash income, income from the sale of agricultural produce, expenditure on food ... and land size".

39. Blankart, D.M., Four Village Surveys in the Coastal Area, Kwale, Kenya.

Expenditure on food absorbs about 70% of income:[40] 60 to 80% in India (town and country), more than 70% in villages, and 70% also in Kenya. No doubt food expenditure increases with income; the choice of foods varies also as income rises. In India, a national survey[41] indicates that, although total expenditure on food is higher for inhabitants in "developmental areas", they consume less grain and pulses than those in "non-developmental areas". Rice replaces millet, wheat sometimes replaces rice. Milk consumption is higher in the "developmental areas"; nevertheless, it also increases, generally speaking, with income in the "non-developmental areas". However, increased income and expenditure is not necessarily synonymous with an improved state of nutrition.

Expenditure on food has clearly increased up to a certain point,[42] which does not necessarily correspond to an adequate intake. Cross-sectional evidence suggests that although as income rises, so does expenditure on food, for families on inadequate diets quite large increases in income may be necessary if income alone is relied on for nutritional improvement.[43] This is the result of prevailing calorie-income elasticities, which may be quite low, in part because families have so many urgent needs, in part because of the substitution of less nutritious foods in the diet as income rises.

---

40. Indian Council of Medical Research, 1964. "Diet Atlas of India", Nutrition Research Laboratories. Hyderabad, Special Report Series, No. 48, 83 p. and Irving, B. Kravis and..., A system of International Comparison of Gross Product and Purchasing Power (These calculations include public expenditures).

41. National Council of Applied Research, 1967. "All India Consumer Expenditure Survey, II, Pattern of Income and Expenditure", New Delhi, 162 p. quoted by Whyte, R.O., in: Land, Livestock and Human Nutrition.

During the national consumption survey, the inhabitants of India were classified in two categories: those in developing areas and those in areas which had not yet reached this stage.

Page 21: "Developmental areas and non-developmental areas, selected respectively on the criteria of population, growth and industrial employment in the case of towns (population over 10,000), and of the extent of use of improved cultivation practices and social amenities in villages (population under 10,000). Given this definition of development, nearly 78% of the population in developmental areas is rural and 22% is urban, while for the non-developmental areas 86% of the population is rural and 14% urban".

42. Sharna, P.P., "Subsistence Crops: Consumption and Marketable Surplus", Econ. Polit. Weekly 3(49), 7th December, 1968, pp. 1879-1883.

Whyte, R.O., op. cit., p. 22, "The most striking result in the developmental areas is the increasing consumption of non-necessities, that is goods other food ... manufactured consumer goods and services".

Korte, R.: The Nutritional and Health Status of the People Living on the Miveatese Irrigation Settlement. "Improvements in economic status were not, however, synonymous with improvements in general health or nutritional status".

43. S. Reutlinger and M. Selowsky, "Malnutrition and Poverty", World Bank Staff Occasional Paper, Washington, D.C., 1976.

Nutrition level, food habits and state of knowledge

The results of different surveys, both nutritional and medical, confirm that malnutrition mainly affects children in the poor areas, but that the fact of living in or near a town seems to have a favourable influence, even among the poor.[44] In towns, such factors as better medical services, and also education, are no doubt the cause of this.

Experience in Kerala invites thought. The State of Kerala in the extreme south of India and Uttar Pradesh in the extreme north may be regarded as the two extremes of health conditions in India. There are considerable differences in the mortality rate as between the two States.

|  | KERALA[1] | UTTAR PRADESH[1] | INDIA[3] |
|---|---|---|---|
| Infant mortality ..... | 55‰ | 162‰[2] | 140‰ |
| Mortality 0-4 years . | 19% of total deaths | 35% of total deaths | |
| Illiterates | Men 33%   Women 46% | Men 78%   Women 90% | Men 61%   Women 84% |

1. Dr. Gopalan, C., "Nutrition and India's Children", Carnets de l'enfance, vol. 29, January, March 1975.
2. Lucknow, K.G., Medical College. Repeat general health survey in a group of villages in the area of rural health training centre, Sarojini Magar, Lucknow (Uttar Pradesh): "Over a period of 10 years (1958-1968) birth and death rates and infant mortality rates remained stationary, while maternal death ... was reduced".
3. India, Office of the Registrar General, Census 1971, Pocket Book of Population Statistics. The infant mortality rate is for the year 1968/69, and would be somewhat lower today.

Food supplies in Kerala are no better than in Uttar Pradesh, and there is little difference in income per head. But factors other than food availability and financial resources can play a part in the health and nutritional situation. A lower rate of child mortality, and particularly a distinctly lower mortality rate under the age of 5, indicate a better state of nutrition among children. This may be connected with the more advanced state of MCH services in Kerala, and educational levels. There are many more illiterates in Uttar Pradesh than in Kerala, especially among women (90% in the former).

---

44. Food and Nutrition in Kenya, WHO unpublished document; and Dr. Bel Haj, on nutrition of young people in Morocco in, Les carnets de l'enfance, Vol. 26, April-June 1974.

Still in India, notwithstanding the poor food situation, many children do not suffer from severe malnutrition; as indicated by Dr. Gopalan[45] this is due to the mothers' ingenuity. There is no doubt that health and nutritional education help them to take better care of their children, and to make better use of their scanty resources to good effect. One should not underestimate the extent to which poor nutrition is due to deleterious food habits, especially lack of understanding of appropriate weaning foods, and of the need for breast-milk supplementation after the second trimester.

This is a somewhat controversial point, many authors believing that poor families make optimal use of their scarce food resources.[46] There is ample evidence, however, of superstitions and folk-lore inhibiting sensible use of food.[47] This, of course, has its economic background - poor parents are commonly uneducated, and may have adopted their food habits because of conditions prevailing in the past. But it may well be possible for poor families through nutritional education to improve their nutrition without the large increases in income implied by cross-section studies of income and food expenditure.

## IV. ANALYSIS OF ACTION PROGRAMMES

### India's experience

Little specific action was taken during the First and Second Five-Year Plans, apart from the "grow more food" campaign. From the beginning of the Third Five-Year Plan, the Department of Food was made permanent: a Nutrition Division was established in the Ministry of Agriculture and Food. Many food surveys were undertaken. In 1965, the Department of Food was renamed the Food and Nutrition Board, comprising representatives of other Ministries concerned with nutrition problems, and made responsible for formulating nutrition policy and co-ordinating activities. In the same way a National Committee for Nutrition was set up in the Ministry of Health. The Third Five-Year Plan also laid the foundations for the green revolution.

Starting from the factual analysis showing:
- insufficiency of food availabilities at national level;
- unbalanced diets, in particular excessive reliance on cereals;
- presence of protein-energy malnutrition;
- presence of many vitamin deficiencies;

---

45. Dr. Gopalan, C., Nutrition and India's Children, op. cit.
46. E.g. Habicht and Butz, in R. Ridker (ed.), Population and Development: the Search for Selective Interventions, Johns Hopkins University Press, 1977.
47. E.g. Government of Haryana/CARE, Punjab Nutrition Development Project, Report, Chandigarh, 1975.

the action undertaken aimed at encouraging production and utilization of subsidiary foods so as to reduce consumption of cereals and raise the nutritive value of the diet. On the other hand, the green revolution aimed mainly at increasing cereal production.

This gave rise to various projects and programmes concerned with production of pulses and vegetables and domestic fruit and vegetable processing; all these programmes included nutrition education, and there were many school meal programmes. A beginning was also made with food research, particularly concerning high-protein foods, and with the preparation of enriched foods. During the two years of very serious drought (1965-1967), the need to give special attention to those hardest hit by the drought - the poorest people - became imperative. A new supplementary feeding programme was started for the vulnerable group of young children, pregnant women and nursing mothers.

With the Fourth Five-Year Plan, the size of the efforts in the field of nutrition became apparent: separate financing of 425.5 million rupees was provided.[48] This effort will be continued on a wide scale in the next Plan. Furthermore, all these programmes benefit from multilateral, bilateral and private foreign assistance.

Fortification of foods

From 1968 onwards the protein composition of bread was improved by the addition of lysine. This broad "modern bakery" programme was developed to increase wheat consumption, as this cereal could be imported, unlike rice. Consumption of bread increased not only in the towns but also in the countryside.

In the same way atta meal,[49] used by the poorest people in preparing "chapattis", North India's basic food, was enriched with minerals, vitamins and proteins (groundnut meal), but only townspeople benefited; the villages have their own mills and grind their own meal.

Realizing that salt was a condiment used by everybody including the poorest, the Government decided to enrich salt with iron (to control widespread anaemia), with calcium, and with iodine in regions of endemic goitre; this operation was feasible because salt production is localized and distribution could be controlled.

Tea, which is widely drunk by both rich and poor, even by children under five, was also enriched in vitamin A; other attempts were also made to increase intakes of vitamin A, deficiency of which often leads to blindness and is quite widespread.

---

48. Not including the programme of assistance to the vulnerable group managed by the Department of Social Affairs.

49. Kymal, P.K. "Fortification of Atta" and Gupta, S.K. "Protein enrichment of bread" in protein fortification of foods, Proceedings of Seminar at Jadavpur University, Calcutta, 15th-16th February, 1969; p. 84-89.

High-protein foods, weaning foods

The food industry, both private and governmental, tried to develop many high-protein foods. These products are increasingly designed to make use of the local basic foods - cereals and pulses. Among them we might mention:[50] balahar, an energy food, mainly used in supplementary feeding programmes; miltone (milk + groundnut milk), a multi-purpose food, protein concentrate enriched in vitamins and minerals; balamul, a pre-cooked food based on cereals and soya meal. These three products are on the market, but part of the production of miltone is distributed to children in health centres. Various other food are prepared, mainly in the form of snacks.

Nutrition education programmes

Nutrition education programmes were set up both to inculcate better principles of nutrition and to ensure consumption of the products developed by the food industry. Posters and films were prepared and radio broadcasting was widely used to give nutritional advice. In the education field a programme[51] on preserving fruit and vegetables was devised outside the school structure. Its aim was to fight seasonal deficiencies by getting women to preserve fruit and vegetables in the high season. A cookery course to permit them to prepare better balanced recipes was also designed for these women.

Supplementary feeding programmes

School meals, meals for children of pre-school age, pregnant women and nursing mothers.

While we do not consider the population coverage of the programme as an indication of its efficiency, there were, in 1970, 17 million beneficiaries from distribution of meals, of whom 15 million were children - not many, of course, compared with the total child population.[52] The originality of these programmes is to use local products at reasonable prices, such as balahar.

Many programme evaluations were attempted, mainly to measure the effects of the food supplement on the children's growth. They are of unequal value and do not always give any real measurement of the effect of the programme, and the reasons for failure have not always been examined.

For both young children and those of school-age, the results are unequal; in certain programmes the food supplement had an effect on

---

50. Mondot-Bernard, J., "La malnutrition fléau de la petite enfance", in Options méditerranéennes, nutrition et alimentation, No. 29, p. 78.

51. Fruit and vegetable processing.

52. India in 1971, had 41.9% population 0 to 14 years - 226.5 million.
Source: The population of India, CICRED, series 1974.

growth and in others it had none. Among the causes of failure, mention may be made of:
- evaluation made too soon after the beginning of the programme;
- an intake of k-calories which was insufficient for requirements, even including the supplement;
- the supplement was not entirely used by the children for whom it was intended, as the mother would share it among all her children; this is one of the difficulties met in the new programme of family planning and nutrition.

The experiment in the Punjab,[53] in which the children (0 to 3 years) were divided into four groups: a) control group, b) group with a nutritional supplement only, c) group with medical care and d) group with both medical care and nutritional supplement, was very significant. It led to the conclusion that a food supplement with or without medical care groups (c) and (d) produced:
- a moderate improvement in the nutritional state;
- an increased level of haemoglobin;
- a significant decrease in the mortality rate of children of 12 to 35 months.

On the other hand, medical care had little or no effect other than that produced by the nutrition programme.

Applied nutrition programmes

These programmes are widespread in India; they began in 1959 in Orissa and now exist in all the provinces. As in other countries, the programmes comprise a) nutrition education activities: lectures on the value of foods and cookery demonstrations; b) food production programmes: horticulture, small livestock, fish production; c) supplementary feeding programmes for young children, sometimes pregnant women and nursing mothers, and schoolchildren.

In 1970 the Indian Institute of Management in Ahmedabad was made responsible for the evaluation of applied nutrition programmes in India.[54] The main conclusions of this report are taken from Jean McNaughton.[55] While the number of production units increased regularly, production from community, school and family gardens remained mediocre; teachers did not recognize the full educational value of school gardens.

---

53. Narangwal Rural Health Research Centre, Interactions of Nutrition and Infection (a prospective field study on children in selected villages of Punjab), Final report to ICRM, 1972:

Schofield, Sue, Lambert C.M., Village nutrition studies, op. cit.

54. Desai G.M., and Gaikwad V.R., Applied Nutrition Programme: an Evaluation Study, Ahmedabad, Centre for Management in Agriculture, Indian Institute of Management, 1971.

55. McNaughton Jean, "Programmes de nutrition appliquée, l'expérience du passé au service de l'avenir," in Alimentation et Nutrition, Vol. 1, No.3, 1975, FAO Rome.

Feeding programmes and cookery demonstrations were of unequal value, better cooking methods were not always taught and too often the feeding programme for young children was not designed as a programme for educating the mothers. The evaluation team tried to measure the effects of the programme by comparing the feeding of children in ANP[56] villages and in a village which did not have these programmes. There was no difference and the foods recommended by the ANP were not mire in use in the one than in the other. Nevertheless, it must be recognized that the number of households growing vegetables was higher in the ANP villages. A major problem was coordination between different agencies responsible for separate parts of the programmes.

Government officials considered that the authors of the report had over-generalized on the basis of insufficient data. The evaluation team recommended turning the ANP into a national nutrition education programme for the public at large, which would particularly insist on the inclusion of such education in the school system and on the establishment of a nutrition education service. It recommended that feeding programmes be strengthened, but that they should no longer depend on the ANP.

The officials responsible for the programmes in India are fully aware that, up to this point, their efforts have not always been crowned with success and that it has not been possible to reach the poorest people. There has been a very definite improvement in dietary habits among the middle classes, even their less privileged groups.[57] Furthermore, India has acquired considerable experience in the preparation of weaning foods and supplementary foods based on local products. But it is obvious that the school meals programmes reached only a fraction of schoolchildren, and often the most privileged. There is no doubt that programmes of the "modern bakeries" type are sophisticated and benefit middle-class town-dwellers. Weaning foods are bought by those who can afford them, and free distribution remains small compared with needs.

Lessons to be learned from nutrition action programmes

Programmes of the same type as those in India have been carried out in many countries in Africa, Latin America and Asia. As in India, the results are uneven. Everywhere the school meals programmes and even those for feeding pre-school children have reached only a small number of the children exposed to malnutrition. In 1973-1974 in Kenya

---

56. Applied Nutrition Programme.
57. J. Mondot-Bernard, mission in India, May 1975.

90,000 meals[58] were served to children of school age. In the same year 1,824,220[59] children were attending school. In Thailand in 1968[60] it was not possible to determine how many primary and secondary schools served meals; few primary schools seemed to serve them - in a sample of 340 secondary schools, 248 replied to the questionnaire on this subject and only 105 of them served meals. At the same time 60% of children of 7-18 years were attending school. Could it be otherwise, given the poor resources and the need to train staff?

It is not merely the small number of meals served that must be criticized, but the ephemeral character of the programmes, depending too much on external resources, including foods unknown in the country concerned and difficult to produce; these programmes are then incapable of calling forth individual effort. On the other hand, certain school meals programmes are of undoubted and lasting value in improving the nutritional state of the whole family. They serve well-balanced meals based on local products and are genuinely linked with nutrition education, not only of the children but also of the parents.[61] We might mention among these the programmes in the Philippines and Taiwan.

The criticism levelled at certain school meals programmes applies even more to milk distributions in medical centres, when these are not combined with nutrition education courses for the mothers, showing them how to supplement the ration with local foods.[62] Sometimes the education of the mothers and the health personnel has been too theoretical and nutrition courses have been conducted in a vacuum without any real support;[63] our own experience was that such classes, both for adults and for schoolchildren, were not always suitable.[64]

In Gabon, in connection with a pilot project for a food education campaign, we observed that the results obtained were more significant in areas where there were "maisons familiales" (family centres). This was due to the continuation of remedial action through the young Gabonese women trained in the "maisons familiales" (same method)

---

58. Source: Institute for development studies, University of Nairobi, Food and nutrition strategies for Kenya and WHO document, op. cit.

59. UNESCO Statistical Yearbook 1,816,017 first level, 8,203 second level.

60. Mondot, J.M., Nutrition Education in schools, FAO, WHO, UNESCO, UNICEF. Consultant mission in Burma, Cambodia, Indonesia, Pakistan, Philippines, Taiwan and Thailand, 1968-1969.

61. The parents in this case come to evening school once or twice a week.

62. Bailey, K.V. "Supplementary Feeding Programmes for Pre-School Children (an Overview)". Nutrition Programmes for Pre-School Children (Reports of a conference ...), edited by Derrick B. Jelliffe and E.F. Patrice Jelliffe, p. 187.

63. Fall, Ibrahima, "Matrones et maternités rurales au Sénégal", in Les Carnets de l'enfance, No. 28, October-December 1974, p. 28.

64. Mondot, J.M., Nutrition Education in Schools, FAO, WHO, ... mission already referred to.

who pass on to other village women what they have learned,[65] (alternation of teaching sessions on a given subject followed by application in the village). However, the mothers do not always apply the principles learned, either through lack of resources or because they are not really convinced.

In the nutritional rehabilitation centres the child receives hospital care. Throughout the treatment the mother prepares her child's food and at the same time receives nutrition education. She participates in all the related activities gardening, cookery, etc. This type of programme has given good results. The mother sees the good effect of balanced feeding on her child and therefore knows that it is the food which has cured him. An evaluation made in Haiti[66] showed that in addition to the positive results obtained in the centre itself, the population acquired better dietary habits in their homes. These programmes are not very numerous and exist mainly in Latin America. There are even fewer in Asia and Africa. We might mention the example of the Philippines (Cebu), Dahomey and more recently Upper Volta. Although these centres are less costly than "clinics", the cost is still high when compared with the possibilities of national nutrition budgets and the capabilities of local communities.[67]

The applied nutrition programmes were aimed at promoting coordinated action in education, food production (garden, small livestock, fish production) and child feeding – thus making the community able to feed itself.

Results have been uneven and related very strongly to the specific country conditions. In Mauritania, it was very difficult to promote school gardens owing to the frequent shortage of water. In Gabon the major constraint was perhaps the fact that work on the land is considered of little value, not to say even degrading.[68] In that case the lack of qualified staff makes the launching of the programme difficult. Some programmes only obtained good results when adequate supervision was assured by technical assistance staff.[69] Successful production did not always improve the family diet because the output was sold to the neighbouring town, as indicated by Gjorgy.[70]

---

65. Mondot, J.M., Développement de l'éducation alimentaire et de l'économie familiale, rapport au gouvernement du Gabon, FAO, No. AT2469, 1968.

66. King, K.W., Beghin, I.D., Fougere, W., Dominique, W., Grinker, R., and Foucauld, J. Two-Year Evaluation of a Nutritional Rehabilitation (Mother Craft) Centre, Arch. Venez. Nutr. 18:245, 1969, quoted by K.W. Bailey.

67. Bailey, K.W., "Supplementary Feeding Programmes for Pre-School Children", op. cit., p. 188.

68. Consequence of colonialism.

69. Gjorgy, Paul, "Previous Experience Nutrition Programmes for Pre-School Children", op. cit., p. 33.

70. Ibid.

Among successful projects, the one in the Philippines seems a good example.[71] At each school meal a soup made of garden vegetables was served to the children, who took turns in preparing the meals. Fifty per cent of the flourishing garden production was used by the canteen and 50% sold, the money obtained being used for the improvement of school equipment. Home gardens are numerous and well-kept, and the agricultural instructor from the school acts as adviser to the families.[72] The children leave school early once a week in order to work in the family gardens. There was another very successful experiment in Indonesia.[73] In remote villages, the primary school was transformed into a small farm, 60% of the time-table being reserved for agricultural work (crop-growing, livestock and fish production), and 40% for traditional teaching (the school results of the children in these schools were no worse than those of pupils in traditional type schools).

Concluding remarks on action programmes

a) In their present form many supplementary feeding programmes designed for children of school age and nursing mothers, as well as schoolchildren, have little effect in themselves for one or more of the following reasons:

    i) the number of people reached is small in relation to those in need;

    ii) food supplements do not affect the intake of target groups, e.g. because children fed at school receive less at home;

    iii) insofar as the effort is to improve protein intake, it may fail because energy requirements are not met, and additional proteins are simply consumed in calories. This implies that the distribution of special protein-enriched foods may be ill-considered in itself: provided the protein proportion in the normal diet is adequate, what is essential is to raise the level of intake of that diet, which will usually be less expensive than the specially-prepared foods;

    iv) health factors - especially gastro-intestinal disease - may reduce the efficacy of feeding programmes;

    v) the programmes do not prepare recipients for self-sufficiency and are effective, if at all, only while they last.

b) The "applied nutrition programme" approach combines the appropriate elements of a more effective strategy: nutrition education, increased local production of relevant foodstuffs, and supplementary feeding programmes as demonstration measures and short-term

---

71. Mondot J., Report to the Government of the Philippines, FAO, 1972, CEP report No. 66, p. 12-13.

72. They have one half-day off a week to prepare their report on family visits.

73. Mondot J., Report to the Government of Indonesia, FAO, 1972.

interventions before self-reliance is attained. But these more comprehensive measures have not always been successful either – also for a variety of reasons:
  i) inadequate staff training, and
  ii) related to it, lack of coordination between central and local authorities and between agencies (agriculture ministries, health or education ministries) at all levels;
  iii) inadequate incomes;
  iv) entrenched food habits and the difficulty of gaining acceptance for better nutritional practices even when families can afford them.

(The problems of supplementary feeding programmes listed above naturally also affect such programmes when they are part of more comprehensive strategies. This can be particularly troublesome when they are incorporated for their demonstration effect.)

## V. CONCLUSION – A NEWER APPROACH TO FOOD AND NUTRITION PLANNING AS PART OF RURAL DEVELOPMENT PLANNING

It should be clear from the foregoing that the record of partial intervention is not very encouraging, though, as noted, some limited successes have been achieved here and there. Very clearly the prescription for doing better will vary from country to country.

Nevertheless, also to varying degrees, numerous variables will affect the design of a plan for food and nutrition; they have been pointed out in the course of this paper.

Some examples

As a starting point, two or three examples can be mentioned. They are still at the study stage and have not yet been put into effect.

In Zambia, the Government, desirous of improving the nutritional level of its people, applied to FAO [74] to collect the data needed for the development of its food policy. A household consumption survey and a clinical nutritional survey were undertaken. The results of the consumer survey in rural areas, together with the previous surveys, were used to determine consumption for the base year 1971. Projection of the food demand of the population to the horizons 1976 and 1980 was based on the elasticity of demand, taking account of the analysis of trends in supply of food products (local production and imports) over the previous years and the expected increase in income per head.

The population was divided into five groups with different characteristics:

---

74. National Food and Nutrition Programme, Zambia, April 1970 to April 1973.

Group I. : Non-african population;
Group II. : African urban population;
Group III. : Non-agricultural wage-earners in small townships;
Group IV. : Agricultural wage-earners;
Group V. : Rural population dependent on a subsistence economy.

In this study,[75] evaluation of the nutritional value of projected food consumption shows that there is practically no improvement in the calorie intake for Group V, whose diet will provide only 1,950 k-calories in 1976 and 1,975 k-calories in 1980.

Although the calorie level increases by 9 to 10% for groups III and IV, the intake will still be hardly sufficient in 1980 (compared with the requirements calculated according to the 1973 FAO standards). The intake for the African urban population will also hardly reach this level.

The study came to the clear conclusion that the subsistence farmer is the worst fed, for he does not have the necessary resources to produce enough, and is unable to purchase food. Conversely, the most deprived townspeople can only feed themselves properly if they obtain part of their food through barter or by producing it themselves.

In Algeria, the Government became interested in the problem of planning agricultural development in relation to the food needs of the population in 1967, when it was decided to prepare the First Five-Year Plan (1970-1975). At the request of the Ministry for Industry and Energy, a study[76] was undertaken to determine the growth of the various industrial sectors required by the potential development of agricultural production to the horizon of 1980. There were no specific basic data to determine the food ration of the individual Algerian. The figure of 2,180 k-calories per day per head was adopted, and the study concluded that Algeria imports as many k-calories as it produces. In the final report, forecasts were made for a population of 19,035,000 inhabitants in 1980 on the basis of a ration of 2,600 k-calories per day.[77] In 1973, the base year for the Second Five-Year Plan, the Planning Directorate in the Ministry for Agriculture and Agrarian Reform (MARA) commissioned a study to examine the food situation in Algeria.[78] The study

---

75. National Food and Nutrition Programme, Zambia, op. cit.

76. Algeria: Ministère de l'Industrie et de l'Energie, développement industriel et production agricole. Grenoble, Université de Grenoble, Institut Economique et Juridique de l'Energie, 1969, 2 volumes.

77. Details of ration: Développement industriel ... op. cit. Tables pages 422 and 425.

78. Algeria: Ministry of Agriculture and Agrarian Reform, Planning Directorate, Division for Statistics and Economic Surveys, The Food Situation in Algeria and the Food and Nutrition Objectives of the Second Five-Year Plan 1974-1977 and Short-Term Forecasts to 1980.

defines "a desirable intake" as 2,500 k-calories, 70 g of protein, 60 g of lipids.[79] At a moderate rate of growth, the desirable nutritional targets would not be reached until 1990.[80] Is this objective feasible? The first two agricultural seasons of the Second Plan have been completed. Official statistics are not available. The Algerians are anxious, and in January 1975, the Ministry for Finance declared: "We are eating one-third of our oil (that is to say oil revenue) in food products.[81]

Various surveys to improve the data are still under way, including evaluation of losses between harvesting and storage.

A study by Smith[82] in Nigeria should also be mentioned here. It was not taken into account in the actual Nigerian plan.

Food and nutrition planning

None of these studies did or could include all the relevant variables. Some of them are indeed part of the overall development policy of the countries concerned; these lack essential data. For purposes of food and nutrition planning, the necessary steps would seem to be:

A. Assessment of food consumption at country level in 10 or 15 years

Obviously in any context the first problem is the identification of the nutritionally deprived and the character of their situation. As was noted above, there are considerable problems of measurement and interpretation, and in most countries, research may be required to establish sensitive and practical nutritional indicators. This should not be taken to imply that no action can be taken until better measurement is available. The purpose of better measurement is to make possible more discriminating intervention, but where malnutrition is obviously widespread - as indicated, for example, by high levels of pre-school age mortality - it is not necessary to suspend all activity pending the availability of precise information. The nature and causes of the

---

79. Ibid., p. 14.

80. Annual growth of 4.5 to 6.4% per annum according to the product. In the light of population growth, these represent an improvement of 1-2.9% per annum in the individual ration.

81. Smith, Pamela Ann, "Algeria Stresses Long-Term Objectives for Agriculture" in The Middle East Economic Digest, London, 23 May, 1975.

82. Smith, Victor, E., Efficient resources use for tropical nutrition: Nigeria, Division of Research, Graduate School of Business Administration, Michigan State University, East Lansing, 1975.

nutrition problem must be understood, however, if false remedies are not to be applied.

With due precautions, the next step is:
i) <u>determination as far as possible of a standard intake</u>, based on nutritional needs and taking into account the population characteristics at the given horizon year;
ii) <u>determination of a target ration</u>, calculated not in nutrients but in foods expressed in kg/year supplying nutrients. This <u>intake must be feasible and acceptable</u>. It must take account of the country's food habits (it is better to modify these slightly so as to balance the intake rather than make sweeping changes), and the agricultural possibilities of the country or area considered;
iii) <u>determination of food tonnage needed for the country as a whole</u>. Minimum global supplies should equal: human consumption + losses + seed + livestock consumption. If requirements are only just covered, this implies that the supplies are shared out equally;
iv) <u>applying the global data</u>. To work out the figures reached for each country, further data are essential: specifically, demographic data; food intake and state of nutrition according to regions (urban/rural), socio-economic groups and vulnerable groups; supplies, production and imports; and in most developing countries, ecological areas.

B. Policy decisions

Basic policy choice is the choice between growing food or importing it. The nutritionist intervenes when a decision is being made as to which food crops will ensure a balanced diet for the population;[83] the choice is made with the agriculturalist who assesses the cropping possibilities. <u>However, any increase in local agricultural output is a function of rural development</u>. The objective must be to increase agricultural production or other resources in poor rural areas in developing countries with the co-operation of the people themselves.[84]

Another vital policy concerns food distribution in order to ensure <u>fair distribution</u>. For a long time, nutritional intervention was seen mainly in terms of supplying a missing ingredient; but now that the lessons of attempts along these lines are fairly clear, and the potential

---

83. Bearing in mind the basic food habits of the population.

84. See e.g. U. Lele, The Design of Rural Development, World Bank Research Publication, Washington, D.C., 1976; M. Lipton, Why Poor People Stay Poor. Urban bias in economic development, London, 1977.

failings of "vertical" nutrition campaigns apparent,[85] responsibility for nutrition work still lies uneasily between agriculture, health and education agencies. The planner's problem is essentially to place nutrition objectives for particular groups within the context of overall development planning in these fields and the national plan as a whole.

It would make no sense to attempt to review here all the relevant interconnections; but the illustration of their nature shows an important truth about nutrition planning: it is partly a matter for specific interventions, and partly a matter to be borne in mind by planners when other topics (especially in agriculture and health) are under consideration.

The necessity for such an approach arises in part from the complexity of the nutrition problem as already discussed, but in part also from the dangers of expecting other processes of development to improve nutrition. Income growth is far from being enough. The spread of towns and cities often destroys important agricultural land, market gardens; family gardens, etc.[86] In the great majority of cases, the poor, the unemployed in both town or country, landless peasants and smallholders continue to be ill-fed.

Free food distribution, however indispensable in cases of famines, is no solution to the problem. The solution lies in converging policies. Nutritional progress can only be planned for if the test of its effect on nutrition is applied to all relevant aspects of development, and if specific nutrition interventions are related to the rest of the development. This consideration, together with the connection between nutrition, work capacity, health and fertility decline may provide pragmatic grounds for what should, even without such support, be accepted as a major goal of any economic plan; namely a guarantee of nutritional adequacy for the entire population.

---

85. The main exceptions are cases where minor nutrients observed to be lacking in diets can be introduced into foods of mass consumption, such as iron, vitamin A, etc.

86. See e.g., L. Malassis, "Agriculture et développement", Monde Développement, No. 2, Paris, 1973, for experience in Algeria; National Food Nutrition Programme Zambia, op. cit., p. 55.

# 4

HEALTH

by

Robert Cassen

## I. INTRODUCTION

There can be few fields in which provision has fallen short more severely than in health. While much has been learned in recent years of the progress that can be made with modest resources, many developing countries are not even moving in promising directions. The conditions which have to be coped with are well known: high mortality, especially in the early years of life; the widespread prevalence of malnutrition; poor hygiene, sanitation and water supply; and their concomitants of infectious and parasitic diseases. A great deal of progress has been made all over the world with the control of communicable diseases, though much still remains to be done. But several countries today are experiencing a slow-down in the decline of mortality as some of the relatively simple and inexpensive forms of disease control which have been tried reach the point of diminishing returns, and the more intractable conditions receive little remedy.

The reasons for this state of affairs are many; one should not underestimate the intractability of the problems even if the measures to meet them are exceptionally well designed. But the fact is that health planning in the past has not been well designed in most countries - in relation to the objective of improving the health conditions of the whole population, rather than a part of it, it has hardly even been attempted, except in a few places. In many developing country health budgets, 40, 50 or even 60% of government health expenditures are concentrated on main hospitals in urban centres, serving a small fraction of the population with curative care, while in rural areas such facilities and personnel as there are engage in a virtually hopeless struggle, attempting to cure the sick while doing next to nothing to alter the environment which generates sickness. Much health planning incorporates three basic defects: a neglect of non-medical aspects of health; within medical services, an excessive concentration on curative medicine; and within curative services, a socially and geographically selective bias. As in other fields covered by this book, plans for health often

start from statements about desirable levels of provision for the
population as a whole; these turn out to be beyond the means of the
government, and some elements are then selected for concentration of
resources. The common result is decent services for the few, tolerable
services for the less poor urban dwellers, and grossly inadequate
conditions for almost everyone else.

A plan which started out with the ambition of bringing good health
conditions to the population as a whole would have different priorities.
It would look to the nutritional status of the population above all; it
would concern itself with water supply and conditions of hygiene and
sanitation; it would put preventive medicine on a sound footing; and
it would work towards a structure of skill-levels in health manpower,
and an organisational structure in health facilities, which would have
sufficiently low unit costs to bring curative care within the reach of
all. Nutrition is of such major importance that it is treated on its own
in this book. What are traditionally known as health services are
discussed first, not so much because of their priority but because they
have a major function in coordinating all the activities which should
properly comprise a health plan, and because they are valued in themselves as part of fundamental needs.

## II. HEALTH SERVICES

An appropriate health system must respect both the need for
universal access and the limitations of costs. It will thus require four
main levels of services to which different types of functions, personnel
and facilities correspond. Primary care must be provided both at the
level of the lowest unit, the village or community, and also with somewhat greater sophistication at what (in most developing countries) is
usually called a "health centre" - a facility shared by several communities, where simple operations may be carried out, more advanced
diagnostic tests conducted, and sometimes in-patient treatment made
available. These two levels of services will be responsible for many
preventive, promotive and educational activities. Beyond them should
be found secondary and tertiary care, provided by 'District' and
'Regional/National' hospitals respectively; these also may have further,
non-traditional functions in new types of health systems, as will be
mentioned below.

The question of standards is critical. The higher the "quality"
of urban hospitals, and the closer they approximate in staff and equipment to the most "advanced" hospitals in the world, the more resources they will absorb - and the less will remain for other things.
If health centres or more peripheral facilities have to be staffed by
doctors with six years' training, that too takes resources away from
activities which could reach more people. When suggestions are made

to developing-country governments that their need for training facilities for medical auxiliaries is greater than that for additional places in traditional medical schools, or that there are more urgent needs than the latest in radio-active immuno-assay laboratories, the rejoinder is often that 'second class medicine' is not wanted - why should developing countries not have the best available in modern medicine? But what in fact is the best? If the best medical services are those which make the maximum impact on the health of the largest number of people, that is an entirely different criterion by which expenditure should be guided. Quality in medicine may be judged in terms of technical sophistication; but it may also, and perhaps should more often, be judged in relation to its impact on the health of the population as a whole. Then what matters is not the technology, or prolonged training of personnel, but the appropriateness of the medical system in general to the needs and resources of each country. There are growing doubts in the developed countries about the fitness of our advanced medical technology and forms of health service organisation and professional structures relative to our needs. Their adoption in developing countries has frequently proved to be a real misfortune.

These preliminary remarks make it clear that the place to start for health planners is not a manpower projection related to population trends and to "desirable" ratios of health personnel to population. There will prove to be some such ratios - but they should be discovered from an examination of the character and distribution of services that can be developed within the bounds of existing resources, not adopted from any internationally established norms or the practice of other countries. As far as medical services are concerned, the point of departure must be the method of delivering primary medical care to the mass of the people. Once that has been determined, other things will fall relatively easily into place.

### III. PRIMARY CARE

The health needs of poor, rural populations include attention to nutrition, water supply, sanitation and hygiene, as well as to preventive and curative medicine. But the greater the scarcity of resources, the more important becomes the role of the local community. A relatively rich country may be able to afford all manner of government programmes, financed out of taxation, and bringing services to the population through the activities of government departments. The local authority provides piped water to households, the education department provides educational facilities, health services provide medical facilities, a host of regulating legislation and government inspection ensures the level of sanitation and hygiene; most things that the government does not do, the majority of individuals can afford

to do for themselves. In these circumstances, health conditions - at
least for the majority - are likely to be good; health problems can be
addressed by a network of doctors, clinics and hospitals; and a constant
flow of material through the communications media draws attention to
health risks and methods of self-care. It may be many decades before
the poorer developing countries are sufficiently advanced economically
for government departments to supply the essentials needed for health.
The local community must be involved in measures necessary for its
own health - it possesses, in its own labour, the main resource available for satisfying health needs. A key function of community health
workers must therefore be to involve local people in working to
improve their own health. But the capacity of health workers to
stimulate action is likely to be importantly connected to the services
they provide. An account of everything that is comprehended under
"primary care" therefore begins with the curative activities of the health
personnel who actually treat patients at the local level.

In a far-sighted book published in 1966, Maurice King[1] laid down
some principles for medical services in developing countries. "Axiom
five" was:

> "Patients should be treated as close to their homes as possible
> in the smallest, cheapest, most humbly staffed and most
> simply equipped unit that is capable of looking after them
> adequately".

Curative services based on such a principle would look very
different from those that currently exist in many developing countries.
As noted above, most health planning has not started out with an
objective of giving high priority to provision of services of this kind.
A typical developing-country health service would have hospitals in
some urban centres, some smaller rural district hospitals, and a
scatter of rural health centres manned by doctors and auxiliary staff.
Beyond these would be dispensaries, and other health-service personnel,
some of them located in villages. But, for the common problems of
daily health care, the majority of rural populations would be out of reach
of this public network, geographically or financially or both. In real
emergencies they might travel to the health centre; otherwise they would
tend to depend on traditional practitioners or whatever was available
nearby. Research suggests that the effective radius of a rural health
centre is of the order of 5 miles at most. Rural health centres (RHCs)
are commonly established to serve populations of 10-100,000; their
efficacy as providers of primary care will depend a great deal on the
network of other units and personnel that operate under their supervision. Within the area in which the RHCs themselves provide effective
care there are likely to be social or other forms of selectivity of
access.

---

1. King M., Medical Care in Developing Countries, Oxford University Press, Nairobi, 1966.

From this can be seen the critical importance of the provider of primary care, whom we shall call the "basic health worker" (BHW). If someone is to attend to the daily health needs of a poor population, as well as fulfil other tasks, he or she cannot work satisfactorily for a population greater than 500-2,000. It is immediately clear that a BHW cannot be a doctor, in the sense of a man or woman with several years of medical training at university level. Few developing countries could afford doctors on such a scale; the costs of their training and the pay they can command prohibits it. It is also clear that this person does not have to be a doctor. The great majority of ailments occurring in poor rural areas can be diagnosed and treated by someone of relatively modest training with modest equipment and medical supplies. As far as curative medicine is concerned, the BHW needs to be able to recognize and treat the commonly occurring conditions and to recognize also those he cannot cope with and must refer elsewhere. His or her training should also permit the BHW to provide education and leadership to the local community in matters of nutrition, sanitation, hygiene and other health needs including preventive activities and water supply improvement and maintenance.

A number of countries have had experience with such BHWs, a few comprehensively, some experimentally. The best known are China's barefoot doctors, but there are many different possible types of BHW, and many possible forms of organisation within which they can work. The work of China's barefoot doctors has been frequently described elsewhere. They are chosen from their own communities, selected by their fellows for qualities of energy, skill and commitment. Although they train for an initial period of only three months, frequently in a nearby commune or other local hospital, they return for subsequent short training courses and are also periodically supervised by more highly trained doctors, especially during the first period of their work. They commonly return to their original occupation in the commune, be it agricultural labour or whatever, but they receive "work points" for medical work on the basis of which they are paid, as for any other paid activity. (A similar but slightly different system, both in terms of length of training, nomenclature, etc., operates in offices or factories in urban areas.) Western observers who have interviewed barefoot doctors have been impressed by their capabilities. They are trained in both Western and traditional Chinese medicine, can identify and treat the common ailments in their communities, and competently assess conditions which they cannot treat themselves. They carry simple equipment and supplies of drugs including antibiotics and other preparations only obtainable in the West by doctor's prescription, but excluding highly

---

2. Horn J., Away With All Pests, Monthly Review Press, New York, 1969; Quinn J.R. (ed.), Medicine and Public Health in the People's Republic of China, US Dept. of Health, Education and Welfare, National Institutes of Health, Washington D.C., 1973.

toxic drugs. And, of course, they also have a major role in promoting good community health practices in nutrition, sanitation and so forth.

Many people have questioned how much the performance of these BHWs is related to the social and economic circumstances of contemporary China, and consequently whether the experience is transferable to other countries. The answer is not simple. As already suggested, primary care by itself cannot have much impact on health if it only cures people to return them to a thoroughly unhealthy environment. Many of the successes of China in the health field are attributable only partly if at all to health workers as such. Good general standards of nutrition are to a major extent the result of agricultural productivity and egalitarian income distribution. There have been major campaigns against important health hazards - rats, flies and other pests, for example - and against specific diseases. Health workers have contributed to these campaigns; but their success stemmed mainly from China's form of social organisation and its ability to generate mass participation in public activities. A famous example was the campaign against schistosomiasis in the late 1950's, in which large bands of workers joined forces in areas of endemicity to exterminate snails carrying the disease-parasite. They went to extraordinary lengths to drain large expanses of water, overturn soil-beds, burn vegetation and so forth. Since then the disease has remained well under control, or so it has been claimed.

Obviously there are few countries where the necessary social discipline prevails to achieve such ends. People had first to be instructed in the nature of the schistosomiasis life-cycle and the role of the snail-hosts; then organised over huge areas to work for their elimination; then instructed yet again in the appropriate measures of vigilance to prevent the return of the disease. There have been few examples of such mass campaigns in non-socialist developing countries. It is undeniable that a high degree of social discipline is a great advantage for participatory public health measures. All this does not mean, however, that other countries have nothing to learn from China's experience, or from those other countries that have attempted similar things in different circumstances. We shall give a brief account[3] of Tanzania's experiments, going beyond the primary-care level, and then recount some other examples of promising primary-care systems.

At independence in 1961, Tanzania inherited a post-colonial structure of health services fairly typical for Africa. The population was about 10 million. There were a hundred hospitals, most of them small, with a total of 11,000 hospital beds, and about 1,000 rural dispensaries. On a per capita basis, the inhabitants of Dar es Salaam enjoyed a wholly disproportionate share of health personnel, facilities and government health expenditure.

---

3. Our account is heavily dependent on Gish O., Planning the Health Sector: the Tanzanian experience, Croom Helm, London, 1975. See also Segall M., The Politics of Health in Tanzania, Journal of Development Studies.

Expenditure was also heavily biased towards curative and in-patient care. Despite planning and policy documents which indicated a desire for change, little was actually done to alter these biases until the early 1970's, when a new health plan was developed. Its starting point was the desirable network of basic health facilities and staffing for rural areas; when allowance was made for a reasonably rapid creation of RHCs and associated staff and satellite dispensaries, new hospital expenditure was treated as a residual. A key feature of the new plan was the staffing patterns to be developed which would lead to a radical change in the health service of proportions of manpower to be employed at different skill levels, and incorporate a redefinition of their functions and training.

The four basic tiers of health personnel are the village health worker (VHW), rural medical aide (RMA), the medical assistant (MA), and the university-qualified practitioner, or doctor. The VHW is not yet as firmly established in the official health system as the other grades; they have most often been recruited for work in "ujamaa" villages, though they exist elsewhere. They receive approximately six months training in local hospitals, after which they return to the village: their fundamental activity is supposed to be to promote health education generally and environmental sanitation in particular, as well as first aid work and the dispensing of simple medicaments. The RMA is trained for 3 years, and must have primary education to age 12 to begin training. The RMA "will function as the Tanzanian general practitioner, the health worker who will offer first medical contact to the bulk of Tanzanians when they fall sick, or assist in the preventive and promotive work intended to keep them from becoming ill."[4] RMAs are intended to take charge of dispensaries where, together with maternal and child health (MCH), the following functions will be discharged:

"1. treatment of simple diseases and short illnesses by outpatient care;
2. initial treatment of serious illness pending referral to a rural health centre or hospital;
3. after care, if required, of patients discharged from hospital;
4. participation in immunization and community health programmes, including control schemes for communicable diseases by mass treatment, e.g. tuberculosis, leprosy, etc.;
5. maternal and child health work, including ante-natal, delivery and post-natal care".

The training of the RMA is extremely practical, confined to the knowledge necessary for diagnosis and treatment only of the commonest prevailing conditions; they may use flow charts for diagnosis until they

---

4. Gish, op. cit., p. 107.

gain experience.[5] The emphasis is on the necessity to work accurately and quickly - there may be no more than five minutes for each patient on a busy day. The next grade up is similarly designed for practicality: the MA also has only three years' training, but the previous qualification is a minimum of secondary schooling up to age 15. The MA's work is mainly to direct a Health Centre, whose functions are rather like those of the dispensary, but somewhat more sophisticated, including laboratory testing, and also a limited amount of in-patient care. With an additional 18 months' training the MA can perform simple surgery such as appendectomies or caesarean sections, either in the Health Centre or, more usually, the District Hospital. It is evident that Tanzania has set itself to train and employ health manpower on a basis which reflects the priorities of rural health and the resources available. The university-trained doctor is now seen in a different role: as a supervisor of his less intensively trained colleagues; as a team leader, especially for preventive work; and as a practitioner working in hospitals. The health ministry no longer feels an obligation to train doctors to work in private urban practices though that is what many doctors in Tanzania still do. But the changing shape of medicine can be seen from the following table.

Provided that these health workers can do the job (an important proviso), the economics of such choices makes obvious sense. An RMA cost about £425 to train in 1971 and had a salary scale of £220-415 a year; a fully qualified doctor's training cost £14,250, and his salary was £975-1,685. (The corresponding figures for the MA are £580 and £440-830.) In other words, the training costs (and these figures exclude the cost of prior schooling) of the RMA and MA are a very small fraction of the cost of a doctor's training, and the salaries a quarter to a half that of a doctor. The meaninglessness of the old WHO recommendation for Africa of 1 doctor per 10,000 population is obvious. As we have already suggested, the whole notion of such ratios as pertaining to numbers of countries is misleading. The ratios should arise from a designed health system which on the basis of available resources can provide access to care for the great majority of the people within a reasonably short period of time. The use of these earlier ratios as indices of progress should by now be discredited. (What are needed instead are ratios of services to population.) In Tanzania's case, the lowest level of workers, the BHWs, represents a particular problem in view of the scattered nature of the population - their future development will depend on the progress of the "villagisation" programme. It is no doubt partly for this reason that the main emphasis has been on the hospital/health centre/dispensary network and its associated personnel.

---

5. The development of diagnostic flow-charts is gaining ground elsewhere too, and is the subject of considerable WHO activity.

Table VI. MEDICAL PRACTITIONERS IN TANZANIA: INDEPENDENCE TO 1973

|  | 1961 | 1970 | 1971 | TRAINING INTAKE | 1972 | TRAINING INTAKE | 1973 | TRAINING INTAKE | 1974-1980 PLANNED ANNUAL TRAINING INTAKE |
|---|---|---|---|---|---|---|---|---|---|
| Graduate doctors | 403[1] | 489 | 479 | 48 | 494[2] | 48 | 533 | 64 | 64[3] |
| Assistant medical officers | 32 | 100 | 115 | 22 | 140 | – | 140 | 24 | 35[4] |
| Medical assistants | 200 | 285 | 289 | 115 | 335 | 146 | 335 | 201 | 210–250[5] |
| Rural medical aides | 380 | 473 | 544 | 124 | 578 | 146 | 621 | 338 | 560[5] |

1. Of the total: 35% in government service; 20% employed by the voluntary agencies (missions); and 45% in private practice. Of the 403 medical graduates only 12 were citizens.
2. Of the total: 62% in government service; 23% employed by the voluntary agencies; and 15% in private practice. Of the 494 medical graduates, 195 were citizens.
3. Does not include students going to Cuba for a 7-year course in medicine.
4. Biennial intake.
5. Wastage from training approximately 15%.

SOURCE: Gish, 1975.

We have spent some time on Tanzania because it represents a fairly thoroughgoing attempt to revise the structure of health manpower, and is fairly well documented. There are, of course, a large number of countries where medical auxiliaries are employed in one capacity or another as a deliberate measure to circumvent the shortage of doctors. These have been described in various sources,[6] and we will not discuss them in detail here, but will outline the basic types of manpower and functions, and the apparent lessons that can be learned. Iran in 1964 created the Health Corps, medical-school and high-school graduates performing substitute military service, working in semi-mobile units mainly in remote rural areas. In a few years, this Corps is said to have doubled the number of rural inhabitants with access to outpatient care. Current developments include the fostering of new types of primary health workers, such as rural nurse/midwives and male health workers operating health posts as satellites to health centres where doctors and Corps men provide higher-level services. The BHWs in this case work and train intermittently for 2 years, with a good deal of attention to communicable disease work (malaria, tuberculosis), immunization, environmental sanitation and so forth.[7]

In the Niger, rural health work has been attempted as a form of extension work, with village health workers and "traditional birth attendants" co-operating with rural extension and literacy services in the development od curative and preventive services. The village health workers run "village pharmacies"; and they are chosen by the villagers from volunteers.[8] Supervisory visits are made from higher-level units, especially in the early years of the new pharmacy. Countries where documented schemes similar to some or other of the above have been tried, either in pilot projects or on a wider basis, include Ghana, Ivory Coast and Nigeria; some East African countries; India, Sri-Lanka and Indonesia; Guatemala, Costa Rica, Jamaica and Venezuela. But in most non-socialist countries developments of this kind are extremely limited in coverage.

Most of these schemes have common features, and common conditions of success or failure. The development of personnel with

---

6. See e.g. Newell, op. cit., Fendall N.R.E., Auxiliaries in Health Care: programmes in developing countries, Johns Hopkins Press, Baltimore, 1972; Hughes J.P. (ed.), Health Care for Remote Areas, Kaiser Foundation International, Oakland, 1972; there are also two relevant bibliographies covering this and other topics: Bibliography on Health Planning in Developing Countries, Institute of Development Studies (Sussex), Library Occasional Guides no. 10, 1975; Low Cost Rural Health Care and Health Manpower Training: an annotated bibliography, IDRC Serial 042e, Ottawa, 1975.

7. Asser M. and Jaksic Z., A health services development project in Iran, in Newell (ed.), op. cit.

8. Fournier G., and Djermakoye, I.A. Village health teams in Niger (Maradi Department), ibid.

training adjusted to functions and resources, within public health services, is the main feature. Personnel and facilities typically follow a three or four tier pattern depending on the socio-economic and geographical distribution of population. The literature draws attention to a number of key factors in performance. One is supervision: the motivation and attentiveness of modestly-qualified health workers commonly depends on sustained supervision by more highly-qualified personnel, at least in the early stages until skill and confidence are gained. This carries implications for health planning, as BHWs and higher-level auxiliaries may not be able to function satisfactorily without the prior or simultaneous development of supervisory staff.

A good deal may depend on socio-cultural phenomena. Thus trust between a BHW and the community is an important factor; this is usually enhanced if the community selects the person in question, but even that may depend on the process of choice and its meaning. Much of the work of primary care personnel is intended as educative and collaborative with the members of the community - this is subject to all the well-known difficulties of "community development"; clearly these difficulties are the greater if the community's social and economic structure are not such as to encourage co-operation. The greater the inequalities in the village, the more success will depend on the dedication and persuasiveness of the health workers, and the harder their work is likely to be.

The record does not suggest however that progress is only possible in the aftermath of a successful revolution abolishing all privilege. It is true that community development schemes in the past often foundered on the rocks of inequality. They also had other unsatisfactory features, most notably the selection of inappropriate village-level workers, who were commonly of an entirely different background and education from that of the people among whom they worked, and attempted to impose on villagers alien ideas and values. The history of community development in the 1950's and early 60's was such that for many people it is now written off as a plausible approach to solving problems. Yet there is currently a renewed interest in it (not only in the health field); and undoubtedly community development in the late 1970's and beyond need not resemble past experience. Lessons have been learned both from the failures of the past and from some more recent successes.

These lessons include, most importantly, an understanding of the need to avoid both the imposition of alien ideas (which might not be so suitable in the village as the specialists believe) and the opposite reflex, reliance on responses based on "felt needs": villagers feel the need for health, but not necessarily for the means to health (sanitation, hygiene, insect control, etc.). Many past schemes also assumed too readily that villagers (and community development workers!) would be motivated to promote the communal good rather than their own ends. Here again there was an opposite misconception to be avoided: the idea that only those measures would succeed which were in the individual's own selfish interests. (Though it may well be true that satisfying felt needs and performing services which do cater to immediate individual interests may be an important part of the CD workers' ability to gain co-operation for communal purposes.) In speaking of community-level health workers, one also may avoid another problem of the old CD approach: the overloading of the CD worker. In the past he was often expected to foster developments in agriculture, education, health, and possibly other fields besides, requiring the support of a variety of government departments. Health work as envisaged today should be a more concentrated and manageable task.

It is not just the lessons of the past which have changed the prospects for community development. Villages have themselves changed, with progress in education, communications, and rural technology. And countries have far greater manpower resources to draw on for training village workers. The prospects for evoking community participation in health work today should thus not be judged by the experience of the past. They should not, either, be too comfortably assumed to be simple or likely to yield quick results. It still is the case that a fair proportion of "success stories" are due to charismatic leaders and injections of unusual levels of other resources, though even this complaint is beginning to diminish as "replicability" is increasingly pursued and projects survive beyond the stage of dependency on such things. But attempts to change behaviour in relatively traditional settings are bound to take time, and not bound to succeed. So while community participation is a desirable and in many places increasingly feasible goal, scepticism about the potential extent and pace of attainment remains entirely proper. (For a perceptive review of many of these issues based on nine case studies see UNICEF/WHO, Community Involvement in Primary Health Care.) [9]

Another important factor in the deployment of basic health workers is the temptation of higher pay and rewards away from the posts for which they are intended, once they have acquired experience and skill. This has been one of the difficulties with village health workers even in Tanzania. High rates of attrition of auxiliaries have been observed in the Venezuelan programme. Obviously the more market-oriented the economy, the more likely this is to be a problem. It has been said that a satisfactory career structure for auxiliary medical personnel is part of the answer. In some cases, that might be so. It is arguable, however, that in others, it would be better for the BHW to have no wider horizons but to see himself as continuing to live and serve in the village - this would obviously be most appropriate for those who combined health work with other village employment.

---

9. WHO, Report for the 1977 UNICEF-WHO Joint Committee on Health Policy, Communities Involvement in Primary Health Care: A study of the process of community motivation and continued participation, JCZ1/UNICEF-WHO/77.2, Rev. 1, Geneva, 1977.

Since we have spoken of success and failure, a word is in order about evaluation. Many of the experiments described have not been under way more than a few years; it is probably not possible in most cases to assess them in terms of measurable impact on health in conditions of poverty, hostile environment, and malnutrition. Where the delivery of curative services is designed to be the centre of community activities, many years must pass before judgment is possible. Thus in the early years success may have to be judged simply in terms of whether health workers are meeting needs and are supported by their communities. Not that such schemes must fail to pass conventional tests. Thus diagnoses by Tanzania's RMA's have been allegedly been found to correspond in over 95% of cases with those of university-qualified doctors, and - possibly because they can imagine fewer explanations of the symptoms - they reach their conclusions very much faster. In the circumstances of their work, this is highly desirable. And several of the schemes to which we have referred claim clear and visible improvements in general health and conditions.

## IV. FACILITIES

Just as there are appropriate manpower structures, there are appropriate designs and organisation for the network of a country's health facilities. We have stressed that there must be such a network. Basic health workers must be able to refer patients upwards through the hierarchy of services, and they must receive supervision from above - there is an interdependence of functions. Given their limited radius of effectiveness, health centres cannot provide care successfully without satellite units and personnel. There is now a considerable amount of international experience on design, construction and equipment of health centres, sub-centres, dispensaries, etc. [10] and we shall not go into detail here. There is a great variety of needs and specifications even within a country, let alone across countries - too great for generalization. But the principles are similar to those already discussed. Buildings and equipment can be lavish or simple; the more expensive they are, the fewer the people who will have access to them. A good deal of experience has been gained on the failures of health centres in the past - the reasons include shortage of staff, transport,

---

10. They are discussed in many of the sources already cited. Maurice King has also developed the "health care package", an "integrated set of components assisting the application of a particular group of interventions for the improvement of health care under specific socio-economic conditions", in which the technological details of every aspect of care at a given level are planned. See King, M. Personal health care: the quest for a human right, in Wolstenholme, G.E.W. and Elliot K. (eds.). <u>Human Rights in Health</u>, CIBA Foundation Symposium 23 (new series), Elsevier, Amsterdam, 1974.

drugs and other supplies as well as administrative and design shortcomings.  But the underlying causes are often those to which we have already referred:  a lack of commitment to rural health measures in general, a lack of definition of the purposes of health centres and measures to achieve them;  and the absence of lower-level units through which the health centre can have an impact on the local community.

A reference to hospitals is necessary, since these have been major consumers of developing-country health resources, and among the main distortions of egalitarian distribution in health services.  The point is simply made if one considers that the cost of a modern teaching hospital may be equivalent to that of more than a hundred rural health centres (if, for example, a hospital costs over £2 million, and a health centre less than £20,000, which are fairly common figures).  The daily cost of in-patient care in a modern hospital may also be several times the cost in a health centre.  Nevertheless, countries do need hospitals - so in this case too there is a question of appropriate standards and technology and priority in construction.  Doctors and surgeons - especially if they have been trained in developed countries - will press for ultra-modern equipment and facilities for performing complex and advanced operations.  If they get them, once more for a few who may benefit many will be deprived of simpler care that the country might otherwise afford.  Regrettably, aid funds have often supported the creation of these distortions;  though by the mid-1970s different views were beginning to prevail, even if their logical consequences (aid for recurrent as opposed to capital costs, or for local cost financing) were not always drawn by donors.

Hospitals have been introduced here in the context of a "referral system" - this may not, in fact, be their main function.  Where communications are poor and expensive, few patients may actually make the journey from outlying centres.  In many cities, in fact, hospitals are swamped with demands for primary care from local residents, to an extent which interferes with their intended functions.[11] It may be more important to consider the hospital within the context of institutional change needed in the health system.  Hospitals (especially teaching hospitals) could become involved in health work not only in their urban surroundings but in the rural areas for which they act as a point of referral.  It is noteworthy that the prestigious "Srivastava Committee" in India recommended that each teaching hospital should share in the responsibility for health activities in a fairly large geographical area beyond the urban centre in which it was located.[12]  This was one of

---

11.  This should remind us that, although rural services have been the most neglected, there is still a great need for urban services, especially for the poor.  For the future, of course, the urban poor will be a very rapidly growing section of those in need.

12.  <u>Health Services and Medical Education - A programme for immediate action</u>, Report of Group on Medical Education and Support Manpower, Government of India, Ministry of Health and Family Planning, New Delhi, 1975.

a set of measures proposed to make medical education more "service-oriented". As well as pushing medical education more in the directions of the requirements of rural medical services, the Committee's recommendations were designed to involve the teaching hospitals more closely with rural health work. (Commentators in India on the whole reacted favourably towards the Committee's suggestions, but it remains to be seen whether they will be effectively adopted.) The Report as a whole is an admirable example of a discussion of the role of medical education in future health systems.

The use of mobile units has sometimes been seen as a substitute for various kinds of facility. Experience suggests however that they may be completely ineffective for curative work unless they operate as back-up and supervisory services for primary care workers. Obviously, in remote areas with scattered populations, economics may not justify the erection of permanent facilities of any size. Nevertheless, a mobile clinic which simply appears at fixed intervals in specified places may have relatively very little value apart from providing temporary relief for individual suffering. As a support to peripheral sub-centre or dispensary units, however, it can be both valuable and cost effective. Where communications are exceptionally bad and distances great, a case can even be made out for the use of light aircraft - though again not in curative services, but in supervision of rural health work, immunization campaigns or combat of epidemics.[13]

The case would have to be carefully made out, but aircraft are not so much more expensive to use than rough-terrain vehicles that savings of doctors' time and other factors could not provide economic justification. (The possibilities of the planes being used for unintended purposes, or of their being out of action if maintenance is a problem must also be kept in mind.)

## V. VERTICAL CAMPAIGNS

By "vertical campaigns" is meant health activities with a single aim, such as the eradication of smallpox or malaria, or tuberculosis immunization - they are "vertical" in that they often have their own personnel and may be only loosely if at all integrated with national health services. (Family planning too has this character in some countries.) These have been among the "success" stories of the 1950's and 60's. Smallpox is forecast to disappear from the earth more or less entirely before long - a rather special case. The incidence of cholera has been greatly reduced in many countries where it has been endemic. So had been that of malaria by the mid-1960's, though it has reemerged since then as a major health hazard in many countries. In other cases

---

13. Hughes (ed.), op. cit., p. 33 ff. (including "discussion").

progress has been less spectacular - tuberculosis, for example - or even virtually nil, as with onchocerciasis ("river blindness") in West Africa. The question arises whether vertical campaigns still have a role in the kinds of health services we have been describing.

As long ago as 1965 a WHO Study Group addressed the question of the relation of mass campaigns with other health services.[14] Their conclusion was that while there was advantage in a specific organisation for the early stages of control, the time usually arrives when further progress requires handing over parts at least of the campaign to general health services. Apart from anything else, it eventually ceases to make sense to have a number of single-purpose health workers in employment when their functions, together with other useful activities, can be undertaken by the same person. But in terms even of the control or eradication of particular diseases, the phasing of work has the same requirement. Thus with malaria, many countries have had effective mass spraying programmes to control the vector, but find that malaria is now returning. This has many causes, including the development of DDT-resistant mosquitoes and chloroquine-resistant strains of the disease; relaxation of programmes in mistaken expectation of victory; and others. But the final stages of eradication are different from the initial ones: they require epidemiological surveillance, case-finding and treatment, and continuing vigilance against the vector, operations which require co-operation between health personnel and the local community.

There is an analogous situation with tuberculosis: mass BCG immunization programmes have been undertaken with reasonable coverage. But without a health network to ensure the vaccination of the newly born, the proportion of non-immunized children begins to rise; case-finding and treatment is weak; even where proper treatment is begun, without supervision the patient may give up chemotherapy when he feels better rather than when he is cured. In some countries it has been found that a high proportion of tuberculosis sufferers present themselves for treatment, but if no skilled person is there, they are sent away with something for their "cough".[15] The test for tuberculosis infection is precisely the type of task that a modestly trained auxiliary can perform as part of his regular activities. The problems of controlling this disease should not be made light of; its complex relations with diet and living conditions are well known, as are the difficulties of immunization and treatment. Nevertheless it resembles other diseases which have been the target of mass campaigns in that after useful preliminary activities, further progress depends on the handing over of the

---

14. Integration of Mass Campaigns against Specific Diseases into General Health Services, WHO Technical Report Series No.294, Geneva, 1965.

15. E.g. Banerji D., Tuberculosis: a problem of social planning in India, National Institute of Health and Education Bulletin 4(1), 1971.

campaigns to general health services at the local level - services which in so many countries simply are not there.

Family planning is another case in point, though a slightly different one. (Different not least because procreation is not a disease.) Family planning services can be and are offered independently of health services. Their effectiveness in such circumstances depends partly on the extent to which motivational work is included, partly on the techniques of contraception offered and the degree of their dependence on medical back-up. Where the health programme has the promotion of family planning among its ambitions, this is often found to work best in the context of health services, particularly if the approach is to mothers. When a mother is receiving post-natal care with her child, she may be well disposed to listening to advice which relates to her own health and that of her existing children. Contraceptive advice in general may be more acceptable from someone who has shown ability and understanding in health care. (This is not to say that other forms of motivational activity - mass media campaigns for example - cannot succeed; they frequently do.) The "techniques" point is fairly obvious: condoms, which are simple to understand and to use, and have few significant side-effects, can be distributed through health outlets, or commercially, or otherwise, without problems. But in the current state of the art, most other available techniques require medical follow-up, particularly for consultation in the event of side-effects (real or imagined).

The IUD has proved very difficult to employ among poor, ill-educated rural populations with little access to medical personnel; to a lesser extent the same has been found with sterilization. Thus an important function for the BHW in countries where family planning is promoted could be follow-up work related to particular techniques of contraception.[16]

## VI. WATER SUPPLY AND SANITATION

As with so many possible health interventions, improvement of sanitation or water supply by themselves where other health conditions remain poor may not have any great impact on mortality or morbidity. While a large number of dangerous diseases are faecally transmitted

---

16. It is noteworthy that India has announced plans to convert most of its health personnel in malaria, smallpox and other programmes to "multi-purpose health workers", partly with this family-planning function in view. So far however there appear to be no concrete plans on a national basis to develop lower-level BHWs of the kind we have discussed. While the plans for multi-purpose workers are a step forward, and will provide a needed layer of health personnel, they are not a substitute for BHWs chosen by and working within their own communities. India has had successful pilot schemes in this field, official or private, but as yet that is all.(Note: Since this was written, India has progressed well beyond the "pilot" stage - Ed's.)

or waterborne, just improving the source of domestic water-supply or the means of waste-disposal may only modestly reduce their incidence. A family may have several sources of water and unless all of them are improved, change in just one of them may make little difference. Even if the water comes from a clean source, it may be drawn or stored in vessels subject to contamination. Fortunately there are some diseases for which an increase in water quantity may be beneficial. We shall not enter here into detailed discussion of the effects of improving water supply and sanitation, on which there is a fairly voluminous literature.[17] In some studies, and in the case of some diseases with a distinctive epidemiology which the improvements affect significantly, better water and sanitation have been found to produce desirable change on their own. But except for a few diseases, the general conclusion is that they are a necessary rather than a sufficient condition of better health. At the same time, the diseases which are related to water supply and sanitation are so numerous, so prevalent and so deleterious to health that it is an area where progress is as important as anywhere else, save perhaps nutrition. These diseases are not only the great lethal scourges such as cholera or typhoid fever, but the diarrhoeas which take such a tremendous toll of life among infants and children in developing countries.

Like most of the topics of this section, water-supply too has been the subject of inappropriate standards, often specified in terms of volume, purity and technique of supply without much regard for cost or the alternatives over which choice is possible. The following table gives a useful schema (see next page).

It is apparent from the Table that different forms of water-supply improvement will have different health effects. Thus even with low quality, increase in the volume of water will assist both a variety of skin and eye infections and gastric disorders. Different degrees of water purity will have different effects on different diseases; even a small increase in purity may reduce the "non-classical" waterborne diseases of the table. Purity may be more important the greater the number of people dependent on a given water-source - i.e. especially in urban areas. Altogether there is no unique "best" specification of desirable water supplies for all circumstances. Given the resources available, there will be some choice of water-supply improvement that is the best way to use them, related to prevailing disease conditions, eco-climatic region, density of habitation, and the response of health

---

17. White G.F., Bradley D.J. and White A.V., <u>Drawers of Water</u>: domestic water use in East Africa, University of Chicago Press, 1972; Saunders, R.J. and Warford J.J., <u>Village Water Supply and Sanitation in Less Developed Countries</u>: Economics and Policy, World Bank, Public Utilities Report No. RES 2, Washington D.C. 1975; McGarry M.G., Empirical Relationships between Sanitation and Health, Science Policy Research Unit, University of Susses, 1974 (mimeo): Wolstenholme and Elliot (eds.), <u>op. cit.</u> (papers by Dieterich B.H.; White G.G.; Burton I.; Bradley D.J.); and references cited by these authors.

Table VII. CLASSIFICATION OF INFECTIVE DISEASES IN RELATION TO WATER SUPPLIES

| CATEGORY | EXAMPLES | RELEVANT WATER IMPROVEMENTS |
|---|---|---|
| I. Waterborne infections | | |
|   a) Classical | Typhoid, cholera | Microbiological sterility |
|   b) Non-classical | Infective hepatitis | Microbiological improvement |
| II. Water-washed infections | | |
|   a) Skin and eyes | Scabies, trachoma | Greater volume available |
|   b) Diarrhoeal diseases | Bacillary dysentery | Greater volume available |
| III. Water-based infections | | |
|   a) Penetrating skin | Schistosomiasis | Protection of user |
|   b) Ingested | Guinea worm | Protection of source |
| IV. Infections with water-related insect vectors | | |
|   a) Biting near water | Sleeping sickness | Water piped from source |
|   b) Breeding in water | Yellow fever | Water piped to site of use |

SOURCE: Bradley, in Wolstenholme and Elliott, op. cit.

in these circumstances to increases of water volume and purity. It is really only in the last few years that the problem has begun to be looked at in this way - but it is obviously a completely different approach from saying "every individual must have so much water of such and such purity", and supplying that to as many individuals as possible. Whatever the specifications in such a formulation, following them would be bound to lead to sub-optimal use of resources, not to speak of the by now familiar result under all our headings: full provision for the few at the expense of adequacy for the many.

Water-supply, though itself complex, is a less difficult field for action than sanitation. Developing countries are littered with well-meaning reports on the desirability of rural latrines, and ineffectual projects to stimulate their use. It is one field in which appropriate technology has been designed and available for years. But more than almost any other aspect of health, it is something that requires communal participation quite essentially, and that in a cause whose benefits are often not obvious to the potential beneficiaries, while the costs, if small, may not be negligible. At a minimum, people must be educated to appreciate the health consequences of insanitary waste disposal, to construct or maintain appropriate facilities, and to use them in preference to traditional methods. As such, any programme to advance the cause of better waste-disposal is once more a matter for community development, with all the difficulties involved. And, once more, it is hard to see how progress can be made in the absence of basic health workers to promote this kind of activity at the local level; and at the same time, even with such workers and desirable support, experience warns of the uncertainty of success.[18]

## VII. HEALTH PLANNING

It is evident from all the above that health planning in relation to population growth is not just a matter of "arithmetic" - of counting the number of people there are going to be, and matching those numbers with "required" facilities and personnel on a per capita basis. Nor, equally obviously, is it simply a matter for the health ministry. Planning starts from identification of the problem, of the nature of ill-health in the society in question and its causes, of the limitations on resources and the problem of access to services. Even here there can be an excess of "technification" - some planners may be tempted to feel that they cannot begin to plan without a detailed analysis of cause of death by region or other cross-classification. In fact in most poor countries the scale of mortality in different age groups will be an indication of the main problems: high infant and child mortality is almost always the consequence of the well-known "synergism of malnutrition and infection". In addition, medical practitioners already at work will be able to provide an adequate account of the main health

---

18. In some countries, particularly in South East Asia, waste-disposal is part of a system of productive use of night-soil. It is fairly simple to treat night-soil so as to render it safe to use from a health point of view; it can then be spread as an efficient fertilizer. This is no sanitarian's dream, but perfectly good economics; in Taiwan at certain times of the year there is even a black market in human waste, which is collected, treated and sold by municipal corporations.

problems in their areas. As health systems ramify and master the basic problems, the need for better information to guide further decisions increases. But with infant mortality in excess of 150 per 1,000 live births and a survival ratio from birth to age 10 of 75% or less, or with high female mortality in the peak child-bearing years, the main priority is rarely better cause-of-death statistics. The main priorities are in nutrition, water supply, hygiene and sanitation, preventive and curative medical services, and progress is required in all these more or less simultaneously. The energies of many government departments besides that of health will be needed.

In most planning, an important choice has to be made between what the government must do itself and what it must leave to others. The main point of this paper is that a great deal of government action for improved health must be designed to elicit participatory responses from the public, for that is what economics, practicality and effectiveness dictate. A perfect example is provided by the issue of village water supply in India. Only about 10% of India's half-a-million villages have piped water, though an unknown additional percentage have reasonably safe tube-well water. In 1969 some 150,000 villages were estimated to have particularly acute water problems because of the depth or distance at which supplies lay, or because of pressing water-associated health problems. The cost of supplying water to these villages was estimated at $870 million, and a further $1,630 million was needed for villages less acutely in need - a total of $2,500 million.[19] This is about twice the total plan outlay on health in the whole of India's. Fourth Five-Year Plan period (1969-1974) - clearly a sum which India will find difficult to raise just for village water supply for a very long time. But does that mean that India's villages cannot have decent water supplies in this century? If it is a question of waiting for the Public Works Department to install piped water, economics (apart from other considerations) would suggest the answer may well be no. But if the criteria for improved water supply discussed above were employed, and if the government's role were to assist villages only to the extent that villages could not cope themselves (e.g. with rock-drilling or long-distance supply where necessary), the costs, and the time-frame within which improvement might come, could look very different. Using seasonally unemployed labour, and local materials, and concentrating on those changes which are locally cost effective, many villages could improve their own water situation, provided only that they received the requisite instruction, and would co-operate to put it into practice.

Those last are, of course, important and difficult provisos. But these seem to be the alternatives: an enormous bill for government-provided facilities which cannot be met in the foreseeable future; or a programme having at least some chance of success within a health

---

19. Government of India, Pocket Book of Health Statistics, Central Bureau of Health Intelligence, Ministry of Health and Family Planning, New Delhi, 1973.

system which maximizes community participation. Under the latter, "village water supply" is not just a head of expenditure in the budget of the relevant government department (usually not the health ministry), but an integral part of a concerted set of activities designed to improve health. These activities incorporate much that has not previously been included in the "health sector"; but they are predicated on - and, one hopes, coordinated by - the functions of health personnel, particularly those working at or close to the community level.

This discussion raises the whole issue of financing of basic health services. Naturally a large share of the budget in health must be borne by the state, and there are the usual economic arguments for that. But various schemes in different countries have employed charges for parts of health services - even for primary care - and there is a case for doing so. (This being a sensitive subject, we would point out that the question of charges does not necessarily occur only to the market-oriented economist: there are health charges even in China, albeit modest ones.) We do not refer to a comprehensive, cost-covering insurance scheme - in a poor country, the size of premium that most people could afford, and the expense of recovering it and administering such a scheme as a whole, would probably render comprehensive insurance a pointless proposition. (And a scheme with only partial coverage is likely to compound maldistribution.) But the question of paying a small sum towards the costs of a local facility, or a small fee to a basic-health worker is another matter. People - even very poor people - may in fact spend quite large sums on medical care, either to traditional practitioners, or in travel expenses (and foregone wages) if a trip to a distant health centre is needed.[20] The cost of a fifteen mile return trip by bullock-cart could well be equal to several days' pay. If sporadic large expenses for unsatisfactory services could be converted to regular small payments for satisfactory ones, everybody might gain. In order for this to happen, the services would have to meet the needs of the community; to exact payment for things people do not feel they want is the opposite of the philosophy of health care which has been advanced here. But people might well be willing to pay a small monthly amount towards the upkeep of a dispensary in the village, or a small fee to the BHW for services rendered. Sometimes the very fact that payment is being made adds to the respect people have for the service. We wish only to raise, rather than pretend to settle this issue. It is a difficult one, and the likelihood of its being a good or bad idea will vary

---

20. We have not discussed the role of traditional practitioners here. There is a considerable variety in the quality and effectiveness of what they do. There has also been much examination of, and some experience with, the problems of incorporating them into modern health systems. Since the traditional practitioner often enjoys the trust of the community more than the government health worker, it is tempting to hope that he or she can be trained to become a health worker using scientifically tested practices. Sometimes -as with the retraining of traditional midwives in some countries - this can be successfully undertaken. But all too often such efforts have proved vain.

greatly from one situation to another. But here again the function of curative services will be important if this method of raising revenue is adopted; for while the other things health workers may do have a greater impact on health, it is for individual consultation and dispensing of medication that, in the first instance at least, the villager is most likely to be willing to part with his money.

While the ambition of the health plan will be to make progress on every front from nutrition to curative medical care, it will have to separate out those things which really are the function of other government departments, and those which come specifically under the health ministry. Thus responsibility for a good deal of activity in nutrition and water-supply, while it requires coordination with health activities, will lie with agriculture, irrigation, public works, or information departments. The core of the health ministry's planning will be the setting up of services - the network of facilities and personnel which will carry forward the educational, promotive, preventive and curative work underlying all health-related activities.

## VIII. OBSTACLES

It might be thought that what is being said here is now becoming so widely accepted that it barely requires repetition. Unfortunately that is not so. While the failings of health development in the past are well enough known, the pursuit of alternatives such as we have outlined is far from common. On the contrary. Large, expensive and excessively capital- intensive hospitals are still being erected in the developing world. Several countries are expanding their training facilities for doctors while programmes for auxiliary training are backward or non-existent. One writer claimed in 1973 that only a single country in francophone Africa had plans to train medical assistants.[21] Countries which have plans for auxiliaries have usually yet to make provision for basic health workers - the auxiliaries are commonly aimed at a 1/10,000 population level of work, i.e. not situations in which they can provide primary care for everyone. The more progressive aid donors are now promoting low-cost rural health schemes; but aid is still going to services with no egalitarian effect on distribution.

The "obstacles" are not hard to discern. They are found partly in the political process of developing countries, where power lies in the cities, or politicians can acquire prestige from the construction of hospitals rather than from the less spectacular, patient work that rural health requires. And they are found very importantly in the medical profession itself, who may feel their own interests threatened by the development of paramedical staffs, or whose own self-esteem is related

---

21. Pene P., The Lancet (1) 1047, 1973, cited by Gish, op. cit.

to the modernity of the equipment with which they work or the advanced operations they can perform. They are found also in the medical colleges of developed and developing worlds, where emphasis in training is still largely on the scientific and technical aspects of medicine, with little place in most curricula for the social and economic aspects of health and health planning. More profoundly, if a professional body does not define its own role as serving the whole population, but adopts a position which results in the denial of services to a large class of people, that must be seen not just as part of a certain obsolescent tradition of medicine, but as a result of the existing social structure and the balance of social and economic power.

At the same time, we would be guilty of bias if we did not reiterate that what is being opposed to the unsatisfactory practices of the past rests to some extent on an act of faith. The main "success stories" in low-cost health care have been in socialist countries; what will succeed in other circumstances has yet to be demonstrated. There have been promising experiments, and there have been mistakes to learn from. Each country will have to adapt from this experience to suit its own needs. But even if not conclusively proven, some or other of the methods reviewed here are bound to form the basis of health development in poor countries, if that development is to mean better health for all. There seems to be no other course.

# 5

## HOUSING AND SETTLEMENT
by
Patrick Crooke

### I. HOUSING, SETTLEMENT AND THE URBANIZATION PROCESS

Housing and settlement conditions and needs in Third World countries have to be viewed not only in terms of the massive present-day growth of their populations, but also in the context of the urbanization of these populations' ways of life: a process that includes the movement of country-people to towns and cities, and also the adoption of urban-derived values and practices by rural populations themselves.

While developing regions and countries differ among themselves in their present-day rates of urban population growth, it is estimated that in the Third World as a whole, town and city populations are now increasing by about 5 to 6% each year, and doubling in size in about fifteen years: a growth rate approximately twice as fast as that of Third World countries' total populations.

This overall growth rate for urban populations contains within it rates of population-increase in primary cities that are far higher, in many cases, than those of smaller urban centres. In the twenty years from 1950 to 1970, for example, the population of Cairo increased by 2.4 times and that of Manila by 2.8 times, while that of Karachi increased by 3.3 times and that of Bogota by 3.7 times during the same period: less than one generation.

Such a rapid increase in urban populations is resulting partly from the high birth rates and longer life-expectancy affecting Third World populations as a whole, and partly from the migration of country-people to towns and cities. Rural-to-urban migration is now accounting for about half of the urban population increase in most Latin American countries; rather more than half, in much of Africa; and slightly less than half in India and most of South-east Asia.

Rates of natural increase among both urban and rural populations are now so high that - despite this migration from the countryside - not only urban populations but rural populations too are increasing in the Third World. In fact, in countries that still have a much larger rural than urban population (the case in nearly all the Third World), the demographic effects of migration on rural populations are not very marked, and migrants make up a relatively small fraction of the increase in rural population numbers. United Nations estimates show that while urban populations in Third World countries are increasing fourfold and more between 1960 and 2000 (from 410 to 1,930 million), their rural populations are nearly doubling in numbers during the same period (from 1,605 to 2,740 million).

This means, among other things, that rural population-pressures will continue to affect and change not only the urban but also the rural economies and societies of these countries, during the rest of this century and beyond it.

How are these rural and urban changes affecting the settlement and housing practices of the low-income majority of Third World countries' populations? We can trace some of these effects by examining the differences between various customary and transitional practices, each of them characteristic of a particular stage in the urbanization process.

Customary rural practices

In many rural areas and populations of Third World countries land for farming and settlement, and houses themselves, have not yet acquired a recognized monetary value. In these conditions, particular tribal or village groups commonly have customary rights to the use of particular land areas for agriculture and settlement; while family groups or households belonging to the tribe or village build and use their own houses, they are not accustomed to buying and selling these among themselves. In traditional circumstances they had no need to do so, since families' or individuals' membership of a given rural grouping itself entitled them to their share in the use of land held by their community.

Good examples of settlement and housing practices of this kind are to be found in Central Sudan, in the development of both riverain villages and those in the huge Gezira irrigation scheme. Housing land in these villages is not individually owned, but is distributed among the various sub-tribal and lineage groups that make up a Sudanese rural community. Each of these groups tends to occupy its own zone of the village and of its periphery, where the group's new and future households can establish themselves. This village "zoning" not only provides womenfolk with some valued privacy and seclusion from non-relatives, but also minimizes disputes between groups over the use of new housing land.

Within the housing zone of any one group, however, a high degree of space sharing takes place between neighbouring relatives: guest rooms and animal compounds are usually built and used in common by several related households, whose own rooms may also share one or more open-air yards sheltered from public view. The sharing and interconnecting of these domestic areas provides an infinitely varied and adaptable family environment, achieved by the simplest and cheapest possible means. House construction and renewal is carried out by local labour (and usually by the household itself) and uses mud and other locally available materials at an extremely low cost.

While any family or family group uses its share of village land by building and occupying its private living-quarters there, these use-rights are enjoyed not through ownership of property but through membership of the community concerned. They cannot be realized or liquidated in money terms.

It should be stressed that in this part of Sudan, the rural populations using land and housing in this way are relatively prosperous ones, living in close touch with Khartoum and other important centres and familiar with modern and highly-organised farming and marketing methods. Moreover many young people migrate from this rural area to Sudan's towns and cities, where they quickly adopt very different settlement and housing arrangements. Those who remain in the rural area or return to it, however, are still strongly affected by the social values and practices that have developed over centuries of settlement in this part of Sudan.

Transitional rural practices
---

In other rural areas of the Third World, this and other types of customary use of land and housing are being replaced by the ownership and exchange of property, and both housing land and houses themselves are acquiring a monetary as well as a use value. One of many examples of this can be seen in the Yoruba region of Nigeria where, until fairly recently, the use of land for agriculture and settlement was governed by practices broadly similar to those of Central Sudan. Customary tribal authorities disposed of land-use rights in their respective territories, allocating them among the members of the rural community they governed and arbitrating in disputes between the users of this communally-held land. To a large extent this system still prevails.

During the past fifty years, however, forest land that hitherto had been cultivated only spasmodically (in a system of roving bush-fallow farming) began to acquire a perennial value when planted with oilpalm, cocoa, citrus and other permanent orchard crops. Coupled with the rapid increase in the population needing and competing for land rights, this is leading to a fragmentation of communally-held lands into individual family properties that are often rented out or sold to outsiders. Yoruba rural land is thus acquiring a money value for the first time, and a land market is beginning to operate more or less along urban lines.

Like farming land, settlement land is also beginning to be bought and sold. Many villagers are moving to new settlement sites close to the region's main roads, where they are better placed for marketing their cash crops or transporting them to their distant consumers. This move to the roadside often requires new settlers to occupy land to which they have no customary right: a problem largely beyond the scope of customary land law, and one that is being resolved by the direct sale of settlement land to these outsiders - who thereby become land owners for the first time in the country's rural history.

In this part of Nigeria the siting and construction of houses themselves often show signs of other urban influences. Traditional housing layouts that involve the sharing of rooms and open spaces among large groups of relatives - in arrangements not unlike those of Central Sudan - are being abandoned in favour of individual houses built side by side along the road, in a semi-urban pattern. At the same time rural houses that were previously built, as a rule, by their farmer occupants are now being built increasingly by paid labour: local artisans and small contractors, the forerunners of a rural building industry.

Yoruba villagers, like those of Central Sudan, are relatively prosperous and are closely in touch with events and practices in Nigeria's towns and cities, to which many of their young people migrate. Current changes in their settlement and housing practices suggest, however, that they are much more ready than are their Sudanese counterparts to adopt urban models of land and house ownership, and to place a monetary market value on these assets previously held and used in common.

Transitional urban market practices

Rural people's gradual adoption of market values for their settlement and housing transactions has to take a major step further when they migrate to towns and cities, where land and housing markets already prevail.

Coming to the city with no assets except their contacts and their work capacity, often with no secure income and with little immediate prospect of accumulating any capital through savings, they find themselves not only excluded from legal home-ownership (which has to be paid for) but also ineligible, as a rule, for any of the types of housing assistance that the city's public authorities are providing. Newcomers thus usually have only two housing options open to them: to rent rooms in the cheapest part of the city, or to settle on any urban land for which they can avoid making immediate payment and start developing there whatever house property they can afford.

For many rural newcomers to Third World towns and cities the latter course represents the beginning of their entry to the urban land and housing market - often first as unrecognized claimants, and later as legal (or at least permitted) owners of urban property. We can see this transition towards ownership of land and housing taking place in the peripheral settlements of most Third World towns and cities; in the suburbio area of Guayaquil, Ecuador's largest city, various stages in this process are clearly visible.

Guayaquil's suburbio occupies an area of tidal swampland of little or no commercial value in its natural state, where settlement entails the creation of solid land as well as housing. Already by 1962 some 360,000 people had settled and housed themselves in this part of the city, and the suburbio's present population numbers well over half a million: about 60% of all the city's residents.

The suburbio swamps have been occupied by successive groups of settlers - mainly low-income households from the city's rental slums, where many of them had spent their first years of city life. In claiming a new area of swamp, settlers demarcate their future house pilots in a more or less regular "gridiron" pattern of city blocks resembling that of the rest of Guayaquil. These suburbio sub-divisions have usually been organised not by the city's planning officials but by local political and other leaders of the settler groups themselves. People then build, in their fenced-in plots of swamp, small temporary houses of bamboo and timber standing on poles above the mud and water, and connected to one another and to the nearest dry land by timber catwalks that make the swamp "streets" immediately usable.

Living conditions at this early stage are noxious: the waters of the swamp become more and more heavily polluted, and drinking water has to be purchased and carried over long distances. In Guayaquil's hot and humid climate these conditions quickly bring infections and illnesses of all kinds and an almost overpowering smell of rotting excreta and stagnant water.

During the subsequent years, however, the settled area of swamp gradually gets reclaimed to slightly above the high tide level, with the City Council filling in the streets while households fill in their plots as best they can. Even before landfill many houses have a rudimentary electricity supply; and water, sewerage and public lighting mains get installed once the streets have been filled and consolidated. At this stage a settler can, with some difficulty, register his newly-created property with the city authorities and obtain a legal title to it.

Once the house plot and its building can be legalized, other changes rapidly follow. The initial bamboo houses - some years old, by this time - begin to be replaced by larger and more permanent dwellings that often include shops, small workshops and rental rooms; and the buying and selling of these properties increases. Within a few years these desolate tracts of mud and water have become "normal" parts of the city area and of its housing stock, through a series of undertakings that involve great effort and danger for the suburbio's settlers but which not only provide them with living and earning space, but also provide employment and income for a large part of Guayaquil's growing population.

Urban newcomers and their housing

In the cases described on the preceding pages, the rural populations of both Central Sudan and Yoruba Nigeria send many migrants to their countries' towns and cities; while in Guayaquil's suburbio most settlers are first-generation in-migrants from the countryside. In most Third World countries approximately half of the current increase in urban population is, as we have seen, resulting from rural-urban migration and it is common to find low-income areas in large towns and cities where well over half of the adult residents were born in the countryside.

The migrants show a variety of intentions in their use of town and city opportunities. For some, urban jobs and incomes are primarily a means of support for their rural families; they tend to come to the city not to settle, but to earn and send home money for a relatively short time, during or after which they can return home better off. The sooner they succeed in the town or city, the sooner they can leave it and rejoin their families.

But for others, urban jobs and incomes are primarily a means of gaining a foothold as permanent settlers in the town or city itself. The sooner they begin to succeed there, the sooner they can bring their relatives to join them.

For an individual migrant these differing objectives are not, of course, mutually exclusive: he may change his intentions several times, as his prospects vary at either the rural or the urban "ends" of his migration. But the rapid and continuous growth of urban populations shows that more and more migrants are choosing to settle in towns and cities and to consolidate there (in, for example, Guayaquil's suburbio) whatever foothold they can gain for themselves and their children in the urban economy and society. Settlement and housing practices in the Yoruba region of Nigeria and in Guayaquil's suburbio illustrate the fact that when urbanizing people settle and house themselves on their own account, settlement and housing are themselves important vehicles in this process of economic and social change.

For a low-income household facing the prospect of a precarious future in the town or city, housing entails only one of many spendings and investments that they need to make and to vary in relation to one another, according to the unpredictable "ups and downs" in the household's urban career.

For example, high rents and overcrowding in a tenement slum may be necessary evils in the view of a poor family seeking work, if the slum room they occupy puts them close to job opportunities. But payments for this same room may be a mere waste of good money for the same family once a job is giving them income that increases their mobility, and enables them to develop elsewhere a rent-free house of their own. This home of their own, in turn, opens up other prospects: of using it as an income-earner (from lodgers, a shop or a workshop) or as equity for borrowing money and branching out into other enterprises.

At each of these stages, house accommodation is playing a particular role in the household's current situation and future prospects, and its standards and cost need to be revelant to that role at that time - rather than to the values of public authorities - if it is to be fully useful to its occupants. In conditions of population growth, rapid urbanization and generally low incomes, a useful prediction of the future housing requirements of any national or urban population group is exceedingly difficult. The three main parts of this requirement are generally agreed to be:

i) the dwelling-accommodation needed for future additions to household totals caused by natural increase in population, by decreases in average household size and, in the case of most urban areas, by in-migration of population from elsewhere;

ii) the continuous replacement of housing stock at the end of its expected "lifespan"; and

iii) the replacement or improvement of that part of the current housing a stock officially defined as deficient or sub-standard. A host of uncertainties attends each of these parts of the housing-need calculation.

While certain factors affecting the number of future households needing accommodation (among them, future rates of household-formation indicated by current trends in fertility and in household size) can probably be predicted reasonably accurately, it is far less easy to predict migration as a factor in new-household formation. Whether it takes the form of out-migration from rural areas or in-migration to urban centres, migration is a response to social and economic problems and opportunities that are themselves liable to change relatively quickly and unpredictably - not only between rural and urban settings, but also between urban centres themselves, in any given country, as the result of disparate development. Meanwhile the "lifespan" of housing stock, and hence the speed at which it needs replacing, is largely a function of how much is spent on building and maintaining it. This depends not only on changing economic circumstances, but also on the political and social factors of people's opportunities and readiness to invest in their housing: highly variable and unpredictable matters, in most countries.

Perhaps most important, however, are the difficulties attending the calculation of housing requirements to meet current housing deficits. These deficits are usually calculated by comparing the current number of households with the current number of dwellings deemed by officials to be of a habitable standard, and thus determining the number of "deficient" dwellings needing replacement by new housing stock. This procedure is highly suspect, on two grounds:

i) the definition of dwelling "habitability" is inevitably an arbitrary one, normally based on the values and expectations of middle-income officials rather than on those of the households involved;

ii) moreover, it is assumed, in this kind of calculation, that low material standards of housing are necessarily more critical to its occupants than is the use-value, to them, of the security and opportunities they can find in low housing costs: an assumption which has given rise to all manner of misplaced housing efforts by official "improvers".

## II. GOVERNMENTAL AIMS AND ACTIONS

Present-day problems and shortcomings

These complex, changing and unprecedented housing needs of Third World countries' growing and urbanizing populations are needs that public authorities have, by and large, found themselves unable (or shown themselves unwilling) to meet effectively. Before looking at some of the apparent reasons for this inadequate governmental response, we have to remind ourselves of the massive extent of the failure of public-sector aims and actions that it has entailed - most of all, in Third World primary cities.

Over the past thirty years a steadily-diminishing proportion of the growing populations of these cities has benefited from the performance of urban planning and housing authorities and of the legal housing market as a whole. At the same time a larger and larger proportion of these urban households have had to find or invent settlement and housing solutions for themselves outside the rule of planning and housing regulations that supposedly govern their actions, and outside the reach of both public and modern-commercial sector suppliers of land and of legal "decent" housing.

This does not mean, of course, that public-sector intervention in the urban settlement and housing field has itself been decreasing during this period, in Third World countries. On the contrary, it has increased considerably over the years in virtually all these countries. But the results of this governmental intervention have mainly benefited minority population-groups that have been growing relatively slowly in numbers - that is, urban households with secure employment and relatively high wages or salaries; meanwhile fast-growing low-income groups have been very largely excluded from these housing benefits and - at the best - have been left to their own housing devices.

A clear indicator of this state of affairs is the growth of unauthorized urban settlement and housing practices, as shown by statistics compiled in recent years by the United Nations and the World Bank from a variety of sources. According to these figures the slum and squatter-settlement populations of, for example, Mexico City increased from 14% of the city's total in 1952 to 46% of the total by 1970; in Manila it increased from 20% of the total in 1962 to 35% in 1972; while in Lima the squatter population alone increased from less than 10% of the city's total in 1956 to 40% by 1970. Lusaka's squatter population is estimated to have increased from about 10% of the city's total in 1963 to 42% by 1973 - or, according to World Bank estimates, to 48% of the total by 1969. In Ankara the squatter-settlement population, already 47% of the city's total by 1965, had increased to 60% of the total by 1970: only five years later. Almost every fast-growing town and city in the Third World tells essentially the same story.

While no-one would claim figures of this kind to be fully accurate (based as they are on varying definitions and problematic data-collection) they do show clearly a diminishing trend in the capacity of both public and legal-private institutions to meet the settlement and housing requirements of their most needy urban populations.

Why has this come about?

When most Third World governments undertook their first urban development plans and housing programmes some twenty or thirty years ago (when many of them were just achieving or approaching independence) their aims in this field were generally based on a view prevalent at that time: that planned and orderly urban development of a high material standard must inevitably induce maximum well-being. This is a view that has come under increasingly critical scrutiny since then - and especially so in the light of urban growth realities in Third World countries. Yet it is a view that still often prevails, even though several of its underlying assumptions have to be questioned.

One of these assumptions is that public planning authorities gain sufficient information and understanding of the functioning of their towns and cities to be able to make accurate predictions of future urban events and needs, and to plan for these. In practice, urban development plans and housing policies in the Third World have proved time and again to be based on grossly incorrect and oversimplified interpretations of current demands, and wrong in their predictions of future population-growth and housing events in their towns and cities.

All the shortcomings to which we have referred so far can be seen very clearly in the planned and unplanned development of New Towns undertaken in Third World countries since the 1950's: Brasilia in Brazil, Ciudad Guayana in Venezuela, Chandigarh in India and Tema in Ghana. In all these cases people have engulfed the new town during and even before its development - to take up the employment opportunities that the town's development offered - and have been too numerous and too poor to be accommodated in the town without destroying the assumptions, predictions and preconceptions of its planners.

The history of population projections for third world cities over the past twenty-five years has served to emphasize the extreme difficulties of any high degree of quantitative or qualitative precision in forward planning of housing or other urban provisions in the medium or long term. Even in the case of the larger and longer established cities, especially in Asia and Africa, the high rate of overall population growtn and/or the small relative size of the urban population compared with the rural means that small shifts in rural conditions over quite short periods of time, or equally short-run changes in urban labour demands, precipitate an influx of migrants over time-periods as yet uncalculable in duration or intensity. In a majority of cases decennial forecasts have been shown to be systematically biased towards underrating the actual increases revealed in succeeding censuses; and in others, where a previous period of high growth has been taken as the basis for upward revisions the succeeding outcome has been to confound the expectation by showing a levelling off. However even this is never quite established because of the vital additional complexity of territorial coverage: if the same city areas are rigourously compared this gives statistical regularity but functional discrepancy, since over any five or ten year period a city will very likely transform its spatial and physical size and shape to reflect other changes in its economic base, its urban technology and its social structure.

Even more taxing are the demands of translating quantitative estimates of future households into quantifiable dimensions of demands and needs. These will depend on such ineluctable factors as the changing structure of the city income distribution, the different rates of upward and downward mobility among the major segments of the urban population, the alterations in the balance between newcomers and established residents, and all the unknowable results of interaction between any given composition of urban households and any changing application of urban investment and the provision of specific urban services or access to new resources. This is especially the case in the larger or more multifunctional cities where the sheer variety and complexity of housing needs and demands over time, for example, cannot be approached at present even by the most sophisticated computer-based urban modelling exercises.

Not only have the predictions and plans for settlement and housing in these new towns proved to be totally at variance with subsequent demands; the continued development of the towns in accordance with these official predictions and plans has also proved unable either to meet or to curtail the settlement and housing demands that have actually occurred.

Thus each of these planned towns is now surrounded by vigorously unplanned shanty and other "illegal" neighbourhoods which show every sign of playing a vital (and perhaps a predominant) part in the towns' future productive and social life. This is not necessarily a bad outcome, of course; but it is almost exactly contrary to what was predicted and planned for. Similar events have overwhelmed most public-sector efforts to achieve planned and orderly urban development and decent housing standards in existing Third World cities also, and call into serious question the planning and housing assumptions, predictions and targets on which these efforts have been based.

Another assumption that appears more and more doubtful is that Third World public authorities can count on having sufficient governmental resources - or can exercise control over sufficient non-governmental resources - to ensure that planned urban growth and housing can be implemented on a significant scale. The intention of chanelling as much of the urban housing supply as possible through a Third World country's legally-controlled institutions (such as public housing agencies, building societies, banks and the contractual building industry) presupposes that these institutions can dispose of large enough resources for doing the job.

Yet in many Third World countries where organised industry and commerce are still relatively little developed, and where the governmental tax-base is correspondingly narrow and insecure, scarce institutional resources have many urgent development demands on their use - of which housing is, of course, only one. In the housing sector itself, therefore, institutional capital and other resources have shown themselves to be very scarce indeed in comparison with the resources of the population at large - most of whom, in these countries, are accustomed to financing and organising their own housing activities. Attempts to replace these widespread housing activities and resources by those of centralized public and private institutions have thus tried to replace plentiful housing resources by scarce ones: an unproductive exercise.

A third assumption has been that the cost of high material standards of urban development and housing can be borne (either directly through purchase, or indirectly through taxation) by a proportion of the population large enough to make high and decent standards the norm. In practice, the intention of providing or promoting a significantly large supply of decent standard housing has proved itself to be financially unworkable: housing projects that provide dwellings of this standard have proved time after time to be too costly for the low-income majority of the urban population to occupy without extravagantly large subsidies.

As a result, housing agencies of Third World governments have found themselves faced with the dilemma of amassing huge repayment arrears by low-income occupants of decent housing; or writing off a large part of the repayment cost, and thus losing rather than recovering and reinvesting scarce public funds; or allocating public-sector housing assistance to those few able to repay all or most of its cost, and thus negating the original purposes of public authorities' intervention in the housing sector.

In the event, public housing agencies in nearly all Third World countries have taken the latter course. Only middle and upper income public servants now normally qualify for low-interest government loans for their house building, while publicly-built housing is allocated to regular wage and salary earners in government, commerce and industry. While political advantage and stability may often depend on satisfying these important minority groups in a rapidly-urbanizing country, it is precisely these groups that have the least need of housing assistance.

Present-day innovations and trends

In several Third World countries, and mainly during the past ten years, the mounting evidence of all these difficulties has begun to lead public sector planning and housing authorities to look more carefully at the performance and the output of the unplanned and uncontrolled urban settlement and housing activities that confront them, and to start working out how to influence these activities in ways that can be more productive and more generally popular than those they have tried to apply in the past.

This "rethinking" process cannot be summarized very precisely, as the evidence for it is visible mainly in the gradual and spasmodic undertaking of new types of urban development and housing programmes by these authorities - often reluctantly, and under growing political and other pressures from both above and below the city-management level - rather than in any overt and comprehensive changes in public-sector aims and policies.

The position which prevailed in the planning response to urban growth until a decade ago, and in many countries still prevails in part today, derived from a set of ideas and accepted practices which dictated a static, piecemeal, regulatory view of the urban situation and what was to be done about it. Such a view tended to highlight the causal importance of elements in that situation which are normally impossible to control, such as migration, to pursue planning solutions which were practically unattainable, such as detailed land-use controls, and to confine promising innovations, for example in the provision of low-cost housing and services, to the category of special cases. It reflected an essentially conservative diagnosis of urban conditions, focussing on the supposed difficulties engendered by sheer size and rate of growth, selectively emphasizing physical and environmental conditions as an index of supposed deterioration, accepting a continued under-utilization of land and infrastructure resources on account of established institutional practices and market operations, relying for salvation on expensive large-scale investment in new urban service systems, particularly transportation systems (based firmly on a code of standards and regulatory practices originally devised elsewhere), defining a limited scope for public policy intervention and public sector operation, and enshrining in city government a divided responsibility for urban planning, urban management and local authority accountability. These perceptions and procedures powerfully influenced the view of the urban problem as a problem for a priori definition rather than for empirical judgement. They had a great deal to do with the partial, inefficient and ineffective use of whatever resources were available for urban development, with a particularly baleful effect on housing.

In the last ten years the contemporary urban situation in a majority of developing countries has been subjected to more or less radical reinterpretation, in parallel with the evolution of a new view of the planning process. The elements of this new diagnosis and response include an emphasis on economic opportunities offered by large and rapidly growing urban concentrations, on changes in environmental and physical conditions indicative of processes of adaptation to urban life, on the mobilization of labour and land resources latent in the urban situation, on the use of organisational and management innovations to substitute for massive capital investment, on the use of planning standards and technologies which are adaptable to the capacities and needs of households involved in incrementally improving their occupations and residences, and on the use of a wide range of policy measures and public enterprise activities to reinforce ongoing urban development by direct support. This new view turns the urban problem for planning into a potential opportunity - resource constraints become a spur to local initiative, public enterprise, managerial efficiency, and above all, a search for emerging relationships within the urban economy and society that will release extra resources. The formerly defensive reaction to urban growth has been gradually replaced by an essentially action-oriented, positive strategy for promoting development, in the sense of guiding urban growth through a series of structural changes that can sustain further growth.

This "action planning" approach links back to previous comments on population predictions and rural-urban migration. The new emphasis is on continuous, incremental, flexible and immediate planning responses in situations which, by the nature of things, cannot be preconceived nor effectively constrained in some preplanned blueprint. The city makes itself and its citizens make their opportunities as they go along. What individual households or groups cannot do to cope with largely unpredicable circumstances is to provide a citywide framework within which resources can be matched to the provision of essentially public goods. Traditional urban planning, of which housing and residential area planning was a sub-species, did not relate itself to such matters save in the one-dimensional space of physical appearance and organisation. The new planning is more comprehensively concerned with the application of resources to selected public projects geared to respond to popular demands and needs. The continuing influx of migrants into the city on the basis of chances of improved economic prospects and social conditions can then be absorbed up to that point where the fully mobilized resources generated in and by the city can sustain such improvement, where this is defined by the needs and aspirations of the newcomers rather than those of the established authorities.

Many programmes and projects undertaken in recent years (and referred to in more detail in later pages) illustrate this changing public-sector approach. In crowded inner-city areas and in settlements that have developed illegally, wholesale demolition and redevelopment schemes are gradually being superceded by improvement projects often entailing the provision of various urban utilities and services: water, sewerage and electricity networks, public schools, clinics and transportation.

At the same time the wholesale (and almost wholly ineffective) prohibitions of unauthorized new settlements, intended mainly to control development on the outskirts of a growing town or city, are now being accompanied in many countries by programmes that provide new housing sub-divisions equipped initially with minimal utilities and services. Here settlers can occupy and develop plots relatively cheaply, but with long-term security of tenure and the prospect of a gradual improvement of the area's equipment, as and when they and the town or city can afford it.

Programmes and projects of these kinds do have important policy implications for the future, even when these are not fully appreciated or acknowledged by the public authorities that are undertaking them.

Firstly, they represent a significant change in the aims and the role of urban planning itself, since they show an increasing emphasis on the planner's job of incorporating and consolidating urban development and housing results that have already taken place, and of providing for and safeguarding housing events that are certain to occur in the predictable future. This new emphasis is one that makes urban planning authorities deal very much more closely with the complex realities of the present and near-future urban growth and housing situations that confront them. They can no longer afford to base their work on the sketchy information and simplistic interpretations of present conditions, and the faulty predictions of future needs and demands, that have in the past undermined so many of their attempts to introduce preconceived patterns and standards for development in their towns and cities.

This more action-oriented role for urban planning requires of public-sector planning authorities direct contact, communication and negotiation with their citizen clients, and will undoubtedly bring about some major changes not only in the aims but also in the methods and institutions on Third World planning itself.

Secondly, these new types of programme indicate a growing recognition by public authorities of both the scarcity of the capital and other resources that they dispose of, and the effective parameters for action that they finance and control.

In programmes and projects of these kinds, public funds are used not to displace the housing resources of households and local communities themselves, but to support and complement them: public spending is focussed on securing those elements of urban settlement and housing that do really need a coordinated provision, such as land, housing utilities and urban services. This leaves the way open for much greater freedom of legal choice by low-income households themselves in deciding the standards and costs of their housing - while providing them with a secure and healthy urban environment in which these choices and decisions can be made.

We can see here the gradual emergence of an understanding of "housing" itself as the necessary assembly over time of several distinct elements, brought together at different timings and from public, private and popular resources that are organised in a variety of ways - rather than "housing" consisting of publicly - controlled products of an unvarying standard.

Thirdly, programmes and projects of these new kinds are, in many Third World countries, the first publicly-sponsored settlement and housing provisions that low-income households can afford to accept and pay for. They involve a recognition that, in the low-income conditions prevailing in virtually all the rapidly-urbanizing countries, neither long-term urban security nor popular well-being can be gained by burdening low-income users of housing with costs of urban development and housing that are too high to be recovered and reinvested: in the long run, only higher incomes can lead to costlier housing.

This is of course makes it all the more essential for public authorities to ensure that the provisions they make for low-income settlement and housing generate as much employment and earning capacity as possible among their clients. The new types of programme now being undertaken can represent an important step forward in this direction also, which is referred to in more detail in later pages.

The following pages describe and compare a variety of examples of this evolving approach by public authorities to the settlement and housing needs of their low-income majorities. The examples include both current schemes that are being undertaken within the existing framework of laws and institutions in the city concerned, and longer-term changes and reforms in the structure of urban housing markets themselves: changes that are more and more needed, and that are beginning to be considered and advanced for the nature.

## III. TOWARDS PRODUCTIVE PUBLIC-SECTOR PERFORMANCE

### Present and future programmes and projects

The current re-thinking by planning and housing authorities described in the preceding pages is resulting in an array of new kinds of public-sector programmes and projects aimed much more accurately than were their predecessors at the needs of poor population groups. Some of these programmes are concerned with remedying the worst effects of unplanned urban growth and housing developments that have already taken place, while others begin to anticipate and provide for future low-income demands for land and other settlement needs.

When we examine the present-day variety of these low-income settlement and housing programmes in terms of their objectives and content, some clear programme groupings can be identified. Moreover some urgent questions common to the programmes of each group are frequently presenting themselves to programme organisers and users alike, and these are questions that need to be looked at for the future.

The following pages deal firstly with current programmes and projects that are aimed at remedying the effects of unsupported urban settlement and housing; and secondly with programmes aimed at providing for future demands for urban settlement and housing.

Slum rehabilitation programmes

One important group of programmes and projects concerns the rehabilitation of slum tenements, commonly located in densely populated inner-city areas. In such areas both the ownership and the occupancy of dwellings is usually "legal" in the sense that no property rights are being violated; but the dwellings themselves are often overcrowded and insanitary and sometimes structurally unsafe. Dwellings in these areas are usually rented from an absentee landlord or resident owner, and often consist of only one or two rooms, in a multi-dwelling building. These are often old properties that have deteriorated through subdivision into cheap rental accommodation; but in some cities they include newer properties deliberately built by their owners to extremely low construction and sanitary standards so as to maximize rental returns.

A central question posed by the rehabilitation of this kind of housing is: how can environmental and housing conditions in these rental properties be improved without prejudicing the security of the present tenants? Very commonly these are tenant-households that simply cannot afford to pay the higher rents that dwelling improvement is likely to entail; moreover they tend to be households that are tied to their present inner-city location by having to live close to their jobs there, and by their lack of savings capacity.

One approach to this problem has been to try and ensure that the cost burden entailed in rehabilitation is borne by the landlord-owner and by the city itself, instead of being recovered in higher rents from the tenants of improved properties. In Bombay, approximately half of the cost of the Corporation's Repairs and Reconstruction Programme for inner-city tenements has been met by compulsory surcharges on the taxes paid by all owners of house-property in the city; while the other half of the programme's cost has been met from other city and state revenues.

The rehabilitation of slum properties in this programme is also compulsory, and is carried out under the Corporation's direction. The owner of an improved property is not allowed, under the prevailing rent-control regulations, to increase the rents payable by his tenants.

This programme has, as one might expect, met with stiff opposition from Bombay's property owners; but it achieved some notable results in the early 1970's when some 20,000 dwellings each year were being repaired or rebuilt at an average programme cost of £100 per dwelling. The Corporation's aim was then to complete its first cycle of rehabilitation - aimed at repairing those inner-city slum properties in imminent danger of collapse - by 1977, and to follow this by a second programme-cycle aimed at improving sanitary standards in this part of the city's housing stock.

The house properties dealt with in this Bombay programme are mostly of four or five storeys, and the building densities and dwelling-occupancy rates they entail are extremely high: population densities in the areas occupied by properties of this kind have been estimated to exceed 4,000 persons to the acre. Since the majority of this inner-city population's jobs are close to home, the programme was planned to avoid any large-scale relocation of residents elsewhere.

This is a programme aimed not at any radical redevelopment of the inner city, but at prolonging the life of much of its housing stock by twenty or twenty-five years and rendering it safe to occupy during this period, when its inhabitants must depend on it. Many Third World cities are now in urgent need of practical "emergency" programmes of this kind, if their low-rental housing stock is to survive the intense pressures to which it will be subjected over the coming generation or more.

A different approach to the rehabilitation of slum property in the inner city is being adopted in the improvement and conservation programme for the historic central Medina area of Tunis. Here the housing stock is mostly made up of large multi-roomed courtyard properties of two or three storeys, of a type traditional to many Arab cities.

In Tunis large numbers of these houses in the Medina have been converted by their owners into rental accommodation, the indoor areas being sub-divided among perhaps ten to twenty tenant households in a single property and the original courtyard being either built over or shared among the tenants. Daylight, ventilation and sanitary conditions are extremely poor and (while overall population densities are considerably lower than in the Bombay case) many tenant households occupy only one or two rooms each.

In recent years a number of these tenement buildings have been confiscated by the Tunis Municipality from landlord owners who have failed to pay property or other taxes, and efforts are now being made by the authorities to rehabilitate these properties on behalf of their tenant residents. After confiscation of the building, its tenants continue to pay for their accommodation: not as rent to the landlord, but as purchase instalments to the Municipality for their dwelling. The intention here is to transfer legal ownership of the building and its dwellings to the residents, who may own it jointly as a co-operative or may own individual dwellings within the building itself.  This gradual transfer of ownership from landlord to tenant via the Municipality is to be accompanied by a rehabilitation of the dwellings involved:  work whose initial costs can be met by the Municipality and other public bodies, and recovered from the new owners in their purchase instalments for the building itself.

Like the Bombay programme, this Tunis programme has the advantage of rehabilitating inner-city slum housing without necessarily burdening its present users with high additional costs, and without evicting them from their homes.  While the scope of the Tunis programme is limited, in its present form, to properties confiscated from landlords the supply of housing for such a programme could be greatly increased through compulsory public purchase of deficient buildings, for similar gradual re-sale to their occupants.

While the Tunis programme is still at a very early stage, its potential contribution to long-term urban development is perhaps greater than is that of the Bombay programme;  the transfer of house-ownership that the Tunis programme entails makes it not only a good vehicle for slum rehabilitation, but also a useful testing and training ground for longer-term policies, legislation and methods in urban land reform, where this involves spreading the legal ownership and control of housing over a wider spectrum of the urban community.

Improvement programmes in unauthorized areas

The latter objective plays an important part in another group of these programmes aimed at remedying the effects of past urban growth and housing activities.  This group concerns the improvement of housing areas that originated through popular action and that have developed hitherto without legal recognition or official support.  These areas have usually originated on the periphery of the built-up area of the town or city where vacant land was available at the time of their origin.

Some of these housing areas have been developed illegally, through squatter-invasions of land that has clearly-established public or private ownership;  while other such areas have been developed on marginal desert, swamp (e.g. Guayaquil) or hillside lands that have no clear owners, in a process of spontaneous or informal settlement that cannot accurately be termed an "invasion".  In both these cases, however, the developers of land and houses usually have no legal title to either.

This fact has often been used by public authorities in the past to justify their prohibition or demolition of housing in areas of both these kinds, or to explain delays in their provision of public utilities and services.  The constant risk of eviction and the lack of elementary services have, in turn, often discouraged the residents of these areas from investing time, money and effort in larger and better houses, since this may merely provide more eventual fodder for a bulldozer.

The vicious circle of illegality, insecurity and under-investment clearly has to be broken, in housing areas of this kind, if its residents' own housing resources are to be fully utilized. But what kinds of public-sector support are needed in order for people to bring these housing resources into play?

The most important supportive measure is undoubtedly the legalization of achieved occupancy of the land. Different ways of doing this are being developed in several countries at the present time, and some of them will be examined later in more detail.

Another important incentive for popular housing investment in these areas is the residents' secure prospect of obtaining those urban utilities and services that they need and can afford.

A third form of public-sector support (needed in some, but not all circumstances) is the provision or promotion of loan finance for the capital costs of house building and improvement. In some countries such loans are being provided directly from public funds, while in others public-sector support may take the indirect form of loan guarantees and/or interest-rate subsidies for credit from private commercial sources.

A fourth incentive - especially valuable in housing areas remote from the town or city's main employment centres - is the public-sector promotion of local job and income opportunities, for example by loans and other assistance to individual or co-operative enterprises in the housing area.

At least three of these supportive measures have figured in the improvement project initiated in the mid-1960s in the Las Colinas settlement in Bogota, Colombia. This settlement occupies two very steep hillsides that were privately-owned, and were invaded in the early 1960s. Within three years the area had been totally occupied by squatters, who carved terraced platforms out of the hillside for their first houses built of bamboo, corrugated iron and scrap materials.

By 1969 three main bodies were engaged in the improvement of Las Colinas: the city's low-income housing bank (Caja de Vivienda Popular), the Municipality, and the Las Colinas residents' association. The housing bank purchased the land from its legal owners and proceeded to re-sell it as individual house plots to the plot-occupants, who pay for them in small monthly instalments over fifteen years or less. No evictions could take place during this period provided that plot payments were maintained. The housing bank also initiated a programme of low-interest loans to residents for enlarging and improving their homes, with priority being given to kitchen and bathroom construction; these loans also are repayable monthly. Not all households have taken up the housing loans available, since some did not need them while others could not afford them.

Meanwhile the Municipality provided the area with housing utilities and services: domestic water and sewer mains and public lighting, as well as a school/community centre and a paved road with a bus service connecting Las Colinas to the rest of the city. The Municipality has also provided the residents' association with tools and materials for local infrastructural improvements, notably surface-water drains and paved footpaths to protect the hillsides from erosion.

The residents' association, for its part, has provided manpower for these infrastructural works by organising its members in voluntary sparetime labour, and by collecting members' contributions for the payment of local artisans for these works.

A notable change has taken place in the standard of Las Colinas' housing stock during this improvement programme. Whereas in 1969 approximately 80% of its houses were still built in temporary materials and only 20% in permanent ones, by 1973 these proportions were almost exactly reversed. Most of this housing improvement has required no public finance whatever, and those housing loans that have been provided are largely recoverable. There can be no doubt that a major cause of this housing improvement has been the domestic security obtained through the legalization of the residents' occupancy of the land: security for which they were quite prepared to pay, when given the opportunity to do so in a way that their incomes permitted.

In Bogota and most other cities in Latin America private freehold ownership of land is the norm, and the ambition to achieve this motivates urban settlers and squatters throughout the continent. But in some parts of the world (including Africa, as we have seen) the concepts of land-ownership and of land as a marketable commodity are still relatively recent ones that have not necessarily replaced, in peoples' ambitions, long-established customary rights to the use of land through membership in a landholding group or community.

This reminds us that the legalization of land occupancy, in areas like Las Colinas, does not necessarily entail freehold ownership by individuals. In many countries the leasing of land for housing use may provide a perfectly adequate security-incentive for people to invest in housing improvement. In Lusaka there has been much discussion in recent years over this aspect of improvement programmes in the city's squatter areas, where the land occupied is mostly in public ownership. In this case the leasing out of land to its occupants, instead of transferring its ownership to them, seems to have some long-term advantages for the city as a whole.

If people are granted legal rights of land-use through leasehold occupancy, the lease itself can be an effective tool for coordinating and sanctioning urban land uses of different kinds. Moreover by leasing out public land for a finite period of time, the city authorities can reserve the option of recovering and reallocating (or redeveloping) this land for other purposes, on the eventual expiry of leases.

In some other countries where the formal ownership or leasing of land is not yet widespread, adequate security of tenure may not yet require the granting of any formal titles. Where the land occupied is publicly-owned, or has no clear ownership, the providing of utilities and services by the authorities may in itself be sufficient de facto recognition, for the time being, of the local population's right to live there. This option often has the advantage of postponing difficult decisions on long-term rights to land; but sooner or later these rights have to be resolved, and a postponement will perhaps only be justified when it gives time for examining all the legalization options available, and for developing locally feasible and acceptable land-rights policies and programmes.

Site and service programmes

Many of the land-holding and other questions raised by improvement programmes in existing "illegal" housing areas figure also in a group of programmes of another kind: those aimed at providing new land and urban services at a low public cost, for future housing use by low-income populations. Programmes of this kind, generally known as site-and-service programmes, are being undertaken on an increasing scale in many Third World towns and cities - often with loans and other assistance from the World Bank, the United Nations Development Programme and other international sources. Perhaps the main question that site-and-service programmes have posed so far is this: Who most needs cheap urban land and services?

It has often been assumed that cheap housing land and services are most needed by the poorest members of a population, who cannot afford to pay for more costly public housing assistance. Yet this group tends to be the least mobile part of the urban community, depending very much on living close to whatever work-opportunities they can find in the built-up central or industrial area of the town or city. This means that they often have to live in other people's houses, even when this involves paying rent they can ill afford, for shared accommodation in existing slums or shanty-towns. When urban households of this lowest income category have been allocated new housing sites and services, this has often separated them from their jobs or clienteles by greatly increased journeys and travel costs, while also requiring of them lump-sum spending on house construction that greatly exceeds the rents they have paid (or owed) hitherto.

A common result of this in several cities has been the development of a kind of "black market" in publicly-provided housing sites, with many of the lowest-income clients of a site-and-service programme renting or selling out their rights to speculators or relatively wealthy settlers: that is, to people who can afford to live there and to build their houses to the costly standards too often laid down by the programme organisers.

Experience so far suggests that, by and large, the most appropriate clients for site-and-service programmes tend to be those households that have recently gained relatively secure jobs and incomes - often after some years of renting a room in the inner city - and can now afford to make the longer journeys to work and the gradual housing investments involved in developing a more distant and vacant site. For this part of the low-income population, site-and-service programmes can enable them to achieve the housing transition between room-rental and full home-ownership without hardship, and at their own pace.

It has been shown (for example in Lima, Guayaquil and several other cities) that a high proportion of squatter-invaders of peripheral urban land in fact belong to just this income-category, which might be termed "low-income with good prospects". If site-and-service programmes can gradually supercede land-invasions in meeting the needs of this important part of the urban population, both they and the town or city as a whole will benefit.

Given this kind of clientele for site-and-service programmes, there are several ways in which the actual provision of land and services can hasten both the development of housing in the programme areas, and the recovery of the programme's capital costs. Firstly, by enabling the settler households to earn as much income as possible in the programme area. When households can include shops, small workshops and other enterprises in the development of their house plots, and build rooms for lodgers as well as for family living, the income they gain in this way can enable them to build the house more quickly. Any city planning or zoning regulations that now impede a mixed and productive local land-use of this kind, in low-income areas, need scrutiny and revision.

The same principle can also of course be applied on a larger scale, by allocating to groups of settlers land-areas additional to their own housing needs and earmarked for small industries, markets and other commercial uses - possibly with the proviso that all or part of the rental and other income gained by the group from these areas go towards their repayment of the capital costs of their settlement.

Secondly, the capital costs of providing sites and services can be recovered from the area's residents more easily if the area's development is itself spread over a time period: if, for example, housing utilities and urban services are introduced in stages that keep pace with the development of housing in the area, and with the increase in the area's user-population. Water and sewerage mains can be installed to serve communal water-points and latrines initially, and domestic connections at a later date; public lighting supplies can later be extended to provide indoor electricity; earth roads can be sequentially graded and surfaced to carry increasing local traffic; and land-areas can be reserved for future extensions to initially-small schools and clinics - and can often be used for recreation, markets and other purposes in the interim.

Site-and-service schemes already show a great variety of initial levels and costs of provision. The settlement areas of this kind provided by the Delhi Development Authority in the early 1960s, for example, had communal washing and sanitary areas in their first phase; while the

Chainama Hills project in Lusaka started in 1963 with only communal water points: settlers were required to dig pit-latrines on their house plots before starting house construction. In the same city the Munali project of 1969-1970 provided each house plot with domestic water supply and toilet facilities from the outset. While an initially-low standard of provision can always be improved later, an initially-high standard of provision may never get paid for.

The staging of public provisions of this kind not only allows the capital investment required for them to be spread over a long period of time; it can also ensure that these provisions are made in response to local demand for such services, rather than in accordance with demand-predictions that may well prove to be mistaken.

Site-and-service programmes provide a viable long-term setting for other measures such as public sector loan schemes for the capital costs of house-building and for local manufacturing, commercial and other enterprises. As in the case of improvement programmes in existing housing areas, measures of these kinds can sometimes be a useful support for the residents' own resources, in settling and developing the area. In some cities, however, public authorities have tended to use housing credit programmes as a means for controlling the standard and cost of house construction in site-and-service areas, by imposing strict specifications for the use of their loans. This can all too easily undermine the vital role that site-and-service programmes can play in providing settlement areas for a gradual increase in residents' housing expenditure, and for their incremental and varied adoption of more costly housing standards over time.

It is important, of course, that this gradual and variable development of housing does not contravene any local public health and fire regulations necessary for safety - and in many Third World cities these regulations are grossly inappropriate and ineffective - but beyond this there appears to be no good case for restricting households' choice of builders, standards and costs for their dwellings.

There may be great advantages to be gained, in some countries, by allocating house plots and/or organising housing and related loan-schemes on a collective, co-operative basis. The more responsibility for such matters is assumed by extended-family, community and other local associations, the lower can be the public-sector overhead costs of the scheme. In many Third World countries governmental assistance to housing and other co-operatives is already well established, but has not yet been adapted to the settlement and employment needs of low-income as well as middle-income groups.

Longer term changes and reforms

The supportive types of present-day programmes and projects described in the preceding pages are clear signs of a trend in many

Third World countries towards a more realistic and productive use of public-sector resources, in meeting the settlement and housing needs of their urbanizing populations.

So far, however, these programmes have mostly been undertaken in an ad hoc fashion, in response to growing local political and other pressures in the countries concerned, and they do not call into serious question the land and housing market-structures in which they play a part. Yet these exclusive market-structures have themselves given rise to the massive housing conflicts and deficiencies that programmes of this kind are intended to remedy.

As well as the direct results that such programmes can achieve, their realization itself is providing increasing contact, experience and understanding among all the actors involved in them, and particularly among government agencies and their low-income clients. In the long run, perhaps the most important role of programmes and projects of these kinds will lie in their contribution of this experience to the development of reforms in the structure of national land and housing markets - and in the laws and institutions that these involve - so as make them more responsive to the needs of the low-income majority. While market changes of this kind are most urgently needed in urban areas, where the elements of settlement and housing already have a market value, they will also affect rural populations more and more as urbanization continues to bring them and their transactions into the nation's monetary economy.

There appear to be three principle fields where future changes in the housing market are most likely to be needed in most Third World countries. These are land, finance and technology: the basic elements that have to be combined for the production of any dwelling.

Settlement land

Perhaps the greatest single obstacle confronting low-income urban households in need of housing, in Third World countries, is the scarcity of land for their cheap and legal settlement. Approaches to this problem of course vary greatly, among these countries, according to their land-ownership situations, the political circumstances of the day, and the policy directions and objectives that the country is adopting for the future. But measures that are being considered or undertaken include:

a) Public-sector efforts to reduce the prices and profits at which private land-ownership or use rights change hands. Intervention of this kind in the land market commonly takes the form of compulsory land purchase at regulated prices, and the taxation of land transactions. In Chile and Colombia in the 1960's private land was being compulsorily purchased by the state at the low values quoted in landowners' own tax-declarations of assets, and this is perhaps a practice that could usefully be multiplied.

b) Penalizing owners of private land needed for settlement and housing, who fail to make it available. This type of measure aims to discourage the hoarding of land for speculative purposes, and often needs to accompany measures of type a), if the regulation of profits is not to reduce even further the supply of private land for development.
c) The study and promotion of new land-tenure arrangements other than freehold ownership by individuals: for example, the long-term leasing of land to housing co-operatives. Such arrangements can reduce the cost entailed by individual low-income families, and alternative tenures of this kind-developed in allocating public lands can perhaps be applied later to lands in private ownership, with appropriate changes in law.
d) Modifying the regulations that govern standards of land use and building construction, so as to make legal the initially low housing investments that low-income households can sustain. Official development-standards often now make the legal use of land too costly for low-income groups to undertake. Combinations of measures c) and d) can enable even relatively poor families to start making productive use of an improved land supply.

Settlement and housing finance

Popular investment in urban housing is constrained not only by low incomes, but also by low-income households' difficulties in obtaining housing credit in advance of their earnings and savings. Though capital for housing loans seems certain to remain in short supply in most Third World countries, their governments can do something to improve low-income groups' access to any available public or private housing capital by developing new forms of security or guarantee for loan finance.

The most promising vehicles for this appear at present to be credit unions and similar types of co-operative in which the aggregate of small savings by individual low-income members can be supplemented by loans granted to, and recovered from, the association itself. The outstanding successes achieved by credit unions in Peru, for example, over the past fifteen years shows their value in increasing the financial security of poor families.

In the long run, however, public-sector support of any kind can only succeed - and its costs can only be recovered - if real efforts are made to increase employment and income among the population groups most in need of better housing. While this basic issue of course reaches far beyond the settlement and housing sector, examples given on preceding pages show that governmental provisions for settlement and housing can themselves contribute to higher earnings among low-income households.

Housing technology

Perhaps the most direct way for Third World governments to increase employment and incomes through the housing sector lies in the promotion of labour-intensive house construction. In many rapidly growing towns and cities building construction provides jobs for at least 15% of the labour force; and unskilled and semi-skilled building work is one of the main means of entry to urban employment for large numbers of newcomers from rural areas.

Yet in many Third World countries the use of imported, high-technology building materials, the increasing activities of large, capital-intensive building firms, and the advanced types of construction often demanded by official building programmes and regulations all tend to favour the growth of a capital-intensive building industry: an extremely wasteful trend in countries with plentiful manpower and scarce capital resources. Several kinds of public sector measures can help to halt or reverse this trend:

a) Encouraging the growth of small-scale, labour-intensive building enterprises, both indirectly through tax incentives, selective credit programmes and loan-guarantees; and directly by employing small contractors for publicly-funded construction projects. Bombay's slum rehabilitation programme has been carried out very largely by small building firms local to the programme area - many of whom did not previously qualify for the award of government contracts.

b) Developing local raw materials into cheap building products and components suited to labour-intensive use on the building site. In some cases this involves finding alternatives for traditional building materials that are now in short supply: for example, the need in Egypt for a cheap replacement for the mud-brick traditionally made from the silt of the annual Nile flood. In other cases it involves finding building uses for the waste products of crop-processing, such as cotton-stalks and sugar-cane bagasse in Sudan. In all cases it urgently requires assistance from public funds.

c) Similar research and development is needed for building tools and equipment suited to the needs of small entrepreneurs: cheap and durable, easily transported and maintained, quickly mastered without technical skill, and with minimal fuel and power requirements. A famous product of this kind is the portable CINVA ram, first developed by the Interamerican Housing Centre in Colombia in the 1950's for making building blocks, and now found in many local variants all over the world.

SUMMARY

The new kinds of settlement and housing programmes now being sponsored by public authorities in many Third World countries, and the longer-term changes and reforms in the supply of housing land and finance and in the development of housing technology that these authorities are beginning to consider and promote, are slowly increasing public sector support for housing's essential role as a generator of social and economic change and advance.

This is the way in which the urbanizing low-income majorities in Third World countries themselves make use of their housing, and they need all possible public-sector support in doing so.

REFERENCES AND BIBLIOGRAPHY

A. Publications

Abrams, Charles: Housing in the Modern World; Faber, London 1966.

Brausch, Crooke and Shaw: Bashaqra Area Settlements 1963, University of Khartoum, 1964. El' Kereiba Village 1962. University of Khartoum, 1963.

Breese, Gerald: The City in Newly Developing Countries, Prentice Hall, 1972.

Crooke, Patrick: Rural Settlement and Housing Trends in a Developing Country: An Example in Nigeria. International Labour Review, No. 3, Vol. 96. ILO Geneva 1967.

Crooke, Patrick: El Suburbio Guayaquileno. Revista del Archivo Historico del Guayas, Guayaquil, 1974.

Dwyer, D. J.: People and Housing in Third World Cities: Perspectives on the Problem of Spontaneous Settlements; Longman, London, 1975.

Gaitskell, Arthur: Gezira. A Story of Development in the Sudan; Faber and Faber, Lond, 1959.

Grimes, Orville: Housing for Low Income Urban Families; World Bank Research Publication, Johns Hopkins, Baltimore, 1976.

Koenigsberger, Otto: The Absorption of Newcomers in the Cities of Developing Countries. (Paper for UN Conference on Human Settlements, Vancouver, 1976), London, 1975.

Koenigsberger, Otto: Action Planning, Architectural Association Quarterly, London, May 1964.

Laquian, A. (ed): Rural-Urban Migration and Metropolitan Development; Intermet, Toronto, 1971.

MacIntosh, Duncan: The Politics of Primacy: Political Factors in the Development of Guayaquil. M. Sc. Thesis, Columbia University, 1972.

Mangin, W. (ed.): Peasants in Cities: Readings in the Anthropology of Urbanization; Houghton Mifflin, 1970.

McGee, T. G.: The Urbanization Process in the Third World: Explorations in Search of a Theory; Bell, London, 1971.

Peattie, L.: The View from the Barrio; University of Michigan Press, 1968.

Perlman, J.: The Myth of Marginality: Poverty and Politics in Rio de Janeiro; University of California Press, 1976.

Rodwin, L.: Nations and Cities: The Comparison of Strategies for Urban Growth; Houghton Mifflin, 1976.

Turner and Fichter (eds.): Freedom to Build; Macmillan, London and New York, 1972.

Turner, J. F. C.: Housing by People; Marion Boyars, London, 1976.

United Nations: Growth of the World's Urban and Rural Population, 1920-2000; New York, 1969.

United Nations: Urbanization: Development Policies and Planning: International Social Development Review No. 1; New York, 1968.

United Nations: Improvement of Slums and Uncontrolled Settlements. (Report of UN Interregional Seminar, Medellin Colombia 1970), New York, 1971.

Ward, B.: The Home of Man: Penguin, Harmondsworth (London), 1976.

Wilsher P. and Righter R.: The Exploding Cities, Deutsch, London, 1975.

World Bank: Urbanization: Sector Working Paper. Washington, 1972.

World Bank: Housing: Sector Working Paper. Washington, 1975.


B.  Bodies regularly sponsoring and/or publishing studies in the fields of Third World Urbanization, Settlement and Housing:

Athens Centre of Ekistics, 24 Strat Syndesmou Street, Athens 136. (Ekistics reviews on the Problems and Science of Human Settlements).

Centre for Housing Building and Planning, United Nations, New York.

Development Planning Unit, University College London, 10-12 Percy Street, London W. 1.

Intermediate Technology Development Group, 9 King Street, London, W. C. 1.

International Development Research Centre, Box 5800, Ottawa, Canada.

United States Agency for International Development, Washington DC; especially "Ideas and Methods Exchange" series published for USAID by Office of International Affairs, Dept. of Housing and Urban Development, Washington DC.

World Bank, 1818 H Street, Washington DC; especially Staff Working Papers.

# 6

## DEMOGRAPHIC CONSTRAINTS AND EDUCATION POLICIES

by

Jacques Hallak

and

Ta Ngoc Châu

## I. INTRODUCTION

The decline in mortality, notably infant mortality, during the last twenty-five years in the developing countries is one of the significant events of our time, and its numerous implications and repercussions stretch far into the future.

Unlike the industrialized countries, where a similar decline was observed in the past, the fall was much more rapid; nor was it accompanied, apart from a few exceptions, by a parallel fall in the birth rate. These two tendencies combined led to very rapid population growth, but above all to an age structure characterized by the strong predominance of the younger age groups.

The implications for the development of education systems are clear. More than rapid population growth, it is above all the age structure which makes the same educational objective demand a much greater effort from the developing countries than from industrialized countries which have different demographic characteristics.

In global terms, the problem thus appears simple and all countries have now become aware of this population weight and its effects on the expansion of schooling. But while the demographic factor may have played a dominant role in past trends, it is by no means the only one. The last twenty-five years also cover the period when many Asian and African countries attained independence. The education systems left by the colonizing powers were generally at a fairly low level of development; the proportion of children attending school was low; the severe selection practised throughout their school career heavily reduced the numbers reaching the university. On the other hand, needs appeared enormous, partly owing to the necessity of replacing foreigners in managerial posts and also as a result of the expected economic and social development. Like other rights which were denied to the colonized peoples, the right to education appeared to be one of the great conquests of independence. It was consequently not surprising that there was a strong pressure of demand and that a special effort was undertaken for the development of schooling.

The narrow starting base, the length of the educational process, and the priority given to resource allocation for education managed for a time to conceal the real problems. Moreover, the evaluation of educational systems, based mainly on "educational progress" measured in terms of increased enrolments, prevented certain inherent weaknesses from coming to light.

Very rapidly, however, the dynamic of enrolment growth proved difficult to control. The repercussions of the expansion of primary education on secondary and then on higher education, where costs are considerably greater, led to more and more acute financial problems, as the share of public resources devoted to education cannot be increased indefinitely.

Moreover, the arrival of larger and larger numbers on the labour market, the acceleration of the movement from rural to urban areas resulting partly from the disparity of income levels and living conditions, and the growth of school attendance combined to increase considerably the demand for paid employment - a demand which neither the chosen or accepted model of development nor the methods of production adopted in the modern sector can satisfy. Finding a job on leaving the education system became more and more problematical.

Faith in the outstanding role of education in development thus began to falter and the unsuitability of the education system inherited from the past, notably the colonial past, began to be perceived. The methods of educational planning were questioned and the simplifying assumptions on which it was based strongly contested.

Despite the significant and revealing results of much research work, education demand continued to be regarded as uniform and homogeneous for the sake of convenience, the school-age population constituting the whole of the potential demand. It was in relation to this potential demand that the growth of school attendance was measured. Any increase in the proportion of the school-going population in relation to the school-age population was considered as progress, without looking too closely at the composition of the school-going population and the extremely unequal representation of the various social categories.

Education demand is in fact far from homogeneous. Parents' aspirations regarding their children's future careers, and the perception of the role of education in constructing that future, vary considerably according to the social category. The sacrifice represented by the opportunity cost of school attendance is perceived differently according to family income level, cultural background and socio-occupational category. Lastly, school success and its effects on the decision to continue studies differentiate between children of different origins. If education demand is understood in its broad sense, i.e. as including not only the decision to go to school but also the decisions to continue one's studies and to move into the various streams, it may be said that inequality in education starts even at demand level.

But this inequality is further intensified by the methods of setting up supply. What supply seeks to satisfy is not the individual demand that may come from parents or students, but rather the organised demand which is capable of expressing itself, of exerting pressure, and consequently of being heard. This has resulted in large disparities in education supply, not only in the spatial distribution of supply facilities to the detriment of certain regions or areas, but also in the type of education supplied and the teaching conditions observed.

Accordingly, despite the substantial efforts made to expand education and the considerable resources devoted to this aim, the results are relatively disappointing in relation to expectations or hopes. The developing countries are in fact faced with a dual problem, on the one hand relatively clear and of a demographic nature, i.e. the effort required to serve a rapidly growing and predominantly young population, and on the other hand a much more fundamental issue leading to the questioning of optimistic and doubtless slightly simplistic assumptions concerning the role of education in development and in the reduction of social inequalities. More and more doubt is felt as to the ability of the educational systems - in the form currently existing in most countries - to solve this dual problem.

In this situation, the path to follow and the proposals to recommend depend of course on one's conception of education and the problems involved. We shall adopt two possible approaches, calling one "traditional" and the other "radical". According to one or the other approach, the solutions envisaged or adopted by the various countries will be more or less "credible". It is therefore useful to summarize each approach and comment on some proposals for solving the education crisis.

## II. THE "TRADITIONAL" APPROACH

According to the advocates of this approach, the major difficulties encountered by the education systems of most countries (in particular, the poorest ones) are as follows:

The financial constraint

The material, financial and human resources devoted to education cannot continue to increase at the same rate as in the past in order to cover current requirements due to inadequate and incomplete school enrolment and future requirements generated by the present population structure and the exceptional population growth foreseeable in the developing countries. Except in the case of the oil countries, available means of action are limited to very unsatisfactory alternatives: either to continue to transfer resources from other productive and social sectors of the economy to education; or to maintain the relative share of education in the national product but with greater intensity of resource utilization (temporary doubling-up, for instance), or to reduce the percentage of resources devoted to school education for the benefit of out-of-school educational activities (formal and non-formal).

Common sense tells us that none of the solutions are adequate, acceptable and adapted to the needs of all countries. The rules of arithmetic show that the growth of the budget percentage will ultimately be stopped: in addition, it may give rise to substantial social costs (in terms of health services, security, communications and economic growth).

Despite enormous wastage in the use of school facilities and substantial possibilities of increasing the rate of resource utilization, the demand for education obviously cannot be met by this means alone: admittedly, a dozen school map monographs on countries as different as Ireland, Morocco, Nepal and Costa Rica have shown that in certain situations one can envisage serving 30 to 40% additional students without additional resources,[1] but the magnitude of the deficit may be far greater and the "supply-demand" imbalance is not only quantitative but also qualitative and therefore cannot be met solely through the more rational use of school resources.

This has led many specialists to propose an increased effort in out-of-school activities, and the most radical of them urge the gradual elimination of formal schooling. To take an example, Malcolm Adiseshiah, referring to his own country (India), says that "despite all our padded, misleading statistics, there are more children out of school than in school, starting at 52% drop-outs by class 5 up to 80% who drop out by the SSLC level and 96% of the college-age group which is not in college ... out-of-school-or-college education has an advantage over school or college education ... such out-of-school and out-of-college provision then is made for the same number of young persons as those enrolled in schools and colleges... ".[2] However, despite this argument (and many others) in favour of out-of-school activities, we are bound to recognize with Simmons and others that we know virtually nothing of the cost-effectiveness relationships of these attractive proposals, notably the reasons why they should be more economic than

---

1. See J. Hallak, La mise en œuvre des politiques éducatives: rôle et méthodologie de la carte scolaire, to be published by Ed. F. Nathan.

2. M.S. Adiseshiah, "Education and productive work in India" in Prospects, Vol. IV, No.2, 1974, UNESCO, Paris.

in-school activities and consequently capable of believing the financial constraint.[3]   We shall revert to this later.

We may mention one particularly interesting proposal for reducing the budgetary constraint: the re-allocation of school time. In the education budget, one of the main elements is the cost of time. According to Ayesh, "time in the traditional school is very expensive, but not valuable ... the basic daily load of formal instruction is about five to seven periods of between three-quarters of an hour and one hour; instruction is carried on five or six days a week; the school year lasts eight to ten months...". In short, "time" means "more money and efforts, but also less time for the child to develop its potentialities".[4]

Starting from this, it is suggested that the school year should be shortened, that periods of instruction should be staggered by shortening the long summer vacation, that hours of school attendance should be limited to permit children to learn more from their environment, etc. These proposals are undoubtedly of interest and deserve to be considered by a number of countries.

A "qualitative" imbalance

This takes various forms:

- It is first of all spatial. For any education policy-maker, the most significant sign (because the most apparent) of the inequitable management of educational resources is provided by the data on regional and local disparities in school attendance.[5]   Such disparities are not only high between large towns, small towns and rural areas (as may be expected), but may also be very large within the same urban or rural area. According to a study on the rural district of Chahroud in Iran, expenditure per primary pupil (which gives some idea of school attendance conditions) varies from 1 to 2 or even to 3 times according to the catchment area.[6]   Similarly, a rapid analysis of the apparent attendance rates by administrative district in Peru gives variations which are too great to be due to chance or to be attributable to the trend of that country's education policy which, like many others, has led to favouring some districts at the expense of the rest.

- Above all, the imbalance is social: it is a common-place to say that the school systems of developed and developing countries discriminate

---

3.   J. Simmons, Education, Poverty and Development, IBRD Staff Working Paper, No. 188, February 1974, Washington.

4.   H. Ayesh, "Re-allocating school time in Third World schools", in Prospects, Vol. V, No. 2, 1975, UNESCO, Paris.

5.   Ta Ngoc Châu et al. Projet de recherche sur les disparités régionales dans le développement de l'éducation, (working paper), 1975, IIEP, Paris.

6.   J. Hallak et al., Etude de la carte scolaire : le charestan de Chahroud, Iran, 1975, IIEP, Paris.

by sex (in favour of boys), by ethnic group (in favour of the dominant group - "whites" in the United States, Tutsi in Burundi, Ceylonese in Sri Lanka, descendants of the Spanish colonists in certain Latin American countries, etc.), by religion and especially by socio-occupational category. In this connection, studies of school attendance by socio-economic strata have shown that in the developing countries attendance at secondary and higher educational institutions was practically reserved for children from well-off families. The reasons for this are numerous and well-known: disparities in "level" of access, disparities in family resources for covering direct costs and "loss of child earnings" due to school attendance, disparities in the backgrounds (cultural and other) of the children and their parents, etc.

- Lastly, the imbalance is temporal: the school system operates more in relation with the past than the future; teachers seek to teach what they have learnt, which is often very different from (if not in contradiction with) what the children's environment teaches them. On such different matters as engineering, physics, sex, religion, culture, etc., messages often fundamentally different from those heard in the school-room are proclaimed by the radio, television, the cinema, books, newspapers, or at public meetings.

There is no lack of imagination on how to deal with such disequilibria and various "package deals" have been proposed. The best known or most popular ones are as follows:

- Control of the geographic distribution of supply by the adoption of the school and university map. The aim is to ensure equality in the "volume" of supply, the school conditions (teacher qualifications, standardization of premises and equipment, norms of distance between home and school, etc.) and the variety of training options proposed (specialities map). It is too soon to assess the effectiveness of this type of measure, but it is already possible to discern some obstacles that will have to be overcome and which are due to the attitudes of local communities competing for the allocation of educational resources (the most powerful and the richest may well prevent the implementation of any policy to correct disparities) and to the attitudes of families (creation of "supply" does not mean that demand will follow: in Morocco, in the Gharb region, where attendance rates are very low, several well-situated educational establishments are empty or very poorly attended).

- Adoption of "quotas" for school attendance by social groups. The experience of the Eastern European countries is well known in this field, but is not entirely convincing. It is true that differences in university enrolment rates by social group are smaller than in the industrialized countries of the West and the Third World countries, but the differences seem likely to be maintained at a significant level.[7]

---

7. J. Markiewicz-Lagneau, Education, égalité et socialisme, Paris, Anthropos, 1969.

- Broader programmes of aid and assistance to the poorest families to offset the economic handicaps. Fellowships, free accommodation and canteen services, students loans at low or zero interest rates, etc. undoubtedly help to improve the situation for some children, even if the improvement remains marginal.[8] Correcting the economic imbalances would in fact call for a fundamental review of the educational financing system so as to ensure a real re-allocation of the State budget according to income criteria. This also implies covering not only the direct costs of education but also the "lack of earnings" according to ways and means (to be defined) which take account, in particular, of the share of the "lack of earnings" in the family resources.[9] Unfortunately, while these proposals may be envisaged "on paper", their adoption and implementation raise political, social, administrative and institutional problems of such difficulty that it seems unreasonable (to some people) to take them into consideration.

- Recourse to out-of-school activities to reduce the "temporal" imbalance. Adiseshiah proposed for India "to close our high schools and universities and colleges for two years and induct our students in ... National Service schemes, youth corps and other rural development programmes where they would have the privilege and opportunity of working productively in the farm or factory". In China all universities were closed for three years, during which period students and teachers worked in communes with other members of the production brigades. Other countries such as Tanzania, Ethiopa and Cuba followed similar paths and it would be very useful to evaluate the results of their experience as a possible illustration of the fashionable slogan about replacing the traditional school by the parallel school. (Obviously the state of existing rural employment levels would be an important factor.)

- Deschooling, or less radically "bursting open" educational establishments. The reference is not only to Illich's proposal, to which we shall revert later, but also to North American experiments like the Parkway in Philadelphia where the school is to some extent "in the street" - a museum, a theatre, the Stock Exchange, a railway station, a parking lot ... all available resources serve as a "location" and "argument" for training children. The importance of such enterprises is considerable for they are not limited to solving the problem of the disequilibrium (that we have called "temporal") between school and real life; these experiments have other aspirations, notably the questioning of the social system to which they are attached. From this point of view, they relate rather to the "radical" approach which we shall discuss later.

---

8. J.P. Jallade, Student loans in developing countries: an evaluation of the Colombian experience, IBRD Staff Working Paper, No. 182, Washington, 1974.

9. J. Hallak, A qui profite l'école ? PUF, Paris, 1974.

Educational "stagflation"

In other words, inflation of enrolments and educational costs, combined with stagnation of employment prospects. This difficulty is not characteristic of the poor countries alone; far from it. Apart from a few prosperous enclaves, unemployment is rife everywhere and affects everyone. But it affects young people in particular and consequently the "school-leavers". It is therefore all the more intolerable because education has drawn vast sums from the national income at the expense of so-called productive investment which creates jobs; it has roused hopes of economic progress (incomes) unlikely to be realized; it has been the subject of carefully prepared development plans. Educational stagflation is so politically sensitive that it has provoked a real crisis of confidence in the school systems and favoured the appearance of wildly extreme proposals even if these are justified or legitimised only by the "flight forward" reflex.

Admittedly, the structural (and notably demographic) character of educational stagflation is recognized; admittedly, it is widely known that the solution to the problem of graduate unemployment must be found mainly outside the school, which at best may favour certain economic policies. It is nevertheless the case that several countries, on the basis of pessimistic analyses of their school systems, are launching out into vast programmes for reforming structures, content and methods. Merely to list these programmes would require a work far exceeding the scope of this Chapter. We shall therefore give only a few significant examples.

An example of structural reform[10]

The analysis and objectives of such reforms vary according to the country. In Nepal, the aim is to help to attain the objective of universal primary education (by shortening the duration of primary school from five to three years and limiting its purpose to "making children literate"), to increase the duration of lower secondary school from three to four years (with the ambitious objective of "building the character of the students") and of increasing secondary school from two to three years (in order to provide vocational education for training skilled workers).[11] Thus the new system:

a)   aims at solving problems of equal access to basic education by minimizing the cost of primary school;
b)   seeks to establish concrete links between the various sectors of the national economy and the education system.

---

10.   There is no "pure" reform. For the sake of simplicity, emphasis has been placed more particularly on structure, content or methods.

11.   D. Bhatt, M. Mohsin, "Restructuring the educational system in Nepal" in Prospects, Vol. V, No. 1, UNESCO, Paris, 1975.

It also seeks to limit the emergence of graduate unemployment by deciding that university enrolments must be determined in relation to the country's manpower requirements. Lastly, being aware of the demographic constraint[12] and the need for the country to double its efforts just to keep pace with the increase in the school-age population, the authorities expect that the majority of the population will be unable to benefit from formal education and envisage a vast programme of out-of-school education. This reform, with its many aspects, illustrates the enormous constraints which poor countries have to face: the difficulties of carrying it out are commensurate with its ambitious objectives; the most obvious difficulties relate to the lack of adequate communications, the shortage of qualified teachers, the slowness in setting up an adequate school infrastructure - premises, laboratories, textbooks - and especially the considerable disparities in living conditions between the Terai Plain, the valleys (e.g. Khatmandu) and the mountain region. It is too soon to predict the results of this reform since, according to the plan, the new system will not cover the whole territory until the end of 1976.[13] No doubt progress will be recorded, but will it be due to the reform? And will it be significant enough to legitimise the reform? Will it really be possible to secure cost-savings by reducing primary schooling by two years?[14] Will it really be possible to restrict entrance to the university in a society which attaches great value to higher degrees? Can one really check migration, when considerable disparities in income and living conditions persist between districts, by the mere fact of having decreed that the main objective of the lower secondary school is to establish a link between education and the surrounding environment? Will one succeed in limiting the alarming drop-out rates by "making the learning hours and working days longer" and "more recreation", while in a rural area children form an essential labour reserve for tending domestic animals and doing household chores? Many other questions may be added to the above, foreshadowing the "radical" approach to educational issues which we shall consider later.

Reforms of content

The questions facing policy-makers today are as follows: what is to be done with the thousands of persons invading the labour market?

---

12. Nepal has a high growth rate, accounted for by its young population, the custom of early marriage in rural areas, high fertility and the recent development of health care facilities.

13. This Chapter was written in the summer of 1976 - Editor.

14. A test on the Kaski district seems to show the contrary: the change in the status of 4th and 5th year teachers in the old system who would become lower secondary school teachers in the new system would substantially increase salary costs. See J. McCabe and N.R. Padhye, Planning the location of schools: the district of Kaski, Nepal, Paris, UNESCO, 1975.

Why are they unemployable? What are their "qualifications"? Their reflections generally lead them to the conclusion that it is necessary to look for a better match between educational content and employment requirements. For Brazil, which is trying to catch up with the most highly industrialized countries in the space of one generation, the answer is to include technology in school curricula.[15]

For Sri Lanka, which notes the impossibility of developing jobs in the tertiary sector, the aim is to introduce vocational subjects into the general studies provided by secondary schools. For most countries (notably Peru, Nepal, Zaire, Tanzania, but also several developed countries of the Northern Hemisphere), the challenge to the school system is how to achieve a synthesis between the requirements of vocational activities and technology, ahd the humanism characteristic of modern societies.

It is not our intention to list the difficulties and obstacles to achieving this synthesis; but they are numerous and make most of the efforts envisaged seem low in credibility. What is important here is to bring up three questions. First, is graduate unemployment entirely due to the inadequacy of curriculum content or mainly to the tightness of the labour market and the disparity between the "hopes" of graduates and the real prospects offered in active life? Secondly, should curriculum content really be adapted to the demands of the labour market when this in fact leads to a strengthening of the education system in its role of "reproducing" a basically unfair, unequal and undemocratic society? Thirdly, are we really sure that the productive sector expects the school to train mainly for a trade or that it prefers to provide its own technical and vocational training and uses the school only as a "filter" or "indicator" for grading individuals according to criteria which are more "affective" (attitude, motivation ...) than "cognitive" (technical and vocational ability to perform a given task)? These questions lead on to the radical approach to educational issues and cannot be neglected in any reflections on education policies.

Changing methods

Let us go back to educational stagflation: for many observers of the Third World, one of the causes of graduate unemployment is their inability to do any of the types of productive work required by society. In other words, young school-leavers are unemployed because they are unemployable; that is to say, they have no experience of productive work. Hence the proposal favoured by many educationists: "learn by doing"; each production technique will be learnt by practising the corresponding productive activity. "The best way of learning to ride a

---

15. See N. Sucupira, Rapport entre l'enseignement du second degré, la formation professionnelle et l'emploi, MEC, Brazilia, May 1973.

bicycle is to practise doing it, not to calculate windspeed, bodyweight, number of chain revolutions to make the back wheel turn, resistance to be overcome to propel the front wheel, etc. " Paraphrasing Mao Tse-Tung, one might say that the best way of learning about the pear is to eat it. Consequently, educationally-productive work is a mental process which must be accompanied by experience. The association of theory and practice and learning through practice implies a profound change in the methods used in the traditional schools; and this pre-supposes a transformation of teacher-learner relationships and vast changes in the attitudes of teachers, pupils and parents; more important, it requires as a pre-condition, a radical revision of the system of values of most Third World societies and notably the status, incomes and living conditions of manual and intellectual workers (perhaps even the questioning of this distinction). Otherwise it is to be feared that when we venture to propose "learning by doing", we are thinking of offering it only to the poorest and most deprived peoples.

These remarks lead on naturally to the radical approach.

## III. THE RADICAL APPROACH

While the "traditional" approach to educational problems is not entirely unaware of the complex relationships between social forces and the school, it does nevertheless usually lead to proposing solutions of the unhistorical, reductionist "other things being equal" type. In other words, it is admitted that education policies cannot disregard the social context to which they apply, "but nevertheless ... ", as the psychoanalyst says.[16] Thus, in order to save costs, it is necessary to shorten the duration of schooling; in order to offset financial handicaps, it is necessary to develop the fellowship system; in order to reduce the demographic constraint, expressed in large-scale migration to the towns, it is necessary to re-create a rural school better suited to the surrounding environment and which would no longer make rural children want to go and live in town; in order to equalize opportunities of access to long-term schooling for all social groups, it is necessary to fix "quotas", for study participation according to the parents' occupation; in order to control regional disparities, it is necessary to supervise carefully the geographical distribution of educational resources, etc. (It will be noted incidentally, that some of these proposals are not consistent with others.) These examples provide a good illustration of the reductionist nature of the traditional approach - since only one aspect of the problem is taken into consideration; they disregard the historical dimension since these are proposals

---

16. O. Manoni, <u>Clefs pour l'imaginaire ou l'autre scène</u>, Editions du Seuil, Paris, 1969.

that, a priori, can be offered to any country, whatever its history: in other words, "all other things being equal".

The radical approach, on the contrary, postulates that all other things are not equal. Educational problems (structures, processes, contents, finance and economics, etc.) reflect the social and economic forces of society. Thus the budgetary constraint and its characteristics, the multiple dimensions of the qualitative imbalance, and educational stagflation (to recall the three difficulties identified by the traditional approach) are neither fortuitous nor inevitable, whatever the history, level and type of development of the societies.[17]

The real problem are those raised in a recent publication:[18] What education? For whom? And for what development? According to the advocates of the radical approach, one cannot talk of education without posing the prior question of its function in social reproduction; this is situated on two main levels, ideological production and development of productive forces.

In this perspective, the problems emerge once education ceases to fulfil its role, i.e. when its social reproduction functions are no longer correctly articulated according to the specific requirements of the dominant mode of production in a society.[19] Thus, 19th century European education was not in a state of crisis because it fulfilled its role perfectly: there was the primary school for the masses ("civic" education), and secondary and higher institutions for the middle classes as training for the trades (guilds) gradually disappears with the birth of capitalism and the decreasing demand for professional skills in the labour force. Similarly, colonial education was perfectly coherent and fulfilled its function; the aim was at one and the same time to ensure the destruction of the traditional system of education (some say, in order to destroy the national culture and national consciousness) and to train a subordinate minority; neither the content of colonial education nor the number of men trained should permit any autonomous development of the dominated society.[20] But the situation has changed in Europe and the industrialized countries as well as in the developing countries. Habermas has shown the consequences of the evolution of capitalism: we prefer to confine ourselves here to the case of the developing countries.

With the accession of most of these countries to independence, the thesis "more education, more development" was accepted and it was simply decided to accelerate educational growth. What education? Colonial-type education. As soon as education covered an ever broader

---

17. M.B. Katz, The Irony of Early School Reform, Cambridge, Mass.: Harvard University Press, 1968.

18. J. Hallak, A qui profite l'école ? Paris, PUF, 1974.

19. J. Habermas, La technique et la science comme idéologie, Paris, Gallimard, 1975.

20. See A. Moumouni, L'éducation en Afrique, Paris, Maspéro, 1964.

section of the population, it became obvious that the thesis was not confirmed; on the one hand the "foreign" character of the culture transmitted by the school system was clearly apparent; on the other hand the growth of the school system could not in any way be justified by the real needs of economic progress; and the budgetary constraint, which was concealed for a long time by the fact of starting from zero and considering education the priority sector to develop, was revealed all the more strikingly since foreign aid was not as substantial as had been hoped and the share of irreducible expenditure - wages - was considerable.

It may be noted, in this connection, that as the schools in question were copied from those of the industrialized world, the teachers had to be paid salaries permitting them a level of living having nothing in common with that of the bulk of the rural population.

Adopting the growth model of the industrialized world helped to accentuate wildly the economic dualisation: pockets of prosperity in vast areas of poverty conducive to such phenomena as the rural exodus, discrimination by ethnic groups on the ex-colonial pattern, exorbitant earnings for the first generation of graduates leading to an explosion of the social demand for education with underlying hopes of upward mobility towards the fortunate group; "extroversion" of the economies through the flow and allocation of foreign capital heavily mortgaging the bulk of export earnings through foreign indebtedness,[21] etc. In short, the "dualisation" which was reflected in the increased disparities, the rigidity of the development process, the concentration of growth in a few areas for the benefit of a few individuals,[22] helped to rouse economic expectations that the development model adopted proved unable to satisfy. Hence the crisis and the question: "What development?". Hence, too, the reflexes - the word is no doubt too strong, but we shall use it for want of a better - of "introversion"; even in the so-called industrialized countries there are those who sing the praises of self-centred development strategies and for education those of a genuinely national model, probably completely different from the borrowed models.

Without going as far as the fashionable extremists, we are bound to admit that if the radical approach is right, we cannot talk of education policies without accepting that very considerable economic and social changes must accompany, if not precede, the reforms envisaged. Although we know very little of what is happening in Cuba, China, Peru or Tanzania, these countries provide an outstanding example of this point of view. The broad lines of the "formulae" followed by these countries and proposed by some experts to others[23] are strangely

---

21. On this last point, the case of Sri Lanka is particularly striking. See J. Hallak, Financing Educational Policy in Sri Lanka, Paris, IIEP, 1974.

22. The scenario is valid for several countries and in a world-scale analysis between rich countries and poor countries.

23. See certain chapters of: E. Faure et al., Learning to Be, Paris, UNESCO-Fayard, 1972.

comparable; definition of educational needs by the masses; discussion of educational objectives; participation in mobilization of available resources; equality of access, implementation and control of the education system; forms of popular education for all, associating theory and practice; rejection and suspicion of foreign models, etc. In this context, the concept of educational stagflation must be re-defined (what is an unemployed person?); the concept of financial constraint up-dated (since human resources are mobilized and the price system disturbed), and the significance of the qualitative imbalance much less obvious (since priority goes to the fight against the causes and not the consequences of the imbalance).[24]

It is too soon to evaluate the results of these attempts: it would, however, be biased or naive to think that the obstacles will be overcome and the objectives proclaimed by these countries rapidly attained. But the problem lies elsewhere: it is to understand the historical context of the Third World societies in the last quarter of the 20th century. In other words, are we sure of the "diagnosis"? If not, educational planning must endeavour to clarify it. Even if the answer to our question is in the affirmative, we may wonder what is the legitimacy of any approach leading to proposals. Whatever these proposals, should they not in fact originate in the countries themselves? Otherwise are they not likely to be of little use or to be merely taken over by the social systems to which they are applied?

---

24. These "models" followed by some countries have also been followed to some extent by certain North American communities. Obviously, however, there is a difference in kind - and therefore essential - between the adoption of this type of reform at the level of a country and of a small community. Let us note, too, that they should be clearly distinguished from the "deschooling" proposals formulated by Illich, Reimer and their associates. For a critical analysis of the "deschooling" proposals, see J. Hallak, op. cit. and R. Dore, "Deschool" Try Using Schools for Education First, IDS (Sussex), Discussion Paper, No. 6.

# 7

## POLICIES FOR EDUCATIONAL REFORM
by
Christopher Colclough

### I. INTRODUCTION

The last Chapter presented an analysis of the main educational problems facing most countries in the Third World, and of the policy prescriptions that emerge from "traditional" and "radical" frameworks of analysis. This Chapter attempts to add to our understanding of these problems by adopting a deliberately empirical approach. The questions asked here are primarily focussed upon what countries are doing, and what success has so far been achieved. On the basis of our analysis of country experiences, we return at the end of the Chapter to diagnosis and prescription, and emerge with conclusions that complement, rather than contradict, those of the previous Chapter.

It would be worthwhile, however, to begin by noting some of the aggregate results of educational policy. The decade ending in 1970 can be characterized as one of rapid and unprecedented expansion in the education systems of the developing world. As can be seen from Table VIII, these years witnessed a large increase in enrolment ratios, particularly at first and second levels, and particularly in the poorer countries. In these countries, the fact that enrolments have had to grow by up to three per cent each year merely to keep abreast of population growth makes the increase in these ratios particularly remarkable. In many countries it has involved a doubling of primary enrolments and a growth of secondary and tertiary places of four and five-fold, respectively, over the period.[1]

Though this represents significant progress, it has, if anything, thrown into sharper relief the more fundamental problems for the future. In the ninety poorest countries shown in the first three groups of Table VIII it has been achieved by devoting a high proportion of public expenditure to education throughout the period - a priority also mirrored in the richest countries. But whereas this emphasis in the

---

1. These indeed are the median rates for all Africa, excluding Zimbabwe, Namibia and the Republic of South Africa, for the decade ending in 1970 (calculated from data in UNESCO 1975).

Table VIII. AGGREGATE INDICATORS OF RELATIVE LEVELS OF ECONOMIC AND EDUCATIONAL DEVELOPMENT FOR 123 COUNTRIES, 1960 AND 1970

|  |  | GROUP I | GROUP II | GROUP III | GROUP IV | GROUP V |
|---|---|---|---|---|---|---|
| Per capita income group, US$ | | up to $120 | $121-250 | $251-750 | $751-1,500 | over $1,500 |
| Number of countries | | 29 | 23 | 38 | 9 | 24 |
| Population in 1970 (millions) | | 970 | 287 | 433 | 112 | 623 |
| First level enrolment ratio | 1960 | 41 | 67 | 73 | 90 | 100 |
| | 1970 | 66 | 83 | 97 | 97 | 100 |
| Second level enrolment ratio | 1960 | 8 | 9 | 11 | 33 | 58 |
| | 1970 | 15 | 19 | 25 | 49 | 83 |
| Third level enrolment ratio | 1960 | 1.5 | 2.1 | 1.9 | 6.2 | 17.0 |
| | 1970 | 3.6 | 5.6 | 5.3 | 10.5 | 30.2 |
| Education expenditures:[2] | | | | | | |
| Public expenditure per student | 1960 | 16 | 33 | 43 | 114 | 388[1] |
| | 1970 | 18 | 49 | 57 | 179 | 749[1] |
| Public expenditure as % of budget | 1960 | 6.7 | 20.0 | 15.3 | 6.1 | 12.9 |
| | 1970 | 13.2 | 18.9 | 13.5 | 10.1 | 17.8 |
| Public expenditure as % of GNP | 1960 | 1.8 | 3.6 | 2.3 | 2.1 | 3.8 |
| | 1970 | 2.9 | 3.8 | 3.0 | 3.1 | 5.8 |
| Student teacher ratios: | | | | | | |
| First level | 1960 | 39 | 42 | 37 | 31 | 28 |
| | 1970 | 42 | 43 | 37 | 36 | 24 |
| Second level | 1960 | 19 | 21 | 15 | 17 | 18 |
| | 1970 | 21 | 25 | 19 | 15 | 16 |
| Median drop-outs in cohorts enter- in 1960: | | | | | | |
| Primary | | 57.5 | 49.0 | 45.1 | 45.7 | 9.7 |
| Secondary | | 43.2 | 46.0 | 28.3 | 13.9 | 15.0 |

1. Group V is a multiple of Group I is 42 for 1970 and 21 for 1960.
2. Expenditure figures do not in all cases include all countries included in each income grouping.

SOURCE: IBRD, 1974.

countries of Europe and North America has allowed a big increase in
the expenditure per student enrolled and a decline in student-teacher
ratios, the reverse is true in the poorer countries. Here, as can be
seen from the Table, student-teacher ratios have generally increased,
whilst expenditure per student has grown only at between one and four
per cent per year - far slower than the rate of inflation. Since
technology in formal education has remained largely unchanged, this
is testimony to a real decline in the services provided. Furthermore,
a high proportion of children in these countries continue to leave school
before completing their courses of primary or secondary education.
In aggregate terms, therefore, the rapid growth of enrolments in Third
World countries has been achieved at some cost to the quality of education provided. More fundamentally, the inequalities of access to
education and of progression from the education system to jobs remain
harsh as between different groups in society, the phenomenon of
educated unemployment has either emerged or become entrenched in
almost all developing countries, and the education that is provided in
the school system seems to remain of little benefit for those children
who do not find formal sector jobs. In what follows, drawing particularly
upon African experience, we examine whether progress is being made in
addressing these problems other than in the rather crude quantitative
terms mentioned above.

## II. QUANTITATIVE AND QUALITATIVE REFORMS

For purposes of discussion, and at risk of over-simplification,
it is helpful to recognize the criticisms that formal education in the
Third World has traditionally had to face. These call into question
the social and economic benefits to be derived by the majority of the
population from the schooling process. Though the need for orthodox
education to secondary and tertiary levels may be acknowledged for
those who are to be employed in the formal sector of the economy, its
charge is that schooling creates dissatisfaction amongst the majority
of youths by raising aspirations for jobs that are unavailable, and that
it is of little benefit to the mass of the people who live and work in
rural areas. Whether one agrees with it or not, this point of view has
had profound influence upon both the quantitative and qualitative aspects
of educational planning and policy.

On the quantitative side the aim has been to influence the expansion
of secondary, tertiary and higher education in such a way as to secure
an optimum supply of skills for the growth of the formal sector. Manpower forecasting quickly became the basis for educational expansion.
In Africa, where this approach has been more widely used than elsewhere, the emphasis of planning was mainly placed upon the rapid
creation of unemployment. Some countries, however, most notably

Tanzania, placed great importance upon the need to hold back the
expansion of secondary and tertiary education in line with the limited
needs of the formal sector.

The results of the emphasis placed upon manpower planning over
the last fifteen years, however, are disappointing.[2] In Africa, the
post-independence shortages of skilled workers are now giving way to
growing surpluses of educated job-seekers. In many countries
localization is no longer a critical issue, but in some - Zambia, Kenya,
Senegal, Tunisia and others - educated unemployment of nationals and
a continued dependence upon the skills of non-citizens in technical and
specialist posts exist side by side. More significant, however, is
that the expansion of secondary and tertiary education has often progressed at rates considerably faster than those prescribed by the
manpower plans. Though the Indian or Sri-Lankan conditions of
unemployed university graduates are not yet widespread in Africa,
they will become so during the next twenty years if current expansion
rates for higher education are continued. Thus, the political pressures
to expand have tended to dominate, and now that manpower planning
units tend to recommend a cut-back in expenditure on middle and higher
levels of education, their advice generally remains unheeded, and they
have little political power or administrative influence.

The problems with this approach to planning have not only been
political. The plan and survey documents produced tended to have
technical shortcomings. Too often projections were prepared using
highly aggregated occupational groups which were in turn associated
with three or four broad levels of general education. Technical training and job experience were largely ignored in the projections.
Undoubtedly, the highly simplifying assumptions that were made by
the planners, together with their unwillingness to become involved in
occupational planning, explain some of the continued shortages of
middle-level technicians and of semi-professional personnel in many
African countries ten to fifteen years after independence. But in spite
of these failures, the pressures for the continued rapid expansion of
the schools are so profound that it is unrealistic to place much
confidence in a purely technocratic approach. In many countries in
Africa and elsewhere much could be gained by a more detailed knowledge of present conditions in the labour market, and the case for a
redistribution of educational resources would be strengthened by a
macro-survey approach. But the information from such sources
cannot alone achieve the redistribution. The more important thing
for the future is not so much whether or not particular planning
approaches are adopted, as whether there exists the political will to
implement their conclusions.

The simplest form of "non-quantitative" explanation for educated
unemployment focusses upon the "irrelevance" of the subject structure

---

2. For an evaluation of the African experience see Jolly and Colclough, 1972.

of the curriculum, and it is to policies designed to change the emphasis that we now turn. Since between sixty and eighty per cent of the labour force in developing countries are involved in agricultural work, and since only a proportion of the remainder are absorbed in the formal sector, it seems to make little sense to give children an "academic" education that is of little or no use to most children in their future economic life. The fact that orthodox systems of education use a curriculum that is biased towards the formal sector is held to account for the tenacity with which school leavers seek employment in that sector, and the unwillingness they show to return to agricultural activities.

The debate about curriculum relevance is not a new one, and in some parts of Africa and Asia it goes back to the first half of the nineteenth century. In 1842, for example, a Select Committee of the British Parliament noted that in Ghana no efforts had been made to offer agricultural instruction or to establish school farms, and recommended that this deficiency be made good. Similarly, a report from the Educational Comittee of the Privy Council was circulated to the British colonies in Africa in 1847 recommending the establishment of "industrial schools" with the objectives of teaching the rudiments of health care and sanitation, handicrafts and agricultural training, suitable to the local environment of the schools. The first Education Ordinances for Sierra Leone (1881) and Ghana (1882) included provision for the establishment of such schools, and during the last decade of the nineteenth century many of the mission schools in those countries established agricultural plots, and students spent considerable time each week doing manual work. Similar innovations occurred in East Africa in the early part of the twentieth century, as in Tanzania, where "native authority" schools from 1928 onwards introduced agriculture, carpentry and tailoring into the school timetable. Such initiatives as these were strongly recommended by the Phelps-Stokes Reports - the first comprehensive reports on education in Africa - which, in 1922, emphasized the need for vocational rural education in primary schools.[3] In general, however, these early experiments failed. In most cases, the climate of popular opinion was against them. The examinations were set and administered by bodies in the metropolitan countries, and the modifications to the syllabus by introducing practical studies were seen as a digression, and a threat to standards elsewhere in the curriculum. Over the years, up to 1960 or so, the pattern has been repeated in many countries. Local or even national initiatives in practical education were generally short-lived and ended in a return to the teaching of orthodox subjects as determined largely by the composition of public examinations.

---

3. For a highly critical evaluation of the Phelps-Stokes Reports, and their contribution to policy, see King, 1971.

This is not to say that there has been little progress in curriculum development since that date. On the contrary, and particularly since independence, there has been a significant shift away from the composition and subject structure of curricula that had been imported from Western countries. Many countries have changed the official medium of instruction to the lingua mater, at least during primary school. This necessitates the production of text-books and materials in many different languages - eleven in the case of Ethiopia, and twenty in the case of Zambia, to take two examples. Similarly, the topics treated in subjects like history geography, languages and social science are becoming increasingly localized in most countries. Examinations, now under local, rather than metropolitan, control have been redesigned to reflect these changes in subject-content. This represents significant progress. But the introduction of practical subjects has still not been a great success. In this connection it is useful to distinguish between innovations limited to one or to a group of schools, and those that encompass the whole of the school system. Their lessons are different, and case-study examples of each will be discussed in turn.

With regard to the former group, one of the most significant experiments in practical rural education in the Third World has been in India. A scheme of basic education was promoted by Mahatma Gandhi, who deeply believed in the need for an education system centred around productive work and instruction in simple skills which would be of some direct use to people in rural areas. After the adoption of his proposals as national policy by the Indian Congress in 1938, Basic Schools multiplied quickly in the rural areas. Craft activities and productive work comprised the largest part of each day's timetable, supplemented by study of the social and natural environment, mathematics, drawing, music, language and physical training. Teaching took place in the vernacular, rather than in English, which was used as the medium of instruction in the rest of the primary system. The reaction of rural parents was good for some years since Basic Schools provided an opportunity of educating their children where none had existed before. But this soon gave way to ambivalence and eventually resentment, owing to the fact that urban children in orthodox primary schools were seen to have a much better chance of moving on to secondary schools, and of achieving the social and economic rewards that followed from this. After fitful periods of expansion, about twelve million pupils were enrolled in Basic Schools by 1962-63, which compared with a total enrolment of about fifty million children throughout the Indian primary education system at that time. Since that date there has been little further expansion of Basic Schools, and the principles they stood for have ceased to be an important element in national policy. Though there were many additional difficulties in providing sufficient trained teachers and equipment for the rapid expansion of the movement, one of the most crucial factors in explaining its eventual demise was its failure to command popular political support.[4]

A similar story emerges from the experience of other countries that have attempted to implement a dual education system at primary level. The largest of such schemes in Africa is that of Upper Volta. Established in 1959, this scheme envisaged a small primary school system with the principal function of providing a preparation for those few who would go to secondary school and subsequently find jobs in the formal sector. All other children were to be given three years of agricultural vocational training, combined with basic literacy and numeracy for effective work in agriculture, and for a literate adult life. Though the rural education system did expand considerably over the following fifteen years, to reach a total enrolment of about 24,000 children, the pressures for the provision of orthodox primary schools in rural areas proved irresistible. The people regarded the rural education centres as a second-best solution which discriminated unfairly against them. They failed to win their acceptance, much less their support, and the programme has now begun to collapse.[5]

The lessons of these and other attempts to introduce differentiated education programmes in rural areas as a substitute for orthodox primary schooling for part of the population are compelling. Such schemes run directly against the promotion of more equal opportunity within education, and serve to restrict the life chances and social mobility of a large proportion of the population. Though they are attractive to many governments, since they appear to achieve a more rational distribution of educational resources, their great weakness is that they entrench existing inequalities between rich and poor, or urban and rural families. It is this element of discrimination that has led to the collapse of such programmes in the past, and it is almost certain that future experiments of this kind would fail as a result of similar pressures.[6]

In attempting to change the content of schooling and its usefulness to the majority of the population, programmes which affect all schools, in both urban and rural areas, are prima facie much more promising. Tanzania has had longer experience than most countries with such reforms, and important general lessons emerge from the educational changes that country has introduced.

President Nyerere outlined the new aims of the Tanzanian primary school system in 1967 in the following way:

---

4. For a detailed evaluation of Gandhian Basic Education which gives evidence for this conclusion, see Sinclair 1976.

5. For an evaluation of the Upper Volta rural education programme, see IEDES and Grabe, 1975.

6. A fuller discussion of the problems and dangers inherent in attempts to introduce dual systems of primary schooling is given in Colclough, 1976.

"For the majority of our people the thing that matters is that they should be able to read and write fluently in Swahili, that they should have an ability to do arithmetic, and that they know something of the history, values and working of their country and their Government, and that they should acquire the skills necessary to earn their living. (It is important to stress that in Tanzania most people will earn their living by working on their own or on a communal shamba, and only a few will do so by working for wages which they have to spend on buying things the farmer produces for himself)... Most important of all is that our primary school graduates should be able to fit into, and to serve the communities from which they come. (Nyerere 1967:27).

In the same document he went on to say that curricula throughout the school system would need to be altered to prepare the people more fully for the realities that awaited them after school. Examinations would need to be "downgraded in public esteem", and he talked of combining examinations with pupil and teacher assessments of work done for the school and the community. The total environment of education institutions would need to be changed, and he envisaged that schools and colleges should develop as self-reliant social and economic units.

Accordingly, in 1968 all primary, secondary and teacher training institutions embarked on farming and other "self reliance" activities, and a new agriculturally-biased science syllabus was incorporated in the primary school curriculum. In 1968 "political education" was introduced as a subject at all levels of the education system and Tanu Youth League branches were also established in all schools and colleges. The history of Tanzania, and of Africa, has replaced Commonwealth and European history in importance. Swahili, the national language, is now the medium of instruction throughout primary education and for some subjects in secondary schools, in place of English. The intention is to extend this policy to all levels of education and training, but its implementation will await the availability of Swahili textbooks and teaching materials.[7]

Over the past few years production has become an essential part of the activities of all schools. The activities vary from region to region, though they mostly centre around agriculture. The age of entry to primary school is now seven years, the older children cultivate their own plots while the younger ones do the weeding and other odd jobs. The amount of time spent in vocational work varies from school to school, and an exact time cannot be set nationally. It also has to vary according to the seasons and the rains. The main exceptions to this scheme are in the towns, where schools develop other activities

---

7. These developments are reported in Morrison, 1976, ch. 11 and in Odia, 1973.

such as poultry keeping. Each primary school has a parent/teacher committee which discusses the content of curricula. Parents have government policy explained to them by the teachers, and committee members are expected to pass this on to other parents. A major theme stressed is that primary schools are not there to prepare merely for secondary entrance.

Nevertheless, there have been problems. Judging from the conclusions of Tanzanian observers who have evaluated the results of the self-reliance programme in some schools, the practical activities have so far had little effect upon the attitudes of the student. Studies that have been completed to date suggest that there is much misunderstanding of the reasons for undertaking production in the schools. Teachers tend not to explain the reasons for conducting self-reliance activities, and appear, themselves, to be indifferent to them. With regard to the pupils, one researcher reports as follows:

> "When the pupils were asked, on the other hand, why they are required to undertake self-reliance activities, the applies ... were quite discouraging. Amongst them were: 1) the headteacher says we must do them; 2) we have to raise the school fund; 3) we must have something to show the inspectors when they visit the school; etc. There is not one occasion where pupils indicated that they undertook these activities because ... (they) have to learn to do what their parents do or that it is the policy of the country to train them to be self-reliant in school". (Besha, 1973: 24).

In part, this lack of understandings derives from the fact that in most schools there has as yet been little attempt to integrate the practical subjects with the academic curriculum. Besha (ibid: 23) observes that though children can typically recite sections of the Arusha Declaration and the Tanu Guidelines efficiently, there is no relationship as far as the children are concerned, between what they learn in their political education classes and what they do or learn in other subjects. Similarly, as another observer reports:

> "Although the school was meant to be a productive unit, a farm or crafts workshop in and of itself, and all teachers and students alike were to be productive members of it, instead, "self-reliance" activities are treated as something separate from the rest of the school work, as extra curricular". (Mbilinyi, 1973, cited in Morrison 1976: 287).

In an important sense, however, these disappointing results have been caused by the fact that there has been little attempt to reform the examinations - at least those that separate primary from secondary school. The General Entrance Examinations were restyled "Primary School Leaving Examinations" in 1967. Though symbolic in emphasizing that the primary course was intended to be complete in itself, the mode of selection for secondary school remained unchanged. The formation of Regional Selection Committees in the following year, though a promising development, also resulted in little change. These Committees continued to rely upon children's performance in written examinations, tempered by evaluations of academic ability furnished by headmasters, as the main criterion for selection. No attempt was made to assess a student's commitment to self-reliance activities as a factor in the selection process (Morrison 1976:274). It is perhaps not surprising, then, that students have continued not to give the practical subjects high priority, and have concentrated on academic subjects which are important for secondary entrance.

The case of Tanzania is therefore instructive. The leadership has been notable for its high degree of socialist commitment, and over the last ten years a series of strong social and economic reforms have been introduced. Income differentials on the basis of both education and occupation have narrowed over this period. The development strategy has had a heavy emphasis on rural development, and the crucial role of the peasant in the nation's future progress has been the major message carried by the media, the Party, the speeches made by the country's leaders, and indeed by all levels of formal and non-formal education. But the old labour market structures and conventions have not yet been reformed. People are still hired by employers in both the civil service and the public and private sectors on the basis of the level of education they have attained. Those with higher levels of certification get the better jobs which carry more money and status. In particular, progression within education is still determined by performance in academic achievement tests which bear little relation to the stated priorities and objectives of the reformed cycle of first-level education. As a result, the change in the content of the curriculum has not yet had major effects upon the attitudes of the students who progress through the system, nor upon the attitudes and skills acquired by those who leave after primary school. The new system of education is now very different to that which existed during the Colonial period and viewed from both educational and social perspectives the changes have most certainly been for the better. But the real goals of the reforms have so far not been achieved.[8] The more detailed implications of these experiences will be taken up in the final section of this Chapter.

## III. COSTS AND EQUITY

We now turn to a second basic criticism of education in the Third World. This emphasizes the fact that, using existing technology, the

---

8. For similar conclusions with regard to the effects of the educational reforms in both Tanzania and Cuba, see Dore 1976:107-121.

orthodox system of formal education is too costly. It takes up a high proportion of the budget and yet provides opportunities for only part of the population of school-going age. The substance for these observations is given by the data in Table VIII. It can be seen that the proportion of the budget and of national income spent on education is not very different for countries at all levels of per capita income: developing countries are already spending as much on education as most of the advanced countries of Europe and North America. Thus, at current cost levels, the further expansion of education systems in the Third World is severely constrained by the limits imposed firstly by the growth of national income, and secondly by the growth of government revenues. Almost all countries in the Third World are committed to a policy of providing free primary education for all. In many others the commitment also includes junior secondary education. Table VIII demonstrates how far away from the target many countries were in 1970. We need to ask to what extent these inequalities are being removed, and whether the costs of education are being reduced.

The main determinants of the unit costs of education are the level of teachers' salaries and the pupil-teacher ratio. The main aim of policies to reduce educational costs is thus to influence the magnitude of these variables. Policies aimed at achieving this will be discussed in turn. In theory, variations in the pupil-teacher ratio are a function of the number of student subject options, the frequency of class meetings, the average size of classes, the number of student contact hours per teacher and the length of the teaching week. In practice, however, the opportunities for manipulating these variables are different at each level of the education system.

At primary level the main choices relate to changes in the size of classes and in the frequency of class meetings for a given student body. With regard to the former, research from some developed countries shows that the performance, as measured by examinations, of classes of 25 students, is not significantly better than that of classes of 40. This suggests that some developing countries with primary classes well below world averages could probably increase class sizes in primary schools without any adverse effects upon quality.[9] But for most countries in the Third World in which classes are typically very large, the issue would be how classes of 40 compare to those of 60 or 70 students. Many countries have already pushed class size well beyong the limits usual in the West in efforts to reduce the cost of schooling, and have probably reached the point where further increases would have serious effects upon the quality of the schooling provided. More research is needed in Third World countries on the

---

9. The following developing countries had primary teacher-pupil ratios of less than 35 in the early 1970s: Gabon, Ivory Coast, Lesotho, Mali, Mauritius, Senegal, Costa Rica, Brazil, Paraguay, Venezuela, Iran, Iraq, Lebanon, Malaysia, Oman, Pakistan, Philippines, Singapore, Yemen. See IBRD 1974, Table 3.

trade-off between less efficient learning and the reduction in unit costs that result from larger classes.

An alternative method of raising pupil-teacher ratios at primary level is through double-session teaching, whereby classrooms are used by one group of students in the mornings and by a second group in the afternoons. This is still widely used in some parts of the Third World - though often in areas where the demand for primary schooling outstrips the provision of physical facilities rather than as a general and deliberate policy to reduce costs. Double-session teaching places a heavy burden on the teachers and reduces both the intensity and the quality of education provided by the primary school. Since the areas most often affected are poor and non-urban, many governments have abandoned this policy, since it is obviously discriminatory. Nevertheless, it remains a real policy option for particularly the poorest countries, where primary enrolment ratios are still very low, and where budgetary constraints are most acute.

At higher levels of the education system double-session teaching is not possible, except in rather special circumstances.[10] But a wider range of cost-saving measures can be introduced. At secondary and university levels, careful timetabling, and control of the number of student subject options, and of the teaching load of staff members are necessary. It is not uncommon to find the teaching requirements for academics in rich country universities applied unquestioningly in the Third World. Yet this is often inappropriate when students, particularly during their first two years of study, may be more in need of intensive (and often remedial) teaching, than of the freedom to pursue unguided study. A recent university study in Africa revealed that the average student contact hours per academic staff member were less than ten per week,[11] hardly an intensive use of resources in the light of the fact that entry to that university was on the basis of "0" level results. The same study demonstrated that modest increases in the contact hours of teaching staff, together with strict control over the size of classes and the number of students options offered by the university in given degree courses, could have dramatic effects upon unit costs. Thus the relationships governing the size of the pupil-teacher ratio in higher education are complex; nevertheless, many governments could reduce expenditures in this sector by using a more considered approach to institutional planning. In particular, the autonomy that is often given to universities in conducting their own planning may be unwise since the choices available in securing cost reductions are often not articulated to the governments or other financing agencies concerned.

---

10. As in the case of the proposed Zambian Educational Reforms, mentioned below.

11. University of Botswana, Lesotho and Swaziland, 1974:12.

The other main way of reducing educational costs is by reducing the level of teachers' salaries in real terms. Since teachers' salaries conform closely to those earned by individuals with similar qualifications outside education, such reductions cannot occur in isolation from other salaried groups. There are obviously immense political difficulties in introducing actual reductions in pay for such a large and powerful section of the labour force. This, indeed, has happened in hardly any country. However, in many countries the real earnings of skilled persons, including teachers, have fallen over the past decade, as a result of salary increases less than would be required to fully compensate for inflation. In some cases, as in India, this has been in part a response to growing levels of unemployment amongst skilled and educated workers of all kinds. But in others this has been part of a deliberate strategy to reduce income differentials between skilled and unskilled workers, and more generally between earnings for work done in the formal, informal and traditional agricultural sectors.

Nevertheless, there are two problems with this approach. First, it has effects upon earnings and costs only over a fairly long time period. Second, it leaves the rigid relationships between earnings and the level of education attained by employees untouched. As a result the costs of upgrading the educational level of teachers is very high, and it may indeed be impossible in many countries owing to budgetary constraints, even if the unemployment rates amongst educated persons are substantial. Kenya has recently introduced policies to tackle this problem that have lessons for other countries. Until recently teachers in Kenya, as elsewhere, have been graded and paid in accordance with the educational qualifications they possessed before undertaking teacher training. Thus, irrespective of how well they performed during their training, or indeed afterwards on the job, their school qualifications determined their seniority and the salary they were to receive. Under the new system, persons with at least four years of secondary schooling will be eligible for teacher training. But their grade and salary will be determined during their period of training, partly on the basis of examinations, and partly on continuous assessment, irrespective of the level of education previously attained. Since the proportion of persons in each salary grade will remain constant from year to year this will allow an increase in the educational level of the teaching force without a concomitant increase in costs, and will additionally provide a strong incentive to perform well during their period of teacher training. Promotion within the teaching profession will also no longer be determined by educational certification, but on the basis of evaluations of performance by Ministry of Education inspectors. There are reasons to suppose that elements of this approach could be used to advantage by many other countries.

The high costs of school systems in the Third World also explain in large measure the inequalities that are endemic in their operations.

The fact that not all children have access to primary education, that only a small proportion of those who do have access go on to secondary school, and that the quality of primary education varies substantially between different regions and different socio-economic classes imply that disproportionate advantages are given to certain groups - usually the progeny of richer families - for progression within the system. Thus, policies aimed at reducing costs in order to universalize provision of primary education and to standardize its quality, would help to reduce these inequalities.

There are, however, two other circumstances that at present reinforce inequalities in education to a formidable extent. The first is that the achievement test examinations used as the selection instrument for progression within education discriminates in favour of children from more privileged families, not only because they go to better schools, but also because for the latter there is less conflict between the medium of instruction and the lingua mater, and because of the non-school cognitive benefits gained by children from such families, where a place in the modern sector and its associated family benefits has already been achieved. But the task of removing these biases is difficult. In Kenya the primary school leaving examination comprises mainly a multiple-choice "aptitude" test, carefully designed to avoid questions that would give special advantages to children from particular regions or social groups. But recent research has shown that the results from the high-cost primary schools are markedly better than from low-cost schools.[12] The high success rates amongst children in the former schools is a sign both of being better taught and of having come from richer families. The corollary is that a good number of high-ability poorer children do not succeed in gaining secondary entrance.

One possibility for further reducing this aspect of inequality would be the use of school quotas for progression to secondary school. Under such a system the same proportion of children from each school or area would continue, determined on the basis of either national or local examinations, or exceptionally, on teachers' assessments. Such a system was recommended by the recent ILO employment mission to Kenya, and has been tried on an experimental basis in various parts of the more developed world.

Though it has the advantage of addressing the equity issues raised by conventional selection procedures, it has the unfortunate side effect of making competition for secondary places entirely internal to the school, which may on balance be more damaging from both social and educational viewpoints.

The second aspect of inequality that deserves particular mention relates to the high rewards - both social and economic - accruing

---

12. See Somerset, 1974.

to those who do succeed in staying in education up to tertiary levels.
In very few countries have incomes policies succeeded in transforming
the rewards structure quickly, and in few others have the links between
educational certification and salary structures been broken. The
political realities imply that in most societies only gradual change
can be achieved through these means. But there are possibilities of
significantly increasing the private costs of undertaking secondary
and higher education, and thereby reducing the net benefits. Ghana,
for example, has been considering the introduction of a student loans
scheme which would aim both at reducing the costs of post-primary
education and at encouraging students to enrol in courses leading to
occupations where significant skills shortages still exist. The main
shortages are for workers with science or maths based qualifications
at middle and senior levels in the formal sector. There are also
insufficient qualified teachers of these subjects. The loans scheme
would cover the cost of boarding (where relevant) and tuition for
students who gain admission to secondary schools and universities.
These would be repayable by all students except those who enrol for
courses in approved science-based subjects. It is hoped that this
policy would stimulate the future supply of skilled technical workers,
as well as serving to reduce the costs to the Government of secondary
and tertiary education. A corollary is that the private returns to
undertaking studies in arts and social sciences would be significantly
reduced.

## IV. THE INTEGRATION OF SOCIAL, ECONOMIC AND EDUCATIONAL REFORMS

It will be clear from the above paragraphs that the task of
successfully over-coming the major educational problems in the
Third World is a difficult business. So often the effectiveness of education can be improved only by integrating a range of policies that
include both educational variables, and those that link the education
system to the wider framework of society. True, one can do much
by improving teacher training, by increasing the supply of textbooks,
and by relating subject topics more carefully to local circumstances
— indeed, almost all countries in the Third World need to continue to
place emphasis upon these kinds of improvement. But the more
fundamental variables that affect so much of what goes on in the name
of education appear to be the enormous financial and social differentials
between the rewards for skilled and unskilled work, and the systems
of selection within education, and from education to jobs. Even those
countries that have had the strength to tackle some of these relationships find that the power of those that remain untouched is sufficient
to undermine the results of the reforms. We have come a long way

from the view that controlled educational experiments can be successful, and by example can change the rest of the system. The problem now seems not to be limited to doing something good in one or a few schools, nor even of affecting one or several of the links between education and society, but rather the formidable task of operating upon all these relationships at once. Whatever the truth, some countries have indeed adopted this view. The most recent, and the most interesting, example in this group is Zambia. The reforms currently being considered in that country are comprehensive and fundamental, and it would be appropriate to end this Chapter with a discussion of their nature and wider international significance. Over the last few years there has developed a popular political feeling in Zambia that the education offered by the orthodox school system is unsatisfactory. Though the origins of this viewpoint began before 1971, the emergence of widespread unemployment of leavers from the middle and higher levels of the secondary schools after that date considerably strengthened and entrenched this view.[13] Instead of the criticisms being mainly concentrated upon the primary schools, the whole of the school system now began to be challenged. In addition, however, the ruling United National Independence Party was committed to achieving universal junior secondary education. But there appeared to be two major problems in achieving this. Firstly, with a progression ratio of 22% between Grade 7 and Form 1, an enormous investment in secondary school places would be needed, which at present cost ratios would be impossible to achieve. Secondly, and more fundamentally, there appeared to be little point in rapidly increasing enrolments in a primarily academically-oriented school system when even the current numbers of graduates were unable either to find jobs or to enter self-employment.

    Following a 1974 seminar in Dar es Sallam on Alternatives in Education, organised by the Dag Hammarskjold Foundation, which was attended by a strong Zambian delegation, important initiatives were taken in Zambia to seek a solution to the above conflict. The idea began to gain ground that the key to solving the problem was to see all schools as centres for not only learning but also producing. Thus, fundamental, rather than marginal, reform of education seemed to be required. However, it was recognized by officials in the Ministry of Education that this was a complex task needing exhaustive enquiries and planning if it was to be achieved. Accordingly, it was decided that proposals would be drawn up for reform only after widespread consultation with and participation by officials in other Ministries, by the teachers, the Party and the public at large. Study tours were arranged for three teams of four or five Zambian officials to a group of ten

---

    13.    Data on the growth of the problem of school leaver unemployment are given in Jackman, 1974.

countries in East and West Africa, the Caribbean and China. In parallel with these visits, a series of internal investigations comprising about a dozen studies on different aspect of the education system were commissioned. Following an exhaustive period of consultations, discussions and drafting, a series of comprehensive proposals for fundamental reform emerged which were published in May 1976.[14] President Kaunda immediately launched a national debate on the document. When this debate has been concluded the draft proposals will be revised and submitted to the Party and Government for approval and implementation. The main elements of the Draft Statement on Educational Reform are as follows:

1. The combination of education and production is the main theme of the proposed reforms. All full-time students will have productive work as part of their curriculum, and workers will be expected to continue their education through part-time study. On leaving school all students will join the Zambia National Service for some time before entering the labour force.
2. Full time education will comprise three successive stages:
   a) basic education, which will provide ten years of functionally oriented education to all children from the age of seven;
   b) second stage education, which will incorporate all existing post-primary vocational training and educational programmes; second stage qualifications will be considered equivalent to each other for purposes of entry to third stage education;
   c) third stage education, which will include all the present post-secondary programmes, and will provide a combination of professional specializations and general education.
3. A system of "continuing education" will be developed to become the chief instrument for improving the social, cultural and technical competence of the people. The literacy programme is to be massively increased using unpaid volunteers as teachers. A new formal education component of continuing education will be developed, allowing workers to continue their education by part-time study, and the qualifications of this system will be treated as equivalent to those of graduates from the full-time system.
4. The production programme of the school system will include food production, community projects, provision of infrastructure, manufacture of educational supplies, upkeep of plant and buildings, craft and retail activities. Local production

---

14. Republic of Zambia, 1976.

unit committees will be established for each school to determine priorities and production schedules.

5. In order to secure the continued availability of students for productive work the school calendar will be reorganised. During the basic cycle, holidays will be shortened and there will be four terms instead of three. Similarly, at the second level there will be four twelve-week terms, each week comprising five and a half days. During the basic cycle all students will be involved in both study and productive work throughout the year. In the second cycle, however, each student will follow a programme comprising two terms of in-school education and two terms of out-of-school education per year. This will allow a doubling of the school population at the second level without increasing classrooms, and will ensure a constant labour force for the production projects.

6. The crucial role of teachers for the success of the new system is recognized. Political education will become the core of all courses for new and serving teachers. Teacher training will be restructured to reduce the total amount of full-time residential training and to increase the amount of supervised on-the-job training in the class-room. The supply of new teachers will be increased by the expansion of teachers' colleges, and untrained teachers will be mobilized through the Zambia National Service.

7. New criteria are set out for the development of curricula. The most important of these are, firstly, the creation of a core of essential compulsory subjects with only a limited number of options; secondly, the combination of study and work in all programmes to achieve the maximum integration of theory and practice; and thirdly, the incorporation of political education in all programmes.

8. Finally, the present system of examinations will be abandoned and replaced by a much more comprehensive system of continuous assessment. This will stretch over the whole of a student's school career, and though written examinations will remain as one ingredient, greater importance will be given to teachers' reports on academic performance and ability, to the analysis of production performance in relation to agreed targets, and to assessment of a student's political attitude and commitment by teachers and fellow pupils. Certificates will be awarded to all students who complete Basic, Second and Third Stage Programmes, which reflect the new assessment procedure. Numerical marks or grades will be abandoned in favour of judgements of competence. As a result the certification process will be separated from that of selection for continuation within the school system. Selection will be based not only upon academic suitability but also upon an

assessment of the student's demonstrated commitment to "Humanism" - the social philosophy of the Party.

The proposals described above represent an example of a comprehensive attack upon the main problems facing education in the Third World. If it is implemented, the Zambian Education Reform could be expected to bring the following major benefits. Firstly, the costs of educational expansion will be significantly reduced. This arises in part from the mobilization of student time and labour for the production of food, and services, generating a cash surplus which can be used to subsidize the improvement and expansion of the education system. At the secondary level, average costs will be reduced directly since the student population will be considerably increased without a concomitant increase in classroom accommodation. Total costs, however, will obviously rise because of the increased need for teachers and equipment. Secondly, the integration of education and production is expected to have a positive effect upon the attitudes and the skills of students who remain in the rural areas. According to our analysis, however, the crucial changes in this regard are not merely the re-design of curricula, but also the implementation of the proposed reforms in the examinations and the system of selection. These elements are perhaps more important than any others, in order to achieve the desired liberation of schooling from the certification syndrome. Thirdly, the reforms will promise greater equity, particularly for the poorer groups in society, in a number of ways. The introduction of basic education for all children will re-allocate educational resources from the apex to the base of the system and provide greater equality of access to schooling. Furthermore, the changes in the content of schooling will shift the future benefits of education more sharply in favour of the rural child. Finally, the changes in selection methods will reinforce these benefits, and, in addition, will reduce the current biases in selection techniques that tend to give the children from rich families the best chances of advancement within the school system.

On the other hand, the extent to which the full benefits of these reforms can be reaped will depend upon whether or not a wider set of social reforms are implemented. At present, income differentials on the basis of education in Zambia are considerable. Though a major advantage of the proposed reforms is that, within educational levels, the criteria for selection will be placed firmly upon the employer, it remains the case that the level of education achieved will continue to be an important criterion for job eligibility. Thus, if the new education system is really to combat elitism, and is to give the children who leave after the basic cycle a sense of purpose rather than of failure, the typical income differentials between more educated urban employees and less educated persons who will work mainly in agriculture must be reduced.

The requirement to change the present structure of earnings is acknowledged in the Draft Statement. But in terms of its policy recommendations the subject is given only passing, rather than central importance. In the absence of such proposals, it is not clear at this stage whether or not the pervasive influence of income earning opportunities upon student aspirations has been fully recognized by the Government.

These difficulties are ones of principle. However, the most pervasive problems are likely to be of a practical kind. The proposed reforms will generate immense demands upon the resources of the Government - both financial and human. Though their magnitude has not yet been quantified, and to do so will itself be a major planning exercise, it is clear that a far greater financial provision for education will be required than has been the case in the past. Moreover, the demands upon the teachers will be enormous. The existing curriculum has provided firm guidelines, arbitrary though they may be, for the content of teaching and for monitoring performance. The new programmes, being much more ambitious, will need more diligence, sensitivity and educative skills than most teachers, particularly those with little training and experience, possess. The massive requirements for new teachers implied by the basic education programme will bring great difficulties for many schools, particularly in the early years. Thus a period of transition can be expected, possibly characterized by confusion and even opposition amongst both teachers and those taught, before the new strategy begins to take root.

Arguably, however, these educational problems are no greater than those faced by Zambia ten years ago. As in many other developing countries, a transformation of the school system has since been achieved which, in quantitative terms, is much greater than had been thought possible at the time. The challenge faced now is a qualitative one. The proposed reforms represent one of the most exciting educational developments in the Third World, and, if realized, may pioneer a form of education much better adapted to the basic needs of development.

The case of Zambia has been discussed at some length because it is useful both to understand what would comprise the most important elements of a strategy for fundamental reform, and to demonstrate that at least one government is at present intending to introduce such a package. Zambia is, however, by no means unique. In Ethiopia, for example, a new system of basic education for all children is to be introduced in which the pupils will spend three hours in school for every two hours at work, a ratio which is to be reversed at the secondary level. All schools in rural areas will be allocated ten hectares of land for production, while schools in urban areas will be encouraged to form links with the informal sector. The plan is not merely to provide students with work experience but to turn schools into production units, so that they will become at least partly self-financing. Until now, children in primary schools have been taught in the national language, Amharic, which is a second or third language to many children in rural areas. In the new system, children will be increasingly taught in one of the eleven most commonly spoken languages of Ethiopia. The six-year curriculum will also combine the three 'Rs' with a certain amount of science, as well as a number of work-oriented subjects. New regional centres are to be created to produce educational materials in eleven languages as part of a policy to shift responsibility for textbooks, stationery and the construction of schools to local farmers' associations. And student selection to post-basic education will henceforward combine traditional achievement-testing examinations with continuous assessment of practical manual skills. Structural changes of a similar kind are being introduced in Algeria, which also seem capable of combining reforms of the education system with the necessary changes in its institutional linkages to the labour market.

## V. CONCLUSION

How one deals with a problem, or its symptoms, depends upon what one believes to be their cause. In discussing the experience of policy responses to educational problems we have had in mind two contrasting causal, and therefore analytic, frameworks. The reasons for this duality are firmly empirical. Though it is impossible to do proper justice to the evidence in a chapter of the present length, it should now be clear that the recent history of educational reform in the Third World comprises for most countries a series of ad hoc responses to emerging problems, based upon a rather simplified analysis of causal mechanisms. More recently still, however, a variety of countries with widely different social and political systems have begun to implement more fundamental structural reforms which seek to integrate changes in education with changes elsewhere in society. It is arguable that such approaches are based upon a more sophisticated diagnosis of the root cause of many educational problems, and at present they appear to hold greater promise for the future than the more marginal approaches so widely attempted in the past.

# REFERENCES

Besha, R.: 1973, Education for Self Reliance and Rural Development, Institute of Education, University of Dar es Salaam.

Colclough, Christopher: 1976, "Basic Education - Samson or Delilah?", Convergence, Vol. IX, No. 2.

Dore, Ronald: 1976, The Diploma Disease: Education, Qualification and Development, Allen and Unwin Ltd., London.

IBRD: 1974, Education Sector Working Paper, Washington, December 1974.

IEDES and Sven Grabe: 1975, "Upper Volta: A Rural Alternative to Primary Schools", in Ahmed, M. and Coombs, P. H., (eds.), Education for Rural Development: Case Studies for Planners, ICED, Praeger.

Jackman, M.: 1974, School Leaver Migration in Zambia, Tracer Project, University of Zambia, Lusaka (mimeo).

Jolly, Richard and Christopher Colclough: 1972, "African Manpower Plans: An Evaluation", International Labour Review, Vol. 106, Nos. 2-3, August-September.

King, Kenneth: 1971, Pan Africanism and Education, Oxford Studies in African Affairs, Clarendon Press, Oxford.

Mbilinyi, Marjorie: 1973, Education for Rural Life or Education for Socialist Transformation, paper prepared for the Annual Social Science Conference of the East African Universities, December.

Morrison, David: 1976, Education and Politics in Africa: The Tanzanian Case, Hurst and Company, London.

Nyerere, Julius: 1967, Education for Self Reliance, Ministry of Information and Tourism, Dar es Salaam.

Odia, Solomon: 1973, "Rural Education and Training in Tanzania", in Philip Foster and James Sheffield (eds.), World Yearbook of Education, 1974. Education for Rural Development, Evans Brothers, London.

Republic of Zambia: 1976, Education for Development: Draft Statement on Educational Reform, Ministry of Education, Lusaka.

Sinclair, M. E.: 1976, Gandhian Basic Education, Notes, Comments No. 12, Unit for Co-operation with UNICEF, UNESCO, Paris.

Somerset, H. C. A.: 1974, "Educational Aspirations of Fourth-Form Pupils in Kenya" and "Who goes to secondary school? Relevance, Reliability and Equity in Secondary School Selection", Education, Society and Development, D. Ghai (ed.), Oxford University Press, Nairobi.

UNESCO: 1975, Statistical Tables, Africa, UNESCO, Paris.

University of Botswana, Lesotho and Swaziland: 1974, Report of the Development Team (Devolution), Roma, Lesotho, April.

# 8

## EMPLOYMENT PROBLEMS
by
Denyse Harari

### I. THE ROOTS OF THE PROBLEM

The social meaning of employment

Employment is not in the same sense as food or shelter, a "basic need". But in market economies, people depend on employment, directly or indirectly, for the satisfaction of their basic needs.
Employment is, in a monetised economy, perhaps the most important means by which individuals and their families receive income, and are able to purchase the goods and services they need. But employment also has a less frequently emphasized but no less important aspect: it marks the participation of an individual in the production system, and thus ensures him the recognition of his role in society and the feeling of being engaged in something worthwhile.

New attitudes toward employment planning

The recognition of employment as a major development policy goal is fairly recent. The International Development Strategy for the Second United Nations Development Decade, adopted by the General Assembly of the United Nations in 1970, provided that "each developing country should formulate its national employment objectives so as to absorb an increasing proportion of its working population in modern-type activities and to reduce significantly unemployment and under-employment " (para. 18a)). Six years later, the World Employment Conference issued a declaration of principles: "Underemployment and poverty in rural and urban informal sectors and open unemployment, specially in urban areas, has reached such critical dimensions that major shifts in development strategies at both national and international levels are urgently needed in order to ensure full employment and an adequate income to every inhabitant of this one world in the shortest possible time".
Behind this change in formulation and emphasis lies a dramatic shift in international thinking, prompted by an awareness of the failure of previous strategies.

To a growing number of people in the Third World, employment is proving an elusive goal. According to a recent ILO estimate, 40% of the labour force in developing countries is unemployed or underemployed. While the mass of those unable to make an adequate living on the basis of employment accessible to them is already considerable, population in LDC's is growing at an annual rate of 2.6%. The labour force, which expanded at annual rates of 1.6% in the years 1950-1960 and of 2.1% in the years 1960-1970, is expected to continue growing through the years 1970-1980 at a rate of 2.3%, thus multiplying the need for jobs.

In most traditional economies, there was full employment in the sense that each member had a role which did not necessarily involve full-time "work" but served a function in the society which was recognized by all and justified a share in the economy's product. In such situations, the growth of population meant that scarce land and capital had to be shared with a larger labour force so that both leisure and poverty tended to increase as limited output and restricted employment opportunities both had to be divided among larger numbers of people.[1]

Another solution was found in the industrializing Western world: the expansion of the economy so as to accommodate the increased populations. The establishment of market economies included changes in the scale and structure of production, increased productivity, accumulation of capital, introduction of new technologies and expansion of international trade.

It is far from self-evident, especially to economists, that population growth alone should lead to employment problems. Only a few years ago it was thought that the higher needs associated with the larger population could spark a take-off process, provided that the increased labour supply was accompanied by corresponding inputs of land or other productive factors. Theorists pointed to the record of successful industrialization in the West and elsewhere. Such strategies overlooked the fact that, in most cases, the industrial take-off occurred in societies where both the rate of growth and the relevant socio-economic circumstances were quite different from the ones characteristic of the developing countries. According to Paul Bairoch:[2] "In the first half of this century the population growth rate in the developing countries was already over 1%; it has now reached 2.6% at which rate the population doubles in 26 years and increases 13 times in a century.

Such a rate of natural growth is something entirely new." In traditional economies the long-term population growth was for centuries around 0.1 to 0.2%, and even in the nineteenth century the population of the countries that are now industrialized increased by only 0.8% per

---

1. Edwards, E.O., ed. Employment in Developing Nations, Columbia University Press, N.Y. 1974. p. 3.
2. Paul Bairoch, Urban Unemployment in Developing Countries, ILO, 1973.

year. Only in North America and other regions of recent settlement were growth rates as high as 2.0 to 3.0%.

"In many European countries the early stages of industrialization, corresponding approximately to those which the developing countries are now going through, occurred either in the second half of the eighteenth century or in the first half of the nineteenth century. During those first decades of industrialization the rates of population growth were only around 0.4 to 0.5%.

There was also an enormous territorial expansion as a result of the colonization of the temperate overseas regions in the nineteenth century. Between 1800 and 1900 the geographical area of the developed regions increased from 10.5 million sq. km. (Europe, including the European part of the USSR which alone exceeds 5 million square kilometres) to 43 million km distributed over Europe, North America, Australia and New Zealand.[3]

Thus, at what might approximately be considered similar stages of economic development, the total population in the developing countries is now increasing five to six times more rapidly than in early Western industrialization. This factor is of outstanding importance to the economic problems of the Third World in general and employment and urban unemployment in particular." It should be evident that the problems of change in a society which had 100 years to adjust to a doubling in the number of its members are essentially different from those where there are only 25 years to achieve the same task.

Another consequence of population growth is that it leaves poor countries with no choice but to modernize: development is no longer an option but a necessity.[4] Traditional societies could still hope to maintain some sort of balance between their food production and the number of mouths to feed. Even episodes of pestilence and famine could be considered as accidents in an essentially stable picture. The huge increase in the numbers of people who must be fed creates an exploding demand for food and other material goods that only a rapidly developing capacity for production can meet. Increased - and even increasing - production capabilities have become a matter of sheer survival.

---

3. If account is taken only of agricultural land alone: (a realistic limitation in view of the vast uninhabitable regions in the new territories), the figures for arable land and pastures around 1900-1910 are: Europe (excluding Russia) 180 million hectares; total for North America, Australia and New Zealand, 250 million hectares. Source: International Institute of Agriculture (Rome): International year-book of agricultural statistics, various years, quoted by Bairoch, op. cit.

4. P. Bairoch, La Révolution Industrielle, Soc. d'Ed. d'Enseignement Supérieur, Paris, 1963, Introduction, p. 7.

Urbanization surge in LDC's

Another demographic feature compounds the difficulties. The migration from rural areas is such that urban population in general is growing at twice the rate of the total population. Million of people have moved, either singly or with their families, to urban centres in search of a better life. The rate of urbanization was twice as high in developing countries between 1920 and 1960 as in earlier industrialized nations at the same stage of development. Urban growth is now preceding development insteed of following it, as during the process of industrialization in Western countries.[5]

In and of itself, "rural-urban migration is by no means an undesirable phenomenon. In fact, most of the theories of economic development, which are based largely on the historical experience of Western industrialized nations, emphasize the beneficial transformation of an economy from a rural agrarian base to one with an industrial, urban-oriented focus".[6] In the developing countries, in general, this transformation did not take place and the outcome was the marginalisation of the displaced population.

Thus, developing countries offer simultaneously the picture of a large underemployed rural population and of huge urban concentrations, inhabited with unemployed or marginally-employed individuals.

The wastage of human resources in less-developed regions has long been known, at least in its economic implications. Early development theorists characterized those countries as "labour-surplus economies". What brought the unmanageable nature of the present situation to international attention was the cumulative impact of demographic growth, together with unruly and premature urbanization, on employment and income. "The first awareness of the unemployment problem came from (the observation of) people in the cities who obviously had nothing to do".[7]

Dualism and segmentation in developing nations

The constraints which put a stranglehold on the economy as a whole do not affect every sector or group in the same fashion. Profound

---

5. In most new nations, decolonization has accelerated urban growth. Independence has been accompanied almost everywhere by a market inflation of the administration. In some countries new capitals were created, reducing the influence of the old political centres, which became unemployment areas. Most restrictions of migration have been abolished and political unrest has often led to a new exodus from threatened rural regions. Industrial employment, largely concentrated in urban centres, was favoured by new industrialization policies. The net result has been an even steeper upward swing of the urbanization curve.

6. Todaro, in ILR, Vol. 104, No.5, 1971, p.388.

7. Employment in Africa, ILO, p. 1.

differences in technological advances and in economic productivity persist in all developing economies, and in many cases the gaps which divide different subsectors in terms of modernity, income and life styles become wider with each passing year.[8]

Paaw and Fei underline other aspects of this unequal development. There is technological dualism in agriculture, with a large backward sub-sector affected by population pressure and low productivity and a modernized agricultural enclave. "Surplus population migrates to both the industrial sector and the modern agricultural sector, components of the enclave ... The fact that this migration is pushed by low productivity in the traditional agricultural sub-sector, rather than being pulled by enclave demand for labour means that the migrant labour remains partially or fully unemployed. Thus the surplus population transferred from traditional agriculture to the enclave represents a drag upon development rather than an asset available for productive employment".[9]

It is as if two distinct and separate economies functioned regularly side by side, with countless mutual links but responding to different sets of priorities and values and giving rise to strikingly diverse social structures: a traditional economy which retains the characteristics of pre-modern times, within which the vast majority of the labour force still works outside the wage system, and a modern economy, geared to the market and closely resembling the industrialized model. The relative importance of wage employment increases noticeably as one moves from poorer to richer countries, and for many labourers in the poorer nations wage employment is still a privilege, a title commanding access into the modern world.[10]

---

8. "The process of modernization introduced new productive relationships and new technologies ... (these) were immensely more productive than the traditional ones but ... required far greater quantities of capital per worker. ... Given relatively low incomes ... and consequently low levels of saving, it was inevitable that the application of modern technology would be partial and selective ...

(Economic) growth resulted in the creation of modern sectors of high productivity co-existing with low productivity traditional sectors. Because of the high capital intensity of the productive process in the modern sector, the number of jobs created were relatively small. But the high productivity of the modern technology ensured ... high incomes for the owners of those enterprises. Some of the benefits also filtered down to workers in the form of relatively high wages. The result ... was that while the great masses of the population continued to have subsistence standard of living, a small minority working in the modern sector enjoyed much higher levels of income and consumption". (Dharam Ghai, "Unemployment Crisis in the Third World" SID, European Regional Conference, Doc. 4-e).

9. Paaw and Fei, The Transition in Open Dualistic Economies, pp. 126 and seq.

10. "The gap in levels of consumption and of income, in prestige and in life style between the different economic groups is behind much of the employment problems in most of the developing world. It explains the migration flows and urban unemployment. It is (Cont. next page)

Many authors refer to this lopsided impact of modernization as technological or social "dualism". But although it is true that there is a wide gap between the small minority working in the modern sector and the under-privileged rest of society, there is also an important division within those sectors. The large segments of economic activity geared to ancient values and set in traditional structures, co-exist not only with a series of modern enclaves which share many features with Western economic sectors, but also with an emerging pattern of informal activities which only recently have been recognized as having an independent economic importance. This makes for disjointed socio-economic setting.

In such a setting, strategies which until very recently seemed to be sensible extrapolations from the known facts of the history of Western industrialization result in a whole new set of problems, the dimension and range of which are only beginning to be grasped.[11]

## II. THE SOCIO-ECONOMIC CONTEXT

### The traditional structures

Subsistence economy prevails in most of the agricultural sector which varies in size but is always large. It is characterized by self-employed workers, their families and unpaid helpers in or around the household. The output is for the use of the group and is shared between its members. No such link as money stands between production and consumption.

Work in a subsistence economy is very different from modern wage employment in terms of the self-image of the participants, their interpersonal relationships and the social structure within which economic life takes place.

On the other hand, parts of the traditional economy produce goods and services for the market; frequently, this production is based on family units, where "everyone does the task for which he is most fit or which the culture assigns to him. It need not be full time: the

---

(Cont'd from previous page)

also a key to the problem of the educated unemployed ... The intense demand for education is the result of vast differences in income earning opportunities,... for it is education more than any other factor which controls entry to the coveted positions in (the modern) sector" (Dharam Ghai, op. cit., p. 14).

11. Table IX orders in a simple fashion the main socio-economic structures of production in the developing countries, including sub-divisions by area (rural/urban), economic sector (primary/secondary/tertiary) and type of market (domestic/export). We have signalled with the letters IA (informal Activities) the segments in which spontaneous economic activities have given rise to the marginal informal sector.

Table IX. A CLASSIFICATION OF THE VARIOUS SOCIO-ECONOMIC STRUCTURES OF PRODUCTION IN THE DEVELOPING COUNTRIES

| TRADITIONAL STRUCTURES | | MODERN STRUCTURES | |
|---|---|---|---|
| Subsistence economy: | | | |
| Rural areas: | | | |
|   Primary sector | | | |
|   Secondary sector | | | |
|   Tertiary sector | | | |
|     Domestic market | | | |
| Market economy: | | Market economy: | |
| Rural areas: | | Rural areas: | |
|   Primary sector | |   Primary sector | |
|     Domestic market | Export market |     Domestic market | Export market |
|   Secondary sector | |   Secondary sector | |
|     Domestic market (IA) | Export market |     Domestic market | Export market |
|   Tertiary sector | |   Tertiary sector | |
|     Domestic market (IA) | |     Domestic market | |
| Urban areas: | | Urban areas: | |
|   Secondary sector | |   Secondary sector | |
|     Domestic market (IA) | Export market |     Domestic market | Export market |
|   Tertiary sector | |   Tertiary sector | |
|     Domestic market (IA) | |     Domestic market | Export market |

remaining hours are devoted to family care, education and community obligations".[12]

The allocation of tasks is in part determined by institutional factors strongly dependent on interpersonal structure and hierarchy.[13]

"The dominance of family as a decision-making unit is not a matter of challenge. Thus it may be the family which inventories its human resources, decides who will go to school, who will work for the next-door neighbour, and who will be sent to the city to seek money income for the family. In this way the family may distribute its resources in search of several opportunities for advancement, may spread its risks and hopefully maximize its gains".[14]

The market-oriented segments of traditional agricultures not only involve different systems of land tenure (total or partial ownership, tenancy, etc.), but may also complement the family with hired labour.[15]

## The modern structures

Modern economic activity, by contrast, is essentially based on monetary mediation between producer and consumer. It does not eliminate traditional structures but results in the establishment of a "dual" economy. The new socio-economic structures are based on the interplay of supply and demand, which not only determines the allocation of the outputs but pervades the whole web of labour relationships.

A relatively small number of workers are employed at relatively high wages in three key economic sectors:
a) a small, highly-capitalized industrial sector using up-to-date technology;
b) advanced, agricultural enclaves growing industrial crops and using the tools and production systems of modern agriculture, up-to-date machinery, improved seeds and large amounts of chemical fertilizers, and
c) modern commercial marketing and credit services.

In these sectors, skill requirements are much higher - and more formalized - than in the more traditional ones.[16]

---

12. Employment in Africa, op. cit., p. 2.
13. For an analysis of these factors see André Beteille, Studies in Agrarian Social Structures, Oxford University Press, 1974.
14. Edwards, op. cit., p. 18.
15. The intricacies of labour relationships in this type of traditional agricultural market economy, together with those of its systems of land ownership and exploitation have been extensively studied by Béteille in the case of India.
16. "Modern employments, those representative of a developed labour market, may be thought of as characterized by institutional working conditions, based mainly on employer/employee relationships including contractual or otherwise explicit arrangements in regard to work time and rates of payment. (Only those) whose conditions of work are of this kind (Cont'd next page)

The price of change

The description of traditional and modern socio-economic structures co-existing in a given country and functioning side by side (Table IX, page 175) is only a first approximation to what is essentially an ongoing, dynamic process of widespread economic, social and cultural transformation.

A high price must always be paid for sweeping social change. The employment-related problems which interest us here provide a major example of the social and personal costs of the disruption brought to traditional societies by the impact of a series of demographic, economic and cultural changes which started long before their political independence.

In the words of two observers of the African scene: "The sheer weight of population growth is causing rural life to deteriorate. Farms are being sub-divided into smaller and smaller sizes. At the same time cultural patterns are changing. Many men no longer undertake warrior training or carry spears. Frequently, menial tasks are no longer acceptable. For the first time in African history a sizeable proportion of the rural population finds itself with "nothing to do". [17]

In any society productive activity depends both on the established distribution of tasks and on each member's acceptance of his lot and submission to the requirements of his economic role. Individuals must be given the opportunity to find their roles and be ready to assume them. When tasks were ascribed according to long established custom, the allocation criteria were perceived as being adapted to the known situation and well accepted. The relatively simple social and economic organisation was characterized by a stable and balanced relationship between the size of the population and the personnel requirements of production.

The introduction of more sophisticated methods of production, of personal mobility and individual choice, of a money-based system of economic exchanges and the new values which accompanied it, together with the ever increasing pressure of population growth had begun to upset the traditional equilibrium well before the end of the colonial era. But the effects of those changes have increased starkly after independence, and now, in the view of some observers, threaten the viability of the new nations. Faced with inevitable absorption into a modernizing economy, families which had subsisted by cultivating small holdings for self-support and surplus, were forced to seek cash income by marketing at the expense of their own nutrition part of what they produced or by turning to wage employment, found mostly in urban areas. Although the modern sector was not yet in a position to offer jobs in sufficient

(Cont'd from previous page)
may, with reasonable acouracy, be described as members of a labour force". David Turnham, The Employment Problem in Less Developed Countries, OECD, Paris, 1971, p. 27.

17. Philip Ndegwa and John P. Powelson, in Introduction, Employment in Africa: Some Critical Issues, ILO, Geneva, 1973, p.11.

quantities to this "agricultural reserve army" labour was thus pulled away from its roots. People came to be divided into two groups: the few winners who were integrated in the new system, and the vast masses of the marginal population, unable even to find refuge in the crumbling traditional world.

The inequality of income and of public services and amenities in rural and urban areas stimulated both urban migration and population growth (the more children one had, the greater the chances for one to secure paid employment sufficient to support the whole family). A new hierarchy was based on schooling and new educated groups often remained unemployed up to the limit of their resources in the hope of finding the job they considered suited to their capacities. Finally, the investment of scarce resources in capital-intensive ventures, favoured by policies designed to keep the price of capital artificially low in relation to that of labour[18] created further imbalance.

From a cultural point of view, the impact of Western ways of life has uprooted integrated traditional value systems and replaced them with fragmentary and contradictory cultural structures, ill-adapted to the needs of individuals and groups caught in the cross-currents of cataclysmic social change.

For a long time, many development experts assumed that the problems of population growth, hyper-urbanization, unemployment, food deficits, widespread poverty and political unrest were essentially transient offshoots of the process of change. But the scale of the process, especially in terms of the billions of people involved, was several orders of magnitude bigger than anything that had taken place in Europe or in the rest of the Westernised world, and this difference of scale did make a substantial difference to the nature of the process itself. Equally important, the time scale had no common measure with the two centuries of Western industrialization.

Several factors account for the fast pace of transformation in the developing countries: the demographic pressure, and the series of individual and collective demonstration effects, which result in an unwillingness to wait for an unspecified number of generations to reach modern levels of well-being (measured, in Western fashion, in terms of consumption criteria).

Moreover, the new nations are constantly prodded and preached at by competing politico-ideological mentors. The result is an untold number of pro-industrialization ideologies mixed with national, tribal and religious appeals. If nationalism combined with international technology accounted for the phenomenal rate of capital concentration and industrialization which took place in the Western world in the last two centuries, a new, often "revolutionary" technological nationalism

---

18. Obviously supported by the well-to-do classes and the newly organised industrial workers' unions, defending the already privileged categories of labourers.

is the central ideological tenet of the political elites which in developing nations try to harness, guide and accelerate the rush to industrialization and modernity.

Neither the traditional nor the modern sector is adapted to absorb even a minor proportion of the number of people, energies, needs and hopes they are supposed to channel.[19] The traditional market economy and what, stretching the concepts, may be called its "labour market" suffer from a chronic and increasing incapacity to utilize inputs, create employment and deliver the flows of products and services needed. Even though they are typically labour-intensive, their capacity to create employment opportunities is severely restricted by their low level of activity, caused by permanent shortages of raw materials, land and finance. Their levels of productivity and labour remuneration are exceedingly low, they lack access to the capital markets and to modern markets in general, to education and to modern technologies, and are helpless victims not only of cyclical or seasonal natural conditions but also of administrative vexations and of money lenders and usurers. In the absence of alternative work opportunities, the overpopulated, marginal peasant economies are forced to the solution adopted by many poor countries (Ireland, Southern Italy, Northern Spain, etc.) in the nineteenth century and earlier, when faced with a similar plight: to "export" their workers - often the best among them - to any promising labour market, often their own urban, "modern", partially industrialized one. But the absorptive capacity of both the domestic and export components of this "modern" market typically falls far short of what would be needed to accommodate more than a minimal fraction of the candidates for modern wage jobs.

Their domestic outlets are strictly limited: lacking the mass markets which in Western or thoroughly Westernised countries gave rise to advanced production and marketing techniques, modern sectors in developing countries often cater to small local élites.

Their export outlets are subject to a different set of limiting factors. Agricultural exports are affected by the serious instability of international markets and by the agrarian protectionism of industrial countries. Manufactured exports are obstructed by trade barriers and by a price and quality competition in which new-comers have difficulty asserting themselves.

Capital shortage, although less severe than in the traditional sectors, constitutes another limiting factor. Most capital markets in developing

---

19. As early as 1971, David Turnham emphasized that:
"By simple arithmetic, a manufacturing sector employing 20% of the labour force would need to increase employment by 15% per annum if only to absorb the increase in a total labour force growing at 3% per annum. In addition, because of productivity increase, about 3% growth per annum in output seems needed to maintain a constant labour force in manufacturing". The Employment Problem in Less Developed Countries, op. cit., p. 10.

countries fail to assist private entrepreneurs adequately in the expansion of the various productive activities. In fact, international agencies have often invoked the lack of capital absorptive capacity as a reason to refuse financial aid.

These are only some of the many factors restricting the rate of growth of the modern sectors.[20] Even though they are favoured by fiscal policies, by factor price distortion, by the injection of foreign capital, and, in general, by the whole paraphernalia of orthodox development strategies, their expansion and their labour-absorbing capacities, given their capital-intensive characteristics, tend increasingly to lag behind the employment needs of the society.

The informal sector

In the fringe area between traditional structures and the promised land of modern economy, a whole range of casual and self-generated activities proliferate. These activities have been designated as "informal" ever since the term was coined in the ILO Kenya mission report, Employment, Incomes and Equality.

They were described as a "way of doing things, characterized by:
a) ease of entry;
b) reliance on indigenous resources;
c) family ownership of enterprises;
d) small-scale of operation;
e) labour-intensive and adapted technology;
f) skills acquired outside the formal school system; and
g) unregulated and competitive markets".[21]

Although the extent of these activities is difficult to evaluate[22] owing to their spontaneous appearance and the little attention they receive from official bodies and institutions, this sector is certainly very large.

According to the ILO, by estimates which were based on commercial statistics, the informal sector in 1969 provided 25 to 30% of total urban employment and 28 to 33% of African urban employment in Kenya. In other African countries for which similar data are available, this sector accounts for 37 to 39% of African adult non-agricultural

---

20. The lack of managerial capacity, of trained labour, of social and physical infrastructure, etc. is often invoked in the literature. Moreover, in the modern sector, although wages are high, especially in comparison with the income of less favoured groups, workers are too few to form a relevant internal market and "pull" the rest of the economy to higher levels of production.

21. Employment, Income and Equality, ILO Kenya, p. 6.

22. The ILO has set up a project to collect data on the urban informal sector. See WEP-19.

employment.[23] These figures justify the comment that "casual and self-employment ... is the basis of the economy."

The ILO report observes that "while the income derived from those pursuits in many cases is less than that for wage jobs, it approximates to that earned by peasants on the land, where most of the population is".[24] The favourable level of reward in the informal sector as compared to the cash income received by wage labourers on small farms and by farmers tilling very small plots[25] accounts for its attraction for rural immigrants.

The informal activities on the periphery of the main towns thus serve as a haven for refugees from traditional socio-economic sectors pushed out of their old environment. But whereas in urban surroundings there is some ground for "the popular view that the informal sector is made up of what are considered to be the marginally productive activities of such people as petty traders, hawkers and shoe-shine boys", in rural areas "20% of those covered by the (ILO) survey were in manufacturing and repair activities, and the three largest groups were in tailoring, saw-milling and (posho) (maize) mills".[26]

It is significant that the characteristic feature of this sector should be a "way of doing things", the rationale of which is not accumulation of capital or growth of output, but just modest susbistence and survival.

Local official attitudes toward informal activities may be described as ambivalent. Often ignored, in some respects helped and in some harassed by the authorities, enterprises and individuals within the informal sector operate largely outside the system of government benefits and regulation, and thus have no access to the formal credit institutions and the main sources of transfer of foreign technology. As a result of official limitation of access to legitimate activity, many individuals pursue illegally economic activities similar to those in the formal sector, such as marketing foodstuffs and other consumer goods, carrying out the repair and maintenance of machinery and consumer durables and running transport. The consequence for them is twofold: risk and uncertainty of earnings.

In the agricultural sector the urban division between operators with and without licences is reproduced between those whose wealth enables them to conform to and benefit from standards officially laid down, while others can make a livelihood only by contravening the regulations. The similarity of illegal rural squatters, who move unofficially on to land scheduled for resettlement and face a continual danger of eviction to urban squatters is equally obvious - both are drawn to

---

23. Employment, Income and Equality, op. cit., pp. 224-225.
24. Weeks, Third World Employment, p. 62.
25. Employment, Incomes and Equality, op. cit., p. 223.
26. Ibid., p. 225.

real or perceived sources of wealth, despite legal restrictions of access.[27]

This description of the informal sector brings to mind features of other environments which have proved to be favourable to various types of creativity. Some aspects are especially propitious in the light of what is known of migrants and minorities as agents of change, and of the relationship between processes of acculturation and innovative social behaviour.[28]

- a) The breakdown of the traditional socio-economic and cultural structures liberates individuals and groups from many social and cultural constraints,[29] particularly during actual transition periods, before new values and structures have had an opportunity to "jell" and become again fixed and institutionalised. The co-existence of two - and sometimes more - competing value systems, although it extracts a high toll from individuals, in terms of day-to-day disorientation and conflict, is a permanent "training" in applied heterodoxy and pragmatic eclecticism.
- b) Migrations and mixed marriages amplify those effects, multiplying cross-cultural contacts and interactions, and widening the range of competing cultural models.
- c) High relative stakes - often nothing short of economic survival - constitute an extremely powerful motivating force.
- d) Free horizontal mobility protects individuals and groups from the most extreme consequences of eventual economic and social failure. In some cases, the persistence of the traditional structures, e.g., of tribal or extended-family ties, may provide them with fall-back positions, and with a base for renewed attempts at social insertion.

It is not implied that:
- i) creativity will unfailingly arise in informal-sector environments; that
- ii) if and when it does, it will be channelled into economic activities; or that
- iii) even if this is the case, it will be successful.

---

27. For a more complete description see Employment, Incomes and Equality, op. cit., p. 504.

28. The agents of innovation - in arts, ideology, techniques and social and economic adaptations to new challenges - will not be the traditional groups, oriented to the past, nor the institutionalised "modern" ones, turned "outward" toward the Western world, but, as always in history, the interstitial, marginal sectors which, as main victims of the clash of cultures, have no other way out than the blending of old and new, local and foreign, in a creative adaptation.

29. More forcibly in urban settings, where freedom from the rigid aspects of the traditional structures is much greater.

But there is an enhanced probability of creative innovation in such environments and it should be used to promote self-help and overall social development.

Informal activities are important not only as a source of second-level, relief employment, but as a source of income. In the case of Kenya by the ILO mission reports: "The evidence suggests that the bulk of employment in the informal sector, far from being only marginally productive, is economically efficient and profit-making, though small in scale and limited by simple technologies, little capital and lack of links with the (formal) sector. ... Often people fail to realize the extent of economically efficient production in the informal sector because of the low incomes received by most workers in the sector. A common interpretation has been to presume that the problem lies within the informal sector; that it is stagnant, non-dynamic, and a net for the unemployed and for the thinly veiled idleness into which those who cannot find formal wage jobs must fall. It is hardly surprising that this view should be widespread, for academic analysts have often encouraged and fostered such an interpretation".

The mission concluded that it requires "a leap of the imagination and considerable openness of mind to perceive the informal sector as a sector of thriving economic activity ... but (both) are entirely called for by the evidence".[30]

Inter-relationships between formal and informal sectors are also significant for the total economy: "an increase in the final demand for informal sector products would have a spill-over effect on other sectors because of the intermediate demand of that sector for goods and services coming from other sectors".[31]

Future perspectives - at least in the case of Kenya - underline the increasing weight of informal activities both in absolute and in relative terms: "A rate of increase in the formal sector high enough to reduce the relative size of the informal sector seems to us beyond the bounds of possibility for the foreseeable future. An absolute reduction is much less likely still. On the basis of any reasonable calculation, the urban informal sector in 1985 will include a larger proportion of the urban labour force than it does today. We do not view this inevitable development with dismay, for we see in the informal sector not only growth and vitality, but also the source of a new strategy of development for Kenya".[32]

---

30. Employment, Incomes and Equality, op. cit., p. 5.
31. Strategies for Employment Promotion, ILO Kenya, p. 69. See also pp. 503-508.
32. Employment, Incomes and Equality, op. cit., p. 505.

## III. THE MAGNITUDE OF EMPLOYMENT PROBLEMS

The numerical aspect

According to the latest estimates of the ILO, 40.4% of the labour force of the developing market-economy countries is either unemployed (4.7%) or underemployed (35.7%).[33]

The size of the labour force in those countries, on the other hand, is estimated to have been 450 million in 1950, 530 million in 1960 and 650 million in 1970, with projections of 820 million for 1980 and 1,400 million for 2000.[34] The rates of increase of the working population in developing countries, which were 44% in the 1950-1970 period, and 55% in 1960-1980, are thus expected to reach 71% between 1980 and 2000. Even if the present rates of unemployment and under-employment did not increase, the number of people with "visible" employment problems in the developing world would reach 560 million by 2000, thus exceeding the projected total number of employed persons in developing countries in 1980.

The accuracy of projected figures of employment and unemployment has been questioned on the basis of inadequacy of current conceptual frameworks, measurement instruments and empirical data. Above all, "under-employment" which looms so large in ILO's estimate is obviously not very precise. Moreover, the weight of "invisible" employment problems is so considerable that some authors seek to shift the emphasis: "In developing countries ... the problem is not that man-power is being wasted because of involuntary idleness, but that the vast

---

33. See ILO, Employment, Growth and Basic Needs, Geneva, 1976, p. 18.

34. Data for the period 1950-1980, from ILO Labour Force Projections, 1965-1985, Geneva 1971. A. Bhagwat, "Main Features of the Employment Problem in Developing Countries", IMF Staff Papers, Vol. 20, No. 1, March 1973.

|  | Total | | Urban | |
|---|---|---|---|---|
|  | Nos. | % | Nos. | % |
| Unemployed ............ | 33 | 4.7 | 14 | 8.0 |
| Underemployed ......... | 250 | 35.7 | 41 | 23.3 |
| Total ................. | 283 | 40.4 | 55 | 31.3 |

Table 2. Preliminary estimates of unemployment and underemployment in developing countries, 1975 (in millions). (Employment, Poverty and Income Distribution, p. 18; Source: ILO, Bureau of Statistics).

Page 80. The projection to year 2000, from Employment, Growth and Basic Needs, ILO, Geneva, 1976, p. 19.

majority of urban dwellers are working long hours in a debilitating climate while burdened by energy-draining diseases and parasites to earn a marginal income".[35]

### Difficulties of measurement and conceptualisation

The quality of the plans and strategies for employment depends in part on the accuracy of the measurement of the magnitudes involved. In the case of employment policies, the magnitudes to be determined or estimated are:

- A. The size of the present labour force and its probable future size, within a given time horizon.
- B. The different types of present-day employment problems, and the approximate number of people affected by each.

- A. The size of the labour force. Population and participation rate.

The determination of the labour force depends on two variables:
i) the size of the population of the country under consideration; and
ii) the proportion of the population which makes up its labour force.[36]

This proportion, the "labour-force participation rate" or "activity rate", is of crucial importance for employment planning. Differences in population sizes and/or participation rates explain the differences in the size of the labour forces of the various countries: "While crude participation rates, which apply to the whole populations can differ for a variety of reasons, much the most important arise from differences in age structure and, to a lesser extent, from differences in measured female participation".[37]

As an illustration of differences in age and sex specific participation rates we include a table (page 186) published in Turnham's study on estimates for 1965.[38]

It should be clear that participation rates refer to the total labour force, including not only employed workers but also every person who is looking for a job. This is equivalent to saying that any estimate of

---

    35.    J. Veekes, "Does Employment Matter?" in Third World Employment, p. 62.

    36.    The "labour force does not include persons engaged in activities which do not produce income", The Determinants of Population Trends.

    37.    Turnham, David, The Employment Problem in Less Developed Countries, op. cit., p. 23.

    38.    Turnham, op. cit., p. 24. In the text we will not enter into the complex technical considerations discussed by specialists of labour statistics. In particular, extensive studies are being carried out on the subject at the World Bank.

Table X. PARTICIPATION RATES

| AGE GROUP | MALES | | FEMALES | |
|---|---|---|---|---|
| | LDC's | DC's | LDC's | DC's |
| 0–14 .................. | 6.5 | 1.3 | 4.0 | 0.8 |
| 15–24 .................. | 78.1 | 70.2 | 36.9 | 47.8 |
| 25–54 .................. | 96.3 | 96.1 | 40.1 | 40.3 |
| 55–64 .................. | 86.8 | 82.6 | 29.2 | 30.1 |
| 65 + .................. | 57.5 | 30.0 | 14.5 | 9.2 |
| Total .................. | 53.2 | 58.3 | 22.9 | 26.8 |

the overall participation rate involves a measurement or an estimate of the rate of unemployment in the given population.[39]

But valid data on unemployment are lacking in most developing countries. This deprives employment strategies of a reliable factual basis. The projection of already questionable estimates into a more or less distant future further compounds the difficulties.

B. The measurement of employment problems

Employment planners face an even harder task when they try to estimate the present positions of the various sections of the labour force along other less "visible" dimensions of the situation.

Statistical, "accounting" difficulties and problems: Part of the technical difficulties in gathering meaningful data on employment problems are common to any effort of census taking or survey research in developing countries. Most of the data to be gathered refer to the bottom of the social pyramid in countries often compartmentalised along tribal, linguistic or caste lines, with extremely authoritarian attitudes against destitute individuals or groups, etc.

Conceptual difficulties: It is often hard to decide which groups of the population should be included in the labour force and which ones excluded,[40] which indexes to use to characterize a given type of

---

39. Or, more exactly, of the specific unemployment rates in the various sections of the given population.

40. For instance, whether the large group of females, largely in the rural areas, whose activities often include the provision of services which in more "advanced" communities are purchased, should or should not be included in the labour force.

employment problem, or how to interpret a given finding. Western labour statisticians are not exempt from this type of doubt. But they work inside a more or less consistent cultural context, while their counterparts who try to produce a realistic picture of the employment situation in a given developing country have to add an implicit query which could be worded, "Is the Westernisation of this community such that we may apply our usual conceptual framework?" In industrialized countries, some questions on working conditions, communications, etc., included in censuses or surveys may be difficult to answer, but in developing countries they may be meaningless due to the inapplicability of Western concepts about work, pay, and productivity.

This is not the place to list the weaknesses in labour statistics or to dwell on technical aspects. What interests us is mainly the fact that the cumulative overall result of those methodological problems and errors is to seriously distort estimates of both:
  i) the magnitude of the present and potential labour force;
  ii) the rates of unemployment and underemployment, and, in general;
  iii) the extent of employment related problems.[41]

One important aspect of this situation is the existence of a practically inexhaustible reserve of potential workers. Apparent participation rates in the younger age groups, especially among women, are extremely low in many LDC's. Unemployed members of these numerically very important groups constitute a potential labour force, in which individuals – whether or not they have previous working experience – would enter the labour market if job opportunities were offered. "The implied large overhang of potential workers outside the labour force could very quickly move into it following social or cultural change or improvement in job prospects. And social or cultural change can occur rapidly among young people".[42]

---

41. Large numbers of unemployed say they are "students" or "housewives" when they are in fact candidates to inexistent jobs. Child labour is neglected. "Discouraged" workers do not figure in labour force statistics, "additional" ones only when they work. All kinds of "invisible" instances of insufficient or low-paid work, and countless unsatisfactory and even inhuman conditions of work manage to escape statistical counts and are left to informed guess-work.

42. "The several studies already completed or currently underway on rural-urban migration and open unemployment in the cities suggest that there is substantial substitutability among these several dimensions of underutilization of labour and that one form can easily and quickly be transformed into another. Thus, efforts to relieve open unemployment in the cities seem to create a vacuum which is quickly filled by others from rural areas who in turn become openly unemployed in the cities". Edgar O. Edwards, Employment in Developing Nations, p. 11 (with a reference to a review by Michael P. Todaro, "Rural-Urban Migration, Unemployment, and Job Probabilities: Recent Theoretical and Empirical Research", International Economic Association Conference on Economic Aspects of Population Growth, Valescure, France, September 1973).
(Cont'd next page)

## IV. THE SEVERAL DIMENSIONS OF EMPLOYMENT PROBLEMS

Many different situations tend to be grouped under headings such as "invisible unemployment", "disguised underemployment" and the like. However, the definition of the various employment problems is multidimensional, and their visibility is only one among such dimensions (see below, p. 191). A systematic analysis of the several criteria underlying each concrete issue may make it clearer.

We have isolated ten such criteria or dimensions and used them to redefine in unambiguous terms all the concrete situations which we have come across in a rather extended bibliography. We do not pretend that the set of criteria we present is exhaustive, and that no type of employment problem, including other dimensions, can recur. The ten dimensions we propose are the following:

1. Number of jobs
2. Time spent on job (or jobs)
3. Level of wages (and other retributions)
4. Skills
5. Statistical "visibility"
6. Forced vs. voluntary
7. Security of job
8. Life style and services and goods which may be acquired on the basis of the retribution
9. Status of the job
10. Comfort, health, etc.

1. Number of jobs

The first, and more obvious, dimension of employment problems has to do with the number of jobs held by a member of the labour force. We may conceptualise it as a continuum running from:
   i) zero jobs - "open" unemployment - to
   ii) part of a job - work sharing or of part-time occupations - to the normal situation of
   iii) one-job employment through
   iv) several jobs - multi-employment, including the frequent cases in which an individual has to supplement the income he gets from one job by working at one or more unrelated activities. [43]

(Cont'd from previous page)

To put totally in line Edwards' quote with our terminology we would only need to substitute the words "several dimensions of under-utilization of labour" by "several employment problems defined in terms of the various dimensions of i) work characteristics, and ii) worker/job relationships".

43. Although not exclusively, multi-employment appears more frequently in urban than in rural settings.

2. Time spent on the job or jobs

This is also a continuum, ranging from zero hours, days or weeks to a whole variety of over-extended daily, weekly and yearly schedules, exceeding normal working time. Closely related to this dimension is underemployment, usually defined as "the situation of individuals who are working less (daily, weekly or seasonally) than they would like to work, or than normally employed people work".[44] The usual situations described in studies which explicitly or implicitly refer to this dimension differ according to whether (A) daily, (B) weekly, or (C) longer-term schedules are taken as the basis for the definition.

A. Daily schedules: Situations ranging from zero hours to overtime and beyond include:
   1. Open unemployment (zero hours)
   2. Daily part-time work (which, as we said before, is part of the definition of underemployment)
   3. Full-time employment
   4. Overtime
   5. Over-extended daily schedules (either in one or in several jobs; to be differentiated from occasional overtime, to be found in most full-time occupations and in many part-time ones).

B. Weekly schedules: Here the main situations include:
   1. Open unemployment (which is common to the three schedules)
   2. Weekly part-time work
   3. Full-time employment
   4. Lack of weekly rest periods.

C. Longer-term schedules: Included here are situations of:
   1. Open unemployment
   2. Yearly part-time work
   3. Irregular or occasional work
   4. Yearly full-time employment.

Together with the ones which are a result of economic trends:

   5. Seasonal unemployment caused by more or less regular variations in the levels of activity of certain sectors or industries during given periods of the year
   6. Cyclical unemployment which is a result of the falling-off in demand of the economy due to variations in levels of activity during more extended periods

---

44. Edwards, op. cit., p. 10.

7. Structural unemployment caused by lasting changes in the structure of the economy as a result of such factors as alterations in needs or wants, the discovery of new natural resources, or the exhaustion of existing ones, and technological progress
8. Chronic unemployment which results from a lasting deficiency of the total demand for labour in relation to its supply[45]

Finally cases of:

9. Frictional unemployment[46] also belong here.

3. Level of wages (and other retributions)

Wages can be considered "low", "normal" or "high" using a series of benchmarks which may call into play any other relevant characteristic of the job. Wages for a given type of job will be considered "low" or "high" depending on whether work is secure or not, dull, risky, tiresome, requires a high level of skills, long hours, is of a high or low status, etc. Even the "absolute" amount of local money being paid for one hour of work has to be compared with the standard of living of the local labour force, with the one of workers able and willing to take up such type of work, with the total income of their typical household, etc. The concept of compensation includes not only monetary wages but any economic, social or psychological benefit accruing to the labourer from his occupation.

4. Relationship between the skill requirements of the job and the skill level of the worker

The skill requirements of the job may exceed the capacities and skills of the worker, or of the candidate for a given job, be fairly equivalent to them or be much less than what the worker or candidate can offer. When the skills of the worker are below the requirements of the existing employment opportunities, the situation is often called "structural unemployment". On the other hand, authors include in their definitions of "hidden unemployment" those who are engaged in "second-choice" activities due to the impossibility to find work appropriate to their higher – or different – capacities. On the macro-economic level, this is a case of underutilization of manpower. At the level which interests us here, it is a source of psychological maladjustment, of lower wages and lower standards of living for a part of the

---

45. The definitions of categories 6 through 9 are taken, verbatim, from the Determinants of Population Trends, op. cit., p. 467.

46. Which may be informally defined as the unavoidable time lag needed for the supply of labour to adapt to the demand, and which takes place even in a full-employment situation.

labour force, possibly of political unrest, etc. The origin of this type of problem has been linked to problems of education and training (humanistic vs. technical education, imitation of Western education systems, ill-adjusted to the needs of the economies, indiscriminate transfer of Western values, etc.).[47]

5. Statistical "visibility" of a given employment problem

Behind expressions such as "open" and "visible" or "disguised", "hidden", "invisible", lies another dimension, the statistical visibility of the issue.[48]

Situations in which a person works full-time in a low-paying job, in one well below his level of skills, in low productivity tasks, seems "occupied ... on a full-time basis even though the services (he) render(s) may actually require much less than full time", or is "engaged in 'second choice' non-employment activities, because job opportunities are not available"[49] are often designated as "hidden", "invisible" or "disguised" unemployment or underemployment. Such conditions superficially appear as "normal" full-employment or non-employment situations, and only a sophisticated analysis of census or survey data reveals the underlying employment problems. These expressions refer to visibility or invisibility to what we may call the "statistical naked eye".

6. Forced vs. voluntary unemployment or underemployment

Expressions like "voluntary unemployment" or "voluntary underemployment" are indications of still another dimension. There are, in almost any society, individuals who exclude from consideration certain jobs for which they could qualify, for reasons linked to some other dimension, such as level of skills, level of remuneration, status or prestige of the occupation, etc.

A strong subjective element is evident in this dimension. In Western advanced societies we would not say that a university professor is "voluntarily" unemployed if he does not accept a post as janitor. In other countries, equivalent impossibilities may exist, but would be much more difficult for us to perceive from the outside.

To be "voluntarily" unemployed or underemployed, the individual must have other means of support (savings, pensions, a dole or the support of others).

---

47. See Chapter on Education by J. Hallak in this book.

48. Not to be confused with the social or political visibility of a concrete instance of a given employment problem (see footnote 7, p. 172).

49. Edwards, op. cit., p. 10.

The "voluntary/involuntary" dimension applies to any situation short of full-time, satisfactory, full employment.

In many instances, the "voluntary" or "involuntary" character of unemployment or underemployment is extremely difficult to establish, especially for large categories of people grouped in censuses or surveys according to their responses to simple questions of the type "are you looking for a job?" or "are you satisfied with your present job", "why?".

A certain number of other dimensions occasionally surface in writings on employment problems. Some of the most frequent, or apparently relevant, follow.

7. Job security

It has been repeatedly said that one reason for the attractiveness of urban jobs, besides their high remuneration and a preference for the amenities of urban life, is that urban jobs tend to be more secure than their rural counterparts.[50]

8. Life-style and type of goods and services which the worker can obtain on the basis of his remuneration

Another frequently mentioned dimension is an assumed preference for urban jobs. The city, in this context, is not only a labour market which offers a higher level of wages and more secure jobs, but also a more varied and pleasant consumer market than the country-side.

9. Status of the job

One of the most important dimensions is the social and cultural characterization of jobs. It influences job attraction, discrimination against or in favour of certain categories of the population, and other conditioning variables of employment problems which vary from country to country as a function of their diverse social and cultural contexts.[51]

---

50. "The most salient characteristic of wage employment in the eyes of the urban proletariat is not the absolute amount of income receipts but its reliability". K. Hart, Third World Employment, p. 69.

51. "The status-ranking of occupations varies between social groups and, while some (such as the Islamic community) may accord high prestige to commercial success, others may look down on all informal occupations. An independent variable in this is undoubtedly the degree of exposure to Western-style education, the means by which we may say that many younger Ghanaians are socialized into rejecting opportunities outside the conventional framework of a bureaucratic career. If, to the illiterate ... migrant, informal opportunities offer a ladder out of poverty, to the educated youth with his eyes on conventional

(Cont'd next page)

10. Comfort and health aspects of the job

A whole series of job characteristics seldom find their way into statistical analyses of employment problems, but are frequently mentioned in more impressionistic treatments of those issues and are closely linked to employment-related problems. Jobs can be either comfortable or uncomfortable, safe or risky, clean or dirty, easy or tiresome, healthy or hazardous, the distance from home to workplace may be a positive or negative factor, etc.[52]

Employment as a multi-dimensional situation: After the preceeding analysis it should be apparent that full employment, which at first may seem only a matter of having a job or not having one, is, in fact, a multi-dimensional situation; only those members of the labour force occupying the "normal" or "ideal" position in all ten dimensions can be considered to be fully and satisfactorily employed in the sense of not having any type of employment problem.

A dimension not included here: level of productivity of the job: In a number of definitions of "invisible underemployment" we find references to the situation of "people employed in low-productivity jobs". This situation is sometimes also called "disguised unemployment". It is often difficult to know, when a job is characterized as having "low productivity", whether, as is frequently the case, it only refers to jobs in which the worker's income is low, sometimes exceedingly so. This is especially true in the case of non-wage, own-account occupations, in which productivity and reward are, of course, intimately related.

But the two dimensions should be kept apart. Level of remuneration has already been stressed as a dimension of employment problems, in its own right. On the other hand, only when a difference in productivity is also accompanied by a shift in any of the enumerated dimensions is it also an employment problem. And although there are any number of obvious situations in which low productivity and low remuneration coincide, we cannot consider this to be always the case.

(Cont'd from previous page)
advancement, such employment may be both socially inferior and undesirable". K. Hart, Third World Employment, op. cit., p. 68.

52. "Whether or not the members of a community will be sharply divided into those who work and those for whom others work will depend at least in part on the nature of the work itself. The operations in wet paddy cultivation are on the whole far more onerous and arduous than those in wheat cultivation. It is no accident therefore that in West Bengal, Tamil Nadu and Kerala even small proprietors owning less than five acres of land often have it cultivated by others whereas in the Punjab and Haryana self-cultivation is common even among those who own ten or fifteen acres of land. While observing the actual work of cultivation in Tanjore and Burdwan I felt that had I owned a small holding there I would rather forego one meal in the day than cultivate the land with may own labour. I am convinced that given the technological constraints such a decision would be perfectly rational". André Béteille, Studies in Agrarian Social Structure, op. cit., p. 29.

Although the productivity of any part of the labour force is an extremely relevant dimension of economic problems, it does not in and of itself constitute a dimension of employment problems, and should be excluded from the criteria used to classify them. But since it may be one of the most important determining or conditioning factors of any number of employment problems, it does interest us within a more general context, as does any economic variable which may influence their employment-related difficulties.

## V. POLICIES AND STRATEGIES

National and international experts, faced with the failure of earlier development plans to meet employment needs and with the mounting public reactions against the unforeseen social and individual costs of growth-oriented development efforts, have reacted by looking for new solutions.

One of the very first was a reversal in the direction of factor-price manipulation. While the tendency had previously been to favour capital in a number of ways (subsidies, tax exemptions, etc.), an inversion of the trend was advocated, to increase the share of labour in the factor "mix". Although this solution is highly attractive logically, its range of application seems limited.

Only in the modern sector are wages relatively high and the price of capital relatively low, but the core of the employment problems lies in the masses of people outside the modernizing circuits.[53] Economically, the elasticity of manpower use relative to price changes is usually low. Technologically, in many sectors, the opportunities for trade-offs between capital and labour are very few. Socially, the inertia of established working patterns slows down the substitution process.

Another recommended measure, which proved successful in a few often-quoted examples (Taiwan, Singapore, South Korea, etc.), was a shift from import-substitution to export-led industrialization; it seemed, however, to require conditions which are not generally found in most developing countries.[54]

---

53. Only "in countries where the modern manufacturing sector is large, the effect could be considerable. See, for example, a study of Venezuela by Toneman (1972). However, in most countries the modern manufacturing and construction sectors are relatively small. Furthermore, the consequences of the removal of price distortions on the distribution of income and the pattern of growth will depend crucially on the initial distribution of income and assets". Redistribution with Growth, op. cit., p. 143.

54. "It is likely that the success achieved by Taiwan and Korea in using this strategy is partly explained by the relatively low concentration of asset holdings, especially in agriculture", D.C. Rao, in Redistribution with Growth, op. cit., p. 144.

For a long time, one of the most popular solutions has been the substitution of labour-intensive technologies for capital-intensive ones. As Hsien points out, this tendency is now "favoured in a number of plans, but the way in which this is to be carried out is not always described in detail". A long time is admittedly required to develop the adequate labour-intensive production techniques and an equally long time will be needed before they can be applied on a sufficiently large scale.[55]

While the prior examples were, so to speak, economists' solutions, another was prompted by a mix of economic and social considerations. Emphasis was shifted from the production of capital goods to that of wage goods. The economic rationale was that an expanded domestic market would result in an increase in labour demand, and the social inspiration was the hope of a fairer income distribution.

Eventually, these macro-economic measures have come to be supplemented, by ad-hoc public-work projects, designed to meet particularly difficult situations.[56]

However, few plans could be said to "contain anything like an integrated development strategy. The emphasis was still on the expansion of output, with the involvement of people as a by-product. Most plans consisted of sector projects and programmes loosely tied to a core strategy in which total capital investment needs were estimated on the basis of assumptions about the growth of output,

---

55. C. Hsien, "Approaches to Fixing Employment Targets in Developing Plans", in Third World Employment, p. 391.

56. Public works programmes are used as an instrument to create employment at all stages of development planning. They present the following evident advantages: the speed with which they enable the government to organise the unemployed and to direct their labour to the construction of needed public facilities; their flexibility, both as to location and to timing (in principle they can be phased to coincide with peak and slack employment seasons); finally and most important politically, their highly visible impact. But whereas public works programmes have been mostly used as purely stop-gap measures by earlier planners and have generally remained unrelated to growth strategy and therefore detached from the overall plan at that period, at a later stage they tend to be included in the overall development strategy: between 15 and 18 developing nations have established special public works programmes with employment as the primary objective in the last two decades, according to J.W. Thomas (see Employment in Developing Nations, p. 297). However, besides their advantages, public works programmes may also, as pointed out by the same author, have adverse effects such as resulting in augmenting the rent of already well-provided groups to the detriment of their intended beneficiaries when the former succeed in reverting expected benefits towards themselves as happened in 1968-69 in Pakistan. His concluding remarks is: "the nature and objectives of the regime undertaking the public works programme has an important relationship to how (it) is designed and its ultimate outcome" (op. cit., p. 229). We shall see below that, currently, public works programmes are considered as main political instruments linked to the overall ends and means of development planning.

with employment derived later by using crude assumptions about labour productivity".[57] But, as pointed out by Edwards (op. cit., p. 14), "the employment problem is so complex and pervasive that it is unlikely to yield to relief measures directed at any one sector ... even when so called multiplier effects are taken into account".

Present trends in employment policy

It is clear by now that there are no such things as employment strategies or employment plans separate from plans and strategies for development. This is why it is necessary to make some general observations about present-day development strategies.

Some of the dissatisfaction with previous strategies is due to a clash of values, of a basic incompatibility in the formulation of ultimate goals for society. The fundamental difference between partisans of market-oriented competitive development and proponents of community-oriented co-operative socio-economic organisation goes beyond the local scene of any LDC. The political nature of the objectives, goals, options and choices is increasingly asserted. Previous planners are criticized for having disguised fundamentally political decisions in the technical and "apolitical" language of economic reports. It should be clear that such criticism is not limited to previous development efforts, nor to the process of modernization in LDC's. They are part and parcel of a much more general and widespread critical current against industrial culture. They included such disparate elements as Illich's criticisms of "oversize" technology, schooling and other features of life in developed countries, the projections of Meadows,[58] and the Club of Rome, the ideas of E. F. Schumacher,[59] the various movements against pollution and for the protection of natural resources, zero population growth and anti-consumerist philosophies, as well as the political criticisms voiced by Third World countries in various international fora.[60]

In addition to such ideological criticism, however, there are a number of new approaches that could be described as reformist. This is not the place to discuss them in detail, but much of this new thinking is reflected in recent contributions by the ILO and the World Bank.[61]

---

57. C. Hsien, op. cit.

58. Meadows: The Limits to Growth, and related literature (not the one which is centered on technical criticism to the mathematical models and other secondary aspects of the controversy, but the one on the substance of the projections, extrapolations and predictions, together with their implications for present models of development in the West and in LDC's).

59. Small is Beautiful.

60. UNCTAD, FAO, the Bucharest Conference on Problems of Population, the North-South dialogue, etc.

61. The World Employment Programme.

The various missions of the ILO within the framework of the World Employment Programme have resulted in a wealth of empirical data together with some stimulating theoretical analyses and a few concrete proposals to deal with the employment problems of developing countries. The mission to Colombia resulted in the notion of "contrived dualism" and a programme of selective subsidies to small farmers without jeopardizing export-oriented modern agriculture as a source of hard currency. The mission to Kenya put great emphasis on the informal sector as a possible "engine" for employment, for the fight against extreme poverty and for overall development.

The ILO basic needs programme

As a direct off-shoot of the empirical and conceptual studies sponsored by ILO in the framework of the World Employment Programme, that Organisation has put increasing emphasis on a new programme which focuses not only on employment, but also on income distribution, poverty, and the situation of groups unable to meet their basic needs. Basic needs strategies are characterized by direct attacks on those problems rather than by priority for growth.

Redistribution with growth study

This World Bank study advocates "stabilizing the incomes of the wealthiest sections in order to use the resources which would otherwise accrue to the wealthy, for investment designed to raise the incomes of the poorest sections of the population above specified poverty lines".[62]

To achieve those results, it was deemed necessary to change the focus of development policies toward different homogeneous target groups, the relative weights of which would necessarily be different in different countries.

Specific forms of assets which could improve the conditions of each target group would have to be identified for specific countries, and a typology of countries was established.

Policy instruments included land reform, public works programmes, aid to small farmers, tenure reforms and the stimulation of demand for landless labourers tailored to local situations.

These policies, however, none of which was strikingly new or radical, except for land and tenure reform, should necessarily form part of a comprehensive plan to suit the country profile. The novelty resides in the "package" approach and in the specificity of the mix. Structural changes would have to be progressively brought about, to create the suitable institutions.

---

62. Strategies for Employment Promotion, op. cit., p. 27.

# 9

## EMPLOYMENT POLICIES
by
Frances Stewart

One obvious and critical effect of rapid population growth is the consequent growth in the labour force. In a situation where productive employment opportunities are already manifestly inadequate – as shown in the last Chapter – this growth in numbers presents a major problem and challenge. The aim of this Chapter is to review strategy and policy measures that have been suggested to deal with the employment problem in Third World countries. But before doing so, it may be helpful to present some background analysis within which the various measures may be identified and discussed.

### I. BACKGROUND ANALYSIS

It is now generally agreed that there is no unique "employment problem" in LDC's. Rather there is a syndrome of problems. The ILO Colombia Mission[1] identified three "distinct but related dimensions to the employment problem": lack of adequate employment opportunities may be a source of frustration among job seekers, a source of impoverishment and inequality, and may represent a waste of potential productive resources. Later Sen elegantly paraphrased these three dimensions as the recognition, income, and production aspects of employment.[2]

The employment situation in any country may be satisfactory or unsatisfactory to a lesser or greater extent in any or all of these respects. Despite substantial overlapping in the categories, each aspect needs to be separately identified: both cause and cure differ

---

1. Recent analysis of employment problems in poor countries owes a lot to the reports of a succession of missions organised by the ILO World Employment Programme, referred to here as ILO Colombia, ILO Ceylon, ILO Kenya and ILO Philippines. Some lessons from some of these missions are helpfully discussed in Strategies for Employment Growth, ILO, 1973.

2. See Sen (1975). Note: For details on authors cited, please refer to the bibliography at the end of the Chapter (Ed.).

between the categories and much confusion in analysis and policy is due to failure to separate them.

The employment problem may then be defined as consisting of inadequate opportunities for productive employment, where inadequate is defined in relation to all three aspects. Obviously with this definition the problem extends far beyond the openly unemployed, whose incomes are often in excess of those of many working people, including some working long hours.[3] Precise measurement, with this definition, is essentially somewhat arbitrary, because the dividing line between what is to count as adequate and what inadequate, is itself somewhat arbitrary.[4] In most poor countries a considerable proportion of the population of working age - generally the majority - are not employed by an employer, but are "self-employed" in family enterprises. It must be emphasized that in discussing the adequacy or inadequacy of employment opportunities, the concept of employment extends to all those who are working, irrespective of the mode of production.

The failure of the economic system to generate adequate employment opportunities may then be viewed as the outcome of five factors: technological dualism; the rapid rate of population growth; sectoral imbalance; the system of prices; and the payments system. Views differ as to the role and significance of each, with corresponding differences in policy recommendations.

Technological dualism

Two distinct technologies are in use in Third World countries. Modern technology, transferred from the advanced countries and requiring high levels of investment per man, is typically designed for relatively large-scale production, generates high labour productivity, and produces modern products initially designed for production and consumption in the advanced countries. Traditional technology is small-scale, uses relatively few investment resources per man, and is associated with low labour productivity and simple products. Technology in use in the informal sector is here classified along with traditional technology. The capacity of the modern sector to absorb labour is determined by the size of the capital stock in that sector,

---

3. For example, ILO Colombia found that 33% of the urban work force had inadequate incomes, of whom over one-third were working. In India Krishnamurty showed a relatively low rate of open unemployment (2.6% in 1966-67) but that nearly a third of the work force were working long hours (over 35 hours) for very low incomes (Krishnamurty, 1975).

4. For example, Turnham (1971) suggests including as underemployed all those whose incomes fall "below some reference level - say one third or less of average full time earnings of the employed population". In more recent reports (e.g. ILO Kenya and Philippines) no precise identification or measurement is made.

which is a function of past rates of investment, and levels of investment per employee in the sector. In general, because of the very high requirements for investment per employee, and the relatively low investment rates, the modern sector can only employ a fraction of the total labour force.[5] The high productivity in this sector permits - and to some extent requires - relatively high wages: management is in general amenable to passing on some of the fruits of the high productivity in the form of wages so as to secure an efficient, stable and cooperative work force. In the rest of the economy, in contrast, rewards are low: there are few investment resources available; given the enormous appetite for investment of the modern sector; the technology is fairly primitive with virtually no research backing. But, because of the low employment absorption of the modern sector, this part of the economy has to provide the majority of the jobs.

Open unemployment emerges as people try to shift from the traditional/informal sector to the modern sector. The level of open unemployment is determined by various factors, including income differentials, the probability of acquiring modern-sector employment, access to subsistence while unemployed, and whether access to jobs in the modern sector is only open to the openly unemployed.

This picture is static in three respects:
a) over time, investment occurs which raises the modern sector's absorptive capacity;
b) over time, technological changes occur, mainly concentrated in the modern sector, which raise labour productivity and reduce labour requirements for a given level of output and increase capital requirements per employee.[6] Hence the rate of increase of employment in the modern sector is less than the rate of increase of the capital stock and less than the rate of increase of output;
c) over time, population growth increases the number of people of working age.

The net effect on employment of the various changes depends on their relative magnitude.

---

5. The industrial labour force accounted for 22% of the total labour force in Latin America in 1970; 29% in the Caribbean, 10% in Africa, 14% in South and East Asia and 24% in West Asia (UNIDO, 1974, Table III.1). This represents a much lower fraction of the population of working age.

6. See Salter (1966) for an analysis of technical change in advanced countries, Stewart (1977 a) Table 3.6 and 3.7 for figures showing changes in capital per head and labour productivity in advanced countries; Baer and Hervé (1966), Gouverneur (1971) for figures showing how similar trends of rising capital per head and labour productivity are to be found in underdeveloped countries.

## The rate of growth of population

Arthur Lewis, in his basic model,[7] assumed that steady expansion of the modern sector would gradually absorb the whole of the work force in that sector, thus eliminating the employment problem. But two factors have, in many cases, invalidated this assumption. First, with technical progress the expansion of employment has lagged behind that of output. Secondly, rapid population growth has meant that employment expansion in the modern sector, even with quite respectable growth of output, has not kept pace with the additional numbers coming onto the labour market. The numbers (and sometimes the proportion) of those outside the modern sector has actually increased over time, instead of declining. This is largely a matter of simple arithmetic, as Lewis himself has pointed out. With a small modern sector - say employing 10% of the work force - the growth in employment in that sector has to be a multiple of the growth in population if all extra people are to be absorbed in the modern sector. With a modern sector of 10% of the total work force, and a growth in population of 2.5% per annum, modern sector employment would need to grow at 25% per annum to employ all additional workers. Since output normally grows about twice the rate of employment, this would require an annual output growth of 50%. Yet, apart from one or two extremely exceptional cases, growth in output in the modern sector of 10% per annum is a considerable achievement, with a corresponding annual employment growth of 5%. The growth in population therefore invalidates a simple growth strategy. It also contributes to increasing impoverishment as more people are added to the traditional/informal sector, which experiences little gain in resources, and little technical progress. Marginal and average product and incomes in that part of the economy decline. The gap between the sectors therefore widens, accentuating the employment problem, when viewed as an income distribution problem.

## Sectoral imbalance

In the model of technological dualism, the modern sector could be identified with the industrial sector, with its high capital labour ratio and imported technology. According to this interpretation, one source of dualism and unemployment lies in the neglect of agriculture. The industrial sector cannot absorb all the extra population coming onto the labour market because of the high level of investment per job in that sector and the large number involved. Many of the additional employment opportunities must therefore come from agriculture. However,

---

7. Lewis (1954).

the agricultural sectors potential for employment absorption is limited in a static appraisal, without reference to changes in technology or institutions.[8]

But the sectoral balance between industry and agriculture is of greater significance in relation to the dynamics of output growth. It has been argued that the overall rate of expansion of output and employment is closely related to sectoral resource allocation. Thus Mellor's proposed strategy is largely concerned with the need for agriculture to lead with consequent effects on the potential for rural and urban industrialization and on labour use. Similarly, the ILO Philippines Report places major emphasis on sectoral imbalance as a source of employment problems, and it points to sectoral balance as a cure. It is argued that lack of dynamism in the rural sector (agriculture and industry) and concentration on growth in the urban industrial sector led to a form of development which eventually became unsustainable, as it gave rise to large income differentials and rural impoverishment. Sectoral balance would require faster growth in productivity outside the modern large-scale urban sector, reducing differentials between the sectors. By supplying markets and surplus to the urban sector, it would also provide a healthy stimulus and produce more rapid growth of output and employment in the modern sector as well as outside it.

## The system of prices

Some economists have placed heavy emphasis on the price system as the source of the employment problem.[9] According to this view, the gap between the technology in the modern and the traditional sector is not in itself the problem. Such a gap may appear because of distorted prices and markets, but with market-determined equilibrium prices, undistorted by governments or by other powerful groups, such as trade unions and industrialists, the market would equalize marginal products in different activities and do much to reduce the employment problem. According to this view, the price system is both cause and cure of employment problems. Others see the price system as one aspect of the problem and its use as one way of improving the situation. An account of the way the price system may be used is contained in the policy discussion below.

Here it is worth making three points. First, the emphasis on prices implies a view of technology. That is to say, it assumes a very great flexibility in choice of technique, so that very labour-intensive techniques may efficiently be used, and the choice of techniques is exclusively (or at least predominantly) determined by prevailing prices.

---

8. See Dovring (1959) and Johnston (1966).
9. See, for example, Ranis (1971) and Bruton (1973).

Secondly, the equation of wages in different occupations may be
inconsistent with the hypothesis that fairly high wages are required, in
certain occupations, to secure an efficient work force. Thirdly, for
this view to be of operational significance the price system has to be
within the control of the government as a policy variable - and not, as
some would hold, largely determined by various interest groups.

The payments system

The level of employment and earnings from employment depend
not only on technology and prices, but also on the institutions which
determine how people acquire access to work and to assets, including
education, with which to work; and how income from work is determined.[10] These institutions are here described as the payments system.
The payments system plays a significant role in determing income
distribution from work, and the extent of different types of work.
Compare, at a micro-level, the way in which income and employment
are determined in a family firm, a capitalist wage labour firm, and
a co-operative. In a family firm, work may be offered to all,
irrespective of productivity, while in a capitalist firm, employment
is only offered if a workers' productivity is expected to exceed his
wage. In a family firm, the distribution of income is determined in
a way that may be unrelated to individual productivity at work, whereas
in a wage-labour firm, earnings are related to productivity. A co-operative, although it shares some features of both, comes nearer to
the family firm in the determination of distribution of work and of
income. If there are substantial inequalities in productivity from work,
a system of family firms, or of co-operatives, is likely to generate a
much more equal distribution of work and of income - and therefore
by our definition much less of an employment problem - than one
consisting of wage-labour firms. A similar contrast is offered between
three types of economy: in traditional economies, all are entitled to
work and to access to communally-held assets, and income is distributed according to varying conventions related to family connections, age,
and so on. "Involuntary unemployment" - i.e. the denial of access to
working opportunities to those willing and able to take them - is
unknown. Similarly, destitution through low productivity or lack of
work may occur communally as a result of various vicissitudes but it
is not an individual phenomenon. In capitalist societies access to work
is determined by those who own or control productive assets; profit
maximization ensures that only if a workers' productivity is expected
to exceed his wage will he be offered employment. If productive assets
are unevenly distributed and hence worker productivity is unevenly

---

10. This view is elaborated in Stewart (1977 b).

distributed, the system leads to a situation of inequality in opportunity to gain access to productive assets and to earnings.

With alternative systems of payment, a similar technological situation may be accompanied by quite different work and income distribution consequences. In some socialist systems for example, some parts of workers' incomes are regarded as a social overhead, which society has an obligation to meet. This part of the wage need not therefore be taken into account in determining whether to employ people. People are then employed so long as their productivity is positive. The employment problem - defined in any of three ways, income, production or recognition - may thus be largely eliminated if workers' employment and income is divorced from their marginal productivity. This is illustrated in the cases of both Cuba and China, where the employment problem is very much less than that in most underdeveloped countries.

## II. APROACHES AND STRATEGIES

This brief discussion of different analyses of the employment problem suggests the following different approaches.

A. Raising the rate of growth of output and labour absorption in the modern sector was the major strategy in most of the early models and development plans.[11] Despite some success in raising output, the employment problem got no better. Indeed, in some countries, it worsened as employment growth lagged behind output growth (see Table XI), and as the number of people of working age increased. In most countries, employment in the modern sector increased less than the work force, and in quite a few cases the proportion of people employed in the modern sector actually fell, despite the emphasis on output growth.

Moreover, in many cases growth in output and productivity in the modern sector was associated with high growth in real wages per employee in that sector, increasing the differential between the sectors, and accentuating the desire for modern sector employment.[12] There were only one or two exceptionally fast growing countries, where the strategy of output growth worked - notably Taiwan and South Korea - and where the proportion employed in the modern sector steadily rose.

The exclusive emphasis on output growth therefore became discredited.[13] But most alternative strategies continued to require

---

11. For example, Lewis (1954) and Fei and Ranis (1961).

12. Turner and Jackson (1970) provide some evidence on movements in real wages in manufacturing in a number of countries.

13. David Morse (1971) used the term "dethronement of growth".

Table XI. ANNUAL % GROWTH RATE, IN GDP CONSTANT PRICES AND EMPLOYMENT

|  | 1960-1970 | | 1970-1973 | |
|---|---|---|---|---|
|  | GDP CONSTANT PRICES | EMPLOYMENT | GDP CONSTANT PRICES | EMPLOYMENT |
| Eastern Africa | 5.9 | 2.0 | 5.8 | 1.9 |
| Middle Africa | 5.1 | 1.4 | 5.0 | 1.3 |
| Western Africa | 4.0 | 1.9 | 3.5 | 1.3 |
| Northern Africa | 5.5 | 1.8 | 7.0 | 3.1 |
| Southern Africa | 5.6 | 1.8 | 6.0 | 1.9 |
| Tropical South America | 5.2 | 2.4 | 6.0 | 2.5 |
| Temperate South America | 3.8 | 1.3 | 3.5 | 0.2 |
| Middle America | 5.2 | 2.7 | 5.5 | 2.9 |
| Caribbean | 3.8 | 1.9 | 5.0 | 2.0 |
| East Asia | 5.3 | 2.2 | 5.8 | 2.2 |
| Middle South Asia | 4.3 | 1.9 | 4.5 | 2.1 |
| South East Asia | 5.1 | 2.0 | 5.5 | 2.3 |
| South West Asia | 7.0 | 2.2 | 7.3 | 2.6 |
| All developing countries | 5.0 | 2.0 | 5.4 | 2.2 |
| Unemployment, all developing countries % increase p.a. | 3.0 | | 3.5 | |

SOURCE: Sabola (1975).

high growth in output both to contribute towards the absorption of labour and to help finance alternative strategies. For example, and perhaps most notably, the ILO Colombia Report which led the way in discrediting output-oriented planning in favour of emphasis on employment, itself required a growth in output considerably in excess of previously achieved growth rates. The redistribution-with-growth strategies also rely on growth in the modern sector to finance their strategy.

 B. Efforts were then concentrated on raising the labour intensity of output, or increasing the employment associated with any given output in the modern sector. This could be achieved in a number of ways: firstly, by changing the choice of technique towards more labour-using methods; secondly, by changing the sectoral composition of output towards sectors which are more labour-using; and thirdly, by changing the characteristics of products within each sector towards greater labour use.

 Approaches concentrated exclusively on expanding modern sector employment may, even if successful in terms of raising the rate of growth of employment in that sector, be unsuccessful in terms of the overall employment problem. If differential earnings between the modern sector and the rest of the economy are maintained or increased, expanding employment in the modern sector may raise desires and expectations of getting a modern sector job among the rest of the work force faster than they can be met. This is not likely to be true of economies which manage to secure a very rapid and sustained increase in modern sector employment, but such success is rare, as shown by the earlier figures. Kenya's two Tripartite Agreements (described in ILO Kenya Technical Paper 26) provide good examples of the futility of policies which are solely concerned with expanding modern sector employment by a moderate amount. In two agreements the government and employers agreed to expand employment by a certain percentage (10% in 1970), and books were immediately opened for the registration of those who would like a job under the agreements. In both cases, there was an overwhelming response and the books had to be prematurely closed. In 1970, registrations amounted to nearly half the total employment in the modern sector. The Agreements clearly had more effect in raising expectations than in realizing them (in the event they had little long term effect on employment); and indicated the almost bottomless nature of the pool of people who would, like to take up relatively well paying jobs in the modern sector.

 Any approach aimed at increasing modern sector employment needs to be supplemented by:

 C. Reducing income differentials between the sectors by holding down incomes in the modern sector, thus reducing people's desire to shift to the modern sector and reducing open unemployment; and

D. Raising productivity in the rest of the economy. If successful this would contribute towards a reduction in differentials; it would also help reduce the extreme poverty associated with maldistribution of employment opportunities.

Many of the strategies towards employment represent some combination of these approaches. India, in her early Plans, intended to deal with the employment problem by a rapid growth of output in the modern sector, of a fairly capital intensive type, to be followed by a rapid growth in employment as output growth accelerated. Simultaneously she pursued policies to promote the incomes and productivity of the traditional sector. China's walking on two legs "involves a similar strategy: again in the modern sector, the emphasis is on output growth, while in the rest of the economy efforts are devoted to improving the productivity of labour intensive techniques. The Kenya ILO redistribution through growth and the Institute of Development Studies/World Bank redistribution-with-growth strategies place prime emphasis on raising productivity in the informal sector by shifting resources from the modern sector to the traditional one. The role of the modern sector, in these strategies, is to provide resources to finance the shift of resources, not primarily to create employment directly - a marked departure from earlier models. Incomes in the modern sector are to be held down in order to finance the redistribution, thus reducing the income differential between the sectors.

The redistribution-with-growth strategies were inspired by the failure of growth-oriented strategies in relation to employment. The ILO strategy for the Philippines (and Mellor's) is similarly inspired; but the main emphasis is somewhat different. The growth-oriented strategies were seen to have failed in terms of growth as well as of employment. The growth achieved, although respectable in the short term, was thought to be non-sustainable in the long run, because it was not based on a balanced relationship between the urban and rural sectors. Their strategy, then, is to promote sustained growth based on a correct balance between the sectors; this sustained growth, it is argued, would be more labour-using and would involve a fuller participation of all parts of the economy.

Finally, another approach is that of changing the payments system, with the prime emphasis on changing the institutional structure which determines distribution of employment and income. It would thus use institutional change to transform the employment situation.

## III. POLICIES

Any discussion of policies[14] tends to suggest that governments have the freedom to choose policies more or less at will. In practice,

---

14. Moaly and Costa (1974) provide a very useful detailed survey of policies towards employment in developing countries.

such freedom is severely limited both by administrative and political factors. Many policies which would appear to be rational are difficult or impossible to put into effect, given the constraints operating in the system.[15] These limits, which vary according to the political, historical and economic circumstances of the country and with the policy under consideration, should be borne in mind in the discussion that follows.

Policies directed at raising the level of investment

An important part of a strategy for employment based on increasing the labour absorption of the modern sector consists of increasing the rate of investment. For any given ratio of investment to employment, the policy will increase modern-sector employment proportionately. Early national plans placed considerable emphasis on raising investment. This required a parallel increase in savings, as well as in the ability and determination to invest. One important source of savings and investment was thought to be the foreign sector, and consequently a significant aspect of this strategy, for many countries, lay in a policy to attract foreign direct investment, by provision of tax incentives related to investment, guarantees of security, tariff protection, appropriate infrastructural investment, and creating the right sort of climate.[16] It is not clear how much this policy contributed to raising foreign investment for LDC's taken as a group, but individual countries increased their share of the total (or avoided a loss in share) by the use of such incentives. The increased rate of foreign investment was not always parallelled by an increased inflow of finance as many foreign companies borrowed much of their finance locally,[17] while remittances overseas on past investments proved a drain on current resources.

From an employment point of view, the results of such policies was often disappointing because of the capital-intensity of much foreign investment,[18] so that any percentage addition to the capital stock brought a less than proportionate increase in employment. However, the relationship between foreign direct investment and employment

---

15. See Stewart and Streeten (1976) for a more extended discussion of these issues.

16. See the references in Lall (1975), especially Chapters 7 and 14 and ILO Kenya, Technical Paper 16.

17. See Herman (1971) for evidence in Kenya.

18. The results of research into the relative capital intensity of foreign as against local investment seen to show that foreign investment is not markedly more capital-intensive for the production of a specified product - and indeed is sometimes more labour intensive - but that it is more heavily concentrated in sectors which use relatively capital intensive techniques, so that the overall effect is to raise capital intensity. See e.g. ILO Kenya, Technical Paper 16, Wells (1973), Morley and Smith (1974).

creation depends on the nature of the foreign investment. The capital-intensity of much foreign investment was partly due to the climate in which foreign companies operated - the relative prices of labour and capital they faced, the nature of the markets and therefore of the products they produced and so on. Where foreign investment takes place in a different climate - as with the location of labour intensive parts of the productive process in low wage countries - their operations tend to be much more labour-using.[19] However, the foreign investors themselves contribute to the climate which favours the use of capital-intensive techniques. The investment incentives and protection they require to attract them are part of this climate. Foreign companies tend to pay above-average wages. Their products and technology are designed in the advanced countries, and are more sophisticated and capital-intensive than would have been appropriate if designed for much poorer countries. Consequently, a strategy which relies heavily on foreign investment tends to produce excessively capital-intensive investment.

The main source of domestic savings is through taxation. However, this source is limited by political acceptability. An alternative way of raising savings is through the choice of technique.[20] More capital intensive techniques may generate more savings, as wage labour and therefore consumption is curtailed. Hence a policy of raising savings and investment may in certain conditions be in direct conflict with a policy of raising short-run employment.[21]

Raising savings is a necessary but not sufficient condition for raising investment. Policies towards investment include raising government investment, which increased substantially during the 1950's and 1960's in many countries, and demand and taxation policies favouring private investment. The effects on employment then depend on the type of investment that occurs. In many countries the nature of the demand and taxation policies followed primarily in order to induce a high rate of investment, and, it was hoped, a high rate of expansion of employment, actually led to increasingly capital-intensive technology.

On the whole, developing countries were successful in raising the rate of investment: for all developing countries the ratio of gross domestic investment to gross domestic product rose from 16.8% in 1955 to 20.3% in 1973.[22] But employment lagged behind both output growth and growth in the capital stock. In part, at least, this lag was due to the nature of some of the other policies followed.

---

19. Described and discussed by Helleiner (1973).
20. See Sen (1968).
21. The conflict is explored in Stewart and Streeten (1972) IBRD.
22. World Tables 1976, Table 3.

### International trade strategy

Many countries in the first stages of industrialization followed an import-substitution strategy in the belief that heavy protection was necessary to secure a guaranteed home market for investors, and that such a market was essential to persuade firms to start industrial operations in countries with little or no previous industrial experience. The important substitution strategy has been described as import reproduction rather than substitution because it involved, for the most part, an exact replication domestically of items that had previously been imported.[23] Hence, on the whole, the same companies, directly or indirectly, were responsible for production after import substitution as before, changing the location of their activities but not their nature. Even the location only changed partially, as, at least at first, local "production" consisted largely of the assembly of imported parts. The strategy as it was widely pursued, therefore, involved the transfer of technology from advanced countries to reproduce products that had been designed in and for advanced countries. Consequently, the technology used reflected the factor availability of the advanced countries and was relatively capital intensive in nature.

The slow growth in employment which accompanied the strategy has been attributed to the protection policy followed.[24] By introducing a wedge between local and international activities the policy removed incentives to international efficiency, which might have encouraged more labour-intensive techniques and products following LDC's comparative advantage. The protection enabled firms to pay fairly high wages without fearing the consequences, and then to adopt capital-intensive techniques in response to these high wages. While it gave favourable terms to the protected industrial sector, it discriminated against the rest of the economy. The agricultural sector lost in terms of trade, and was consequently relatively impoverished;[25] similarly, the traditional sector suffered, with the exchange rate biased against its exports, while it obtained any inputs it required from the industrial sector on unfavourable terms.

Hence, this policy, although it led in the short run to expansion of output of the modern sector, failed to absorb labour in that sector on a sufficient magnitude, while it biased the system against the rest of the economy which had to cater for the majority of the work force. It has even been argued that the policy was a dead-end one and could not lead to sustained growth over a long period.[26] As the first easy stage of imports substitution becomes exhausted, with substitution for the main items of consumption, production of parts and of machinery

---

23. By K. Marsden.
24. E.g. by Little, Scitovsky and Scott (1970).
25. The bias against agriculture is described fully by Lipton (1977).
26. ILO Philippines.

has to follow. But these are more difficult to substitute for, as it tends to involve complex technology and short production lines. Excess capacity tends to worsen at this stage, while market expansion tends to peter out. Sustained growth requires some external source of sustained demand - such as might be provided by growth in the agricultural sector or in export demand. But the import substitution strategy discriminates against both of these potential sources, leading in the end to a form of involuted development.

Employment expansion, therefore, requires export orientation which secures a product and technology mix more suited to countries' factor endowment, and generates sustained expansion of output and of employment. Thus numerous commentators have recommended a move towards trade liberalization and the promotion of labour intensive manufactured exports.[27] Policies required involve dismantling import restrictions, lowering tariffs, devaluing the exchange rate and pursuing policies to promote the production and marketing of exports. Taiwan and South Korea are often quoted as successful examples of this strategy. In some countries, there are obvious political and economic difficulties about the immediate dismantling of the structure of protection, and here gradual policies and the creation of tariff free zones have been suggested.

But some doubts about this proposed "free trade" strategy have been voiced. Firstly, there is the question of whether some import substitution phase is not an essential precondition to build up the necessary industrial capacity and entrepreneurial ability. This, for example, appears to be the view of Fei and Ranis in their work on Taiwan and South Korea.[28] Secondly, there is the difficulty of obtaining markets for labour-intensive manufactured goods in view of the restrictive policies of developed countries. It is often argued that the policy offers a possible path for a few countries, but that developed countries would not permit it to be pursued on a substantial scale by many countries simultaneously. Thirdly, there are implications for technology of adopting an export-oriented strategy. Exported manufactures have to be of high, sophisticated and often changing quality to keep up with trends in world demand. This imposes requirements for a fairly capital-intensive and increasingly sophisticated technology. While, therefore, in the short run, the export orientation might offer a more labour-intensive pattern of production, in the long run it would involve capital-intensive technological change, as compared with an appropriate technology strategy.

Most analysis of the relative merits of export orientation compared with import substitution take the existing style of import substitution as the standard of comparison. But countries may pursue more genuine

---

27. Notably Little, Scitvosky and Scott (1970), Mellor (1976) and ILO Philippines; it also forms part of the strategy of ILO Ceylon and ILO Kenya.

28. Fei and Ranis (1975).

import substitution policies, in which they substitute different and more appropriate products for those products previously imported. The local substitutes - where they are available - are likely to be simpler, less standardized, using local materials and more labour-intensive (often indigenous) technology, as compared with imported products. This type of genuine import substitution would therefore be likely to be more labour absorbing and to make greater use of the products of the traditional, informal and small-scale sectors, as compared with the import reproduction policy which has required large-scale urban production. A policy of appropriate product import substitution would be consistent with trade between developing countries, pursuing similar strategies, as against the heavy dependence on trade between rich and poor countries.[29]

Technology policy

Technology lies at the heart of much of the employment problem. The earlier analysis of technological dualism suggested that it was the highly productive but capital intensive nature of modern technology, in comparison with the low productivity and incomes generated by traditional/informal sector technology, that was responsible for much of the employment problem. The view is challenged by the price school, which holds that such technical choice in the modern sector is a feature of the distorted price mechanism, rather than of technical rigidity. On that view, it is the choice of technology from within the available range, rather than the range itself, which is of critical importance in creating employment problems.

A considerable amount of empirical evidence has been collected in order to decide between these views of technology.[30] Broadly, the outcome suggests a middle way between the two extremes of complete technological rigidity and complete technological flexibility. In ancillary processes - such as transport and packaging - there are labour-intensive efficient alternatives. In core processes, if the characteristics of the product have been narrowly defined, there is in many cases little choice, particularly at large scale. From a policy point of view, the empirical evidence suggests that changing relative prices may have some effect on choice of technique, but of a more limited nature than the price school suggest. The price policies that flow from this include removing government support for high wages in the modern sector (through, for example, wages councils and minimum wage legislation),[31] removing the fringe benefits which may substantially

---

29. See a more extended discussion in Stewart (1977 a) Chapter 7.

30. See Jenkins' bibliography (1975), Bhalla's collection (1975), Stewart (1977 a), Chapters 8-10, and the work of the David Livingstone Institute in Strathclyde.

31. See Ghai's (1968) discussion of Incomes Policy; however, ILO Philippines wishes to use wages policy "to protect the working class against further erosion of their real incomes", p. 46.

increase the cost of labour into the firm,[32] subsidizing the employment of labour or additions to employment; removing the subsidies on capital and raising interest rates paid in the modern sector.

There are substantial variations in the labour intensity of techniques associated with different products. Altering the balance of production between sectors to increase labour intensity may be achieved by trade policy (discussed above), by indirect taxes and subsidies, by government expenditure and by redistribution of income. The Indian Government has used heavy indirect taxation of such items as consumer durables while subsidizing handicrafts as part of the employment/income distribution policy. Government expenditure on labour-intensive products - notably construction and housing - has also been partly a response to employment problems in many countries.[33] (Public works will be discussed separately below.) The rapid rise in the public sector payroll, observed in many countries, may be attributed in part to employment-creating policies. One observer noted that "Government policies of absorbing new entrants to the labour force in the public service stimulate the development of employment expectations that do not match the economy's manpower requirements".[34]

The Colombia Report emphasized income redistribution as a means of changing the balance of consumption towards more labour-using products. The elite consumed items with a heavy import content, which led to little employment as compared with the consumption patterns of the poor. Since then a fair amount of empirical work has been directed at assessing the employment intensity broad groups of products and the tendency if any, for the rich to consume more employment-intensive goods than the poor. In general, the evidence suggests that little in the way of employment creation would result from income redistribution as the consumption of labour-intensive services by the rich tends to offset their consumption of capital-intensive items.[35]

Most recent work, in this area, however, has been concerned with redistribution of consumption in relation to rather broadly defined product groups. The evidence on choice of techniques suggests considerable variation in labour intensity of techniques between products fulfilling the same broad need and within the same product group. For example, the housing of the poor tends to be more labour intensive than that of the rich; another example is provided by sugar consumption.[36]

---

32. Much emphasized in ILO Colombia (see Chapter 14).
33. The employment implications of increasing expenditure on construction is explored in detail for Sri Lanka by Ganesen (1975).
34. Berouti (1956).
35. See the survey article by Cline (1975); Tokman (1975); Figneroa (1975) finds a small positive employment effect from redistribution in Peru.
36. See (Stewart 1977 a), Chapters 9 and 10 on maize grinding and housing materials, and James on textiles in India (1975) and on sugar processing (study for ILO, 1977).

For some products the relationship works the other way round. One often-cited case is footwear: products consumed by the poor in LDC's (plastic moulded sandals) are more capital-intensive than the leather footwear consumed by upper income groups.[37] Where traditional/ informal sector products compete with modern sector products, the traditional/informal sector products are nearly always more labour-intensive and nearly always consumed to a greater extent by the poor. It follows then that redistribution of income may shift the sort of products consumed within each product group towards more labour-intensive variants.

Taxes and subsidies and government expenditure may also be used to favour the more labour-intensive and appropriate products.[38] Generally speaking, government tax and subsidy policy is directed at modern sector products, but government regulations play a significant (normally negative) role in determining product characteristics. Thus health and hygiene regulations designed for advanced countries and reproduced in poor ones lead to modern sector capital-intensive products. Examples are regulations in relation to building standards, public eating places, and beer.[39] Government expenditure is to a large extent also directed at modern sector products - for example, in its educational and health expenditure and public sector housing. But more recently the need to spread the benefits more widely has led to more appropriate spending patterns - e.g. in relation to health auxiliaries, to site and service housing and so on. The more appropriate patterns of spending have the dual effect of improving income distribution directly through spreading the direct benefits of the products, while increasing employment and redirecting markets towards the small-scale and traditional producers.

Another critical determinant of the nature of technology - both what is produced and how - is the scale of production. Heavy reliance on foreign technology has led to relatively large scale units which tend to inhibit local entrepreneurship besides leading to capital-intensive technology. A deliberate policy to encourage local small-scale entrepreneurs, therefore, can improve the choice of technique as well as the local dynamism of the system. This seems to have happened in some countries more or less automatically in the recent past (e.g.

---

37. See for example McBain's study of footwear in Ethiopia (1977).

38. The appropriate characteristics of products vary with the income level of the consumer, as well as with the environment in which they are consumed. In general the appropriate products for low income consumers differ from those appropriate for high income consumers, being simpler, less costly and incorporating less packaging.

39. Relaxation of such regulations formed part of the proposals of ILO Kenya. In Kenya local beer making, using local materials and indigenous technology, is illegal.

Japan, Taiwan) and has been recommended for many others.[40] However, large-scale units continue to dominate in the access to credit.

The policies discussed above aim at improving the choice of technique from within those available. But the dominance of advanced countries in research and development, and particularly in product development, means that modern-sector technology becomes steadily more efficient (and also more capital-intensive), while the rest of the economy lags behind in terms of efficiency.[41] A critical requirement therefore is for an active policy on technology. A prime need is to develop improved techniques and products for the small-scale and traditional sector; a second requirement is to develop more labour-using techniques for the modern sector. While many countries have elaborate science policies and high rates of expenditure on research and development, a good deal of the efforts are devoted to near duplication of developed country technologies, and too little to the development of appropriate technology. A coordinated international effort is required.[42] Among the many difficulties, there are considerable problems in getting effective communication between small-scale users of technology and those who are responsible for research and development.

Income and asset redistribution

Income and asset distribution are central to the employment problem, as it has been identified as largely a matter of maldistribution of income-earning opportunities. Tackling the income aspect of the employment problem must involve some redistribution of income and assets. Yet this is likely to prove difficult, given that the income and asset distribution are largely the outcome of the economic system in existence.

The dilemma is seen clearly in relation to the sort of economic and technological strategies which are responsible for the emergence of the employment problem. A pattern of investment that involves a relatively capital-intensive modern sector, with high labour productivity, and producing sophisticated products, normally leads to the emergence of high-paid jobs. These income groups then provide the chief market for the goods they produce. The distribution of assets tends to be concentrated in that sector, because of the heavy capital requirements its technology imposes. The income and asset distribution is closely intertwined with the general industrial strategy. Probably the most effective attack on the employment problem is to redistribute income and assets from the large-scale and privileged modern sector elite to

---

40.  For example by Mellor (1976) and ILO Philippines.

41.  A recent OECD survey shows that the developing countries' share of global research and development expenditure was 4% in 1973.

42.  See Cooper (1972 and 1974) for a discussion of some of the difficulties.

the small scale, the rural areas and the informal sector. While this is a prime requirement, and an important part of all recent employment strategies, it will be difficult, it not impossible, to achieve without simultaneous action on the other policy fronts discussed.[43]

The need is not simply for some sort of continuing transfer through the tax/subsidy system, but for a redistribution of earnings opportunities. This requires that the impoverished receive productive assets with which to earn. There must also be a redirection of credit, markets, improvement of technology, and so on, to make these redistributed assets effective. Such a transfer would then not only have the effect of directly improving the income distribution, but would also have indirect effects which would help solve the unemployment problem. The effect on the pattern of consumption has been discussed above: with a greater proportion of incomes earned in the low income small-scale sector, a greater proportion of consumption would be likely to be directed to that sector, thus bringing about a redirection of markets in a labour-using direction. Moreover, the technology used in that sector is more labour-using than that in the large-scale sector, and this too would increase labour use. In agriculture it has been firmly established that small firms, and particularly family farms, are more labour-using and produce more output per hectare than large farms. This is one reason why land reform is a part of most strategies for equity and employment.

There are various ways in which the redistribution of assets and income may be achieved. At one extreme, assets may be confiscated and redistributed. Such a policy cannot transform existing physical assets from factories/machines of a particular design, normally fairly large scale, into the sort of small-scale assets that are needed. To provide the small-scale sector with appropriate assets investment resources must be redirected. (This does not apply to agricultural land which can be sub-divided and parcelled out, and for which therefore straightforward redistributive policies are relevant.) The redistribution-with-growth strategy recommends holding down incomes in the modern sector and transferring investment assets to the traditional/small-scale sector. No direct asset confiscation is recommended - partly in the belief that this would make the policy more acceptable politically. The ILO Philippines strategy towards redistribution is more indirect. The reorientation of credit, markets, and government expenditure is supposed to achieve the required reorientation of investment. While the desirability of these policies is beyond doubt, it must be said that their realism is questionable.

---

43. Especially the redistribution with growth strategies, but also Mellor and ILO Philippines.

Sectoral balance

It has been argued that a more employment-oriented growth path would follow from a strategy which gave priority to agriculture and rural industry. Industrial expansion alone cannot provide employment opportunities for the annual growth in the labour force, given the size of the investment resources required for each extra job and the size of the annual increase in the work force.[44] Agriculture is in itself a labour-intensive industry: a growth strategy which started with agricultural growth would generate rural industry in its wake, if the appropriate rural infrastructure, local entrepreneurs, credit and technology were available. Such rural industry would be more labour-using than large-scale urban industry and would have better income distribution effects. Subsequently, the flourishing rural agricultural and rural industrial sector would provide both markets and food for sustained expansion of the urban sector.

The policies relevant to such a strategy are an amalgam of price and exchange rate and taxation policies favouring agriculture, government expenditure on rural infrastructure and corresponding educational and credit policies. The examples of both China and Taiwan can be cited as cases where successful interaction between agriculture and rural industry led to a labour-using pattern of growth. In Taiwan much has been attributed to heavy government expenditure on rural infrastructure.[45] In China the integrated structure of rural decision-making, within the Communes, together with a strong bias in favour of rural industrialization, may account for the success of achieving a high level of employment.

While there is plausibility in the pattern of development postulated by advocates of sectoral balance, the major difficulty is knowing how to create the necessary and sufficient conditions for the realization of the virtuous growth path they describe.

The agricultural sector

Shifting the sectoral balance towards the agricultural sector would increase income and productive employment opportunities within the sector. Other action may be taken to increase employment absorption of the agricultural sector, such as providing incentives to change the crop pattern to more labour-intensive direction. In Colombia, for example, it has been found that crops for domestic consumption tend to be more labour-using than export crops.[46] One may change the structure of incentives, of institutions, and, notably, of land holdings

---

44. See Cassen (1977).
45. See Fei, Ranis and Kuo (1977).
46. Evidence reported by Ranis.

so that labour-using methods are adopted rather than mechanization. Access to and price of credit, exchange rate and tariff policy and the price of imported machinery help determine the rate and nature of mechanization. The type of infrastructural services provided - including roads, marketing assistance and irrigation - also influence the choice of technique in agriculture. As already argued, the size and nature of land holdings are of great significance in relation to land use with small farms tending to be more labour-using than large, and family farms more labour-using than others.[47] In recent years, the rate and direction of technical change has become of considerable significance in determining the labour intensity of agriculture; concentrating on labour-using technical change could be a potent policy influencing labour use.[48]

Prices and project selection

The use of the price system in relation to an employment strategy has already been discussed in connection with trade and choice of technique. Recommendations for reduced wage rates and raised capital/interest rates, with a realistic exchange rate, form part of most packages. However, it should be noted that where the modern-sector products and services compete with those in the traditional sector, reduced wages in the modern sector may actually reduce total employment by allowing the modern sector to secure some of the markets of the traditional sector.[49] Policy-makers may face severe limitations on their ability to alter prices at will. Wage rates are negotiated by trade unions and firms. Firms often choose to pay fairly high wages in order to secure a stable, co-operative and efficient work force. While there is more freedom of control over capital prices - through taxation and credit control - credit institutions often prove difficult to control at will. Vested interests in tariff protection may make it difficult to dismantle controls. Those countries which have managed to switch from tariffs and import substitution to export promotion (notably Taiwan and South Korea) did so partly in response to external pressure, and with very tough governments. Methods of shadow pricing and project selection provide a substitute for prices, where these are not amenable to control. Shadow prices which place an appropriately low price on labour inputs, and a high price on foreign exchange and interest rates, may therefore be used to select projects in a more employment-creating direction. However, though very sophisticated on paper, such

---

47. See for example evidence collected by Ajit Ghose.
48. See M. Lipton (1977 b) for a detailed discussion of technical change in agriculture.
49. See Stewart and Weeks (1975).

methods have so far rarely affected actual decisions.[50] In both public and private sectors, decisions taken according to shadow prices may lead to severe financial problems, where there are big divergencies between shadow and actual prices. In the private sector, in addition, there is the problem of persuading decision-makers to adopt projects which are not profit maximizing.

## Government expenditure and public works

Government expenditure may be used as a catalyst to promote employment generation - for example, by infrastructural expenditure, supplying finance to local groups which are organising employment-oriented projects, and so on. It may also be directly employment creating. Most governments rely on labour-intensive public works - wholly or partially financed by them - to create employment. Sometimes these works have been designed seasonally to fit in with agricultural labour demands; sometimes to provide emergency relief after some vicissitude such as crop failure; and sometimes to mop up surplus labour on a continuing basis. The record of public works has not, however, been very successful.[51] The magnitude of most efforts has been small in relation to the size of the employment problem. Administrative obstacles have often prevented planned public works employment being fully realized. In India, for example, the Third Five-Year Plan envisaged employing two million people by the final year of the Plan, "In the event the target was not attained, only 400,000 jobs being given in the final year; this was reported due to lack of technical staff, foremen, vehicles and materials and to insufficient planning". One of the most successful public works schemes seems to have been the Tunisian one, which provided jobs for about 300,000 people. Large numbers of those involved were later integrated into the rural economy as permanent agricultural workers.

Apart from administrative problems, finance provides the most serious obstacle to the use of public works on a sufficient magnitude to make a sizeable impact on the employment problem in many countries.

## Education and training

Most government-sponsored or financed education has been concentrated on education for formal sector employment, rather than

---

50. Little and Mirrlees (1974) provides the best guide to one method of shadow pricing and project selection. Their methods are discussed and criticized in a special issue of the Bulletin of the Oxford University Institute of Economics and Statistics, 1972 (Vol 34); see also Stewart (1975) and the special issue of World Development edited by J. MacArthur and G. Anin, November 1977.

51. Mouly and Costa (1974), Chapter 6 provides a good survey of developing countries' experience of public works.

preparation for self-employment or informal sector activities. This type of education may actually impede successful activities in the informal sector, by gearing expectations towards formal sector employment and providing little of relevance to the lives people are actually likely to lead. In Kenya it has been estimated that 50% of the population receive less than 4% of the educational expenditure.[52] Moreover, the type of education received has been criticized; "Not only does the education they receive not equip them in any way for the kinds of life they will inevitably have to lead, but it is alleged to add to social and economic problems by the inculcation of inappropriate attitudes and values and by raising false expectations. All this leads to alienation and frustration of youth and a tragic waste of manpower".[53]

The type of education of relevance to self-employment is to a large extent unknown. To some extent the informal sector provides its own education.[54] Undoubtedly, however, a redirection of educational expenditure, and a substantial revision of syllabuses is required as part of a policy directed at improving productivity in the informal and agricultural sectors.[55]

Within the formal sector, excessive and imbalanced educational expenditure has contributed to the employment problem. Part of the problem is due to the big income and status differentials between different jobs within the formal sector.[56] Education becomes a profitable investment since it ensures access to high status and high income jobs. Thus there is pressure on educational establishments to expand. As they do so, the number of graduates exceeds the number of jobs for which they are traditionally qualified. Many of those who then become unemployed prefer to stay unemployed (possibly acquiring further educational qualifications) to taking a lower status and income job.

Chronic unemployment among the educated emerges, representing a waste of resources as well as a source of frustration and political resentment. Employers' reaction to the queues of applicants which then develop is to raise the educational qualifications of the jobs, thus providing themselves with an easy rationing mechanism, but giving the system a further push towards over-education. The reverse side of the educational deprivation of the majority of the population is that the highly educated receive disproportionate resources - in Kenya, 2% of the population are estimated to receive 34% of the resources. These 2% are over-educated in relation to many of the jobs they are likely to

---

52. Stewart (1977), p. 77.
53. Ghai (1974).
54. See King (1974) for a description of apprenticeships in the informal sector.
55. Aspects of the educational/training reforms required are discussed in ILO Kenya.
56. Hinchliffe (1975) shows substantially higher differentials in relation to education level among a selection of developing countries, compared with differentials in some developed countries.

do; their education is entirely related to employment within the formal sector. At the same time, education for entrepreneurial activities or self-employment is neglected.

Payments system reform

This involves changing the institutions which form the vehicle by which people acquire employment and income. Such reform, if radical enough, can eliminate the employment problem. Employment for all becomes both a right and a duty and is allocated accordingly, and not according to whether an individual's productivity is expected to exceed his wage. Payments of income are then determined according to some sharing principles (which may include some incentive element). Less radical change of the payments system may also make some contribution, changing the way in which access to work and income is determined. For example, co-operatives of family firms are likely to employ their members more fully and distribute the income which results more equally than capitalist firms which maximize profits and employ wage labour.[57] This is because the former institutions regard a large part of the income labour receives as an overhead cost, which they have an obligation to meet, whereas for capitalist firms the whole of the wage is required to be covered by the extra output labour produces. The extent to which institutional change of this kind alters employment and income distribution depends on the magnitude of the changes, and the rules the new institutions follow. Some co-operatives, for example, appear to act in a very similar way to many capitalist firms. Similarly, state enterprises, which in theory may adopt different rules from capitalist firms, often in fact work in a very similar way to them. Change in the institutional structure of employment has both direct short run and indirect long run effects on employment. In the long run, a different institutional structure is likely to lead to a different type of technical change, and also to a different package of infrastructure and government policies. The long run employment effects may therefore exceed the short. Moreover, payments system reform may also change the dynamic pattern of growth and employment by changing the rules determining the accumulation of assets, preventing the heavy accumulation of assets, by some and the complete decumulation by others, which is at the heart of some of the worst aspects of poverty and lack of productive employment.

## IV. CONCLUSIONS

As the analysis of the nature and causes of employment problems has changed, so suggested approaches, strategies and policies, have

---

57. Stiglitz (1969 and 1976) explores some of the implications for employment and output of different institutional arrangements in agriculture.

also changed. The change is partly a matter of emphasis, partly one of direction. With the emergence of unemployment in developing countries as industrialization proceeded, the problem was at first identified with the sort of unemployment problems suffered by developed countries. While it was soon recognized that developing countries' unemployment was not of a purely Keynesian variety, and that Keynesian demand inflation policies would not therefore be appropriate, there was an underlying belief that the fundamental cure for the unemployment problem lay in the creation of more modern-sector jobs, as in developed countries. Nurkse and others recognized that open unemployment represented the tip of the iceberg, and the total potential surplus labour included vast numbers of underemployed or disguised unemployed in the rest of the economy. The rapid growth in population added to the numbers in need of jobs, and therefore to the now seemingly impossible challenge of creating jobs in the modern sector on a sufficient scale to absorb them all. During the 1960's, however, the problem of employment in poor countries came to be identified quite differently as largely a matter of distribution of income earning opportunities. The cure was no longer seen as consisting entirely in expansion of modern-sector jobs: rather improvement in the productivity and opportunities of those outside the modern large-scale sector came to be emphasized. The new emphasis made the problem seem much more tractable in technical terms - a view which was supported by the fact that countries with different institutions seemed to have overcome it. But politically the solutions then offered were more difficult to achieve, with the emphasis on redistribution of income and assets and institutional changes as of fundamental importance.

Although there are significant differences between the various strategies that are currently advocated, there is a greater degree of agreement on the appropriate directions for policy. The main alternative strategies would concur in supporting policies which dilute the privileged position of the large-scale urban industrial sector and redistribute opportunities - markets, credit, technology, investment, education and government expenditure - towards the small-scale, informal, traditional and rural sectors. Increased labour intensity of the modern sector is seen more as a means of reducing the differentials between the sectors than as providing the main contribution to the solution of the employment problem. The strategies concur too about the importance of maintaining sustained growth of output; however, this is viewed as a means of securing satisfactory income earning opportunities for the poorest, rather than as the be-all and end-all of economic activity.

In the discussion of policies relevant to the strategies, the various policy areas were discussed individually, as though they were separable. In fact for the most part they are inseparable and need to be pursued simultaneously. The inseparability arises in two different ways: first, from the point of view of attaining the objectives many of the policies would be unsuccessful if followed singly. For example, a new technology policy which created new appropriate techniques and products would be of little use without simultaneous redistribution of investment resources to those likely to use appropriate techniques, and of income to those likely to provide the markets for appropriate products. Conversely, redistribution of assets with no improvements in technology may make for an inefficient and short-lived pattern of production. The policies may also be inseparable from a political point of view, because, unless pursued jointly, they are likely to break down under pressure of old established interests. This applies particularly to policies concerned with redistribution, which require a simultaneous supporting reform of technology and production structure if they are to be long-lasting. The need to pursue many of the policies in a coordinated way makes marginal reform more difficult. On the other hand, it means that if the policies are pursued jointly, they become reinforcing, leading, it is hoped, to a virtuous growth path, in which the fruits of growth are fairly earned and shared.

## REFERENCES

Baer W. and M. Hervé (1966), "Employment and Industrialization in Developing Countries", Quarterly Journal of Economics, Vol. LXXX.

Berouti L. J. (1976), "Employment Promotion Problems in Arab Countries", International Labour Review, Vol. 114.

Bhalla A. S. (ed) (1975), Technology and Employment in Industry, ILO, Geneva.

Bruton H. (1973), "Economic Development and Labour Use: A Review", World Development, Vol. 1.

Chenery H., Ahluwalia M. S., Bell C. L. G., Duloy J. H., Jolly R., (1974), Redistribution with Growth, Oxford University Press.

Cline W. R. (1975), "Distribution and Development: A Survey of Literature", Journal of Development Economics, Vol. 1.

Cooper C. (1972), "Science, Technology and Production in the Underdeveloped Countries: An Introduction", in C. Cooper (ed.), Science and Technology in Development, Frank Cass.

Cooper C. (1974), "Science Policy and Technological Change in Underdeveloped Economies", World Development, Vol. 2.

Dovring F. (1959), "The Share of Agriculture in a Growing Population", Monthly Bulletin of Agricultural Economics and Statistics.

Fei J. C. H. and G. Ranis (1961), "A Theory of Economic Development", American Economic Review, Vol. 51.

Fei J. C. H. and G. Ranis (1975), "A Model of Growth and Employment in the Open Dualistic Economy: the Cases of Korea and Taiwan", in F. Stewart (ed.) Employment, Income Distribution and Development, Frank Cass.

Fei J. C. H. , G. Ranis and S. W. Y. Kno (1977), Equity with Growth: the Taiwan Case, mimeo.

Figueroa A. (1975), "Income Distribution, Demand Structure and Employment: The Case of Peru", in F. Stewart (ed.), Employment, Income Distribution and Development, Frank Cass.

Ganesan S. (1975), "Employment Generation through Investments in Housing and Construction", Ph. d. thesis, London University.

Ghai D. P. (1968), "Incomes Policy in Kenya: Need, Criteria and Machinery", East African Economic Review, Vol. 4, New Series.

Ghai D. P. (1974), "Towards a National System of Education", in D. Court and D. P. Ghai (eds.), Education, Society and Development: New Perspectives from Kenya, Oxford University Press, 1974.

Gouverneur J. (1971), Productivity and Factor Proportions in Less Developed Countries: The Case of Industrial Firms in the Congo, Oxford University Press.

Harris J. R. and M. Todaro (1970), "Migration, Unemployment and Development", American Economic Review, Vol. LX.

Helleiner G. K. (1973), "Manufactured Exports from Less Developed Countries and Multinational Firms, Economic Journal, Vol. 83.

Herman B. (1971), "Some Basic Data for Analysing the Political Economy of Foreign Investment in Kenya", Institute of Development Studies, Discussion Paper, No. 112, University of Nairobi.

Hinchliffe K. (1975), "Education, Individual Earnings and Earnings Distribution" in F. Stewart (ed.), Employment, Income Distribution and Development, Frank Cass.

ILO, (1970), Towards Full Employment: A Programme for Colombia, Geneva (ILO Colombia).

ILO, (1971), Matching Employment Opportunities and Expectations: A Programme of Action for Ceylon, Geneva (ILO Ceylon).

ILO (1972), Employment, Incomes and Equality, A Strategy for Increasing Productive Employment in Kenya, Geneva (ILO Kenya).

ILO, (1973 a), Employment and Incomes Policies for Iran, Geneva.

ILO, (1973 b), Strategies for Employment Growth, Geneva.

ILO, (1974), Sharing in Development: A Programme of Employment, Equity and Growth for the Philippines, Geneva (ILO Philippines).

James J., (1976), "Products, Processes and Incomes: Cotton Clothing in India", World Development, Vol. 4.

James J., (1977), "Technology, products and income distribution: a conceptualization and application to sugar processing in India", ILO, World Employment Programme.

Jenkins G., (1975), Non-Agricultural Choice of Technique, An Annotated Bibliography of Empirical Studies, Institute of Commonwealth Studies, Oxford.

Johnston B. F., (1966), Agriculture and Economic Development: The Relevance of the Japanese Experience, Food Research Institute Studies, Stanford University.

Krishnamurty J., (1975), "Some Aspects of Unemployment in Urban India", in F. Stewart (ed.), Employment, Income Distribution and Development, Frank Cass.

Lall S., (1975), Foreign Private Manufacturing Investment and Multinational Corporations, An Annotated Bibliography, Praeger.

Lewis W. A., (1954), "Economic Development with Unlimited Supplies of Labour", The Manchester School of Economic and Social Studies.

Lipton M., (1977a), Why Poor People Stay Poor, Maurice Temple Smith.

Lipton M., (1977b), "The Technology, the System and the Poor", World Development.

Little I. M. D., T. Scitovsky and M. FG. Scott, (1970), Industry and Trade in Some Developing Countries, Oxford University Press.

MacArthur J. and G. Amin (eds.) (1977), Special Issue of World Development on Project Selection.

McBain N. S. (1977), "Developing Country Product Choice: Footwear in Ethiopia", World Development, Vol. 5.

Mellor J. W. (1976), The New Economics of Growth, Cornell University Press.

Morley S. A. and G. W. Smith, (1974), "Managerial Discretion and the Choice of Technology by Multinational Firms in Brazil", Programme of Development Studies, Rice University, Paper No. 56.

Morse D. (1971), "The Employment Problem in Developing Countries", in R. Robinson and P. Johnston (eds.), Prospects for Employment Opportunities in the Nineteen Seventies, HMSO.

Mouly J. and E. Costa (1974), Employment Policies in Developing Countries, George Allen and Unwin.

Nurkse R. (1953), Problems of Capital Formation in Underdeveloped Countries, Blackwell.

Ranis G. (1971), "Output and Employment in the '70s: Conflicts or Complements", in R. Ridker and H. Lubell (eds.), Employment and Unemployment Problems of the Near East and South Asia, Vikes Publications.

Sabola Y. (1975), "Employment and Unemployment 1960-90", International Labour Review, Vol. 112.

Sabot R., "The Meaning and Measurement of Urban Surplus Labour in an African Context", Oxford Institute of Economics and Statistics, mimeo 1974.

Salter W. E. G. (1966), Productivity and Technical Change, 2nd edition, Cambridge University Press.

Sen A. K. (1966), "Peasants and Dualism with or without Surplus Labour", Journal of Political Economy.

Sen A. K. (1968), Choice of Techniques, (3rd Edition), Blackwell.

Sen A. K. (1975), Employment, Technology and Development, Oxford University Press.

Stewart F. (1975), "A Note on Social Cost Benefit Analysis and Class Conflict in LDCs", World Development, Vol. 3.

Stewart F. (1977 a), Technology and Underdevelopment, Macmillan.

Stewart F. (1977 b), "Inequality, Technology and the Payments System", World Development.

Stewart F. and P. P. Streeten (1971), "Conflicts between Output and Employment Objectives in Developing Countries", Oxford Economic Papers, Vol. 23.

Stewart F. and P. P. Streeten (1976), "New Strategies for Development: Poverty, Income Distribution and Growth", Oxford Economic Papers, Vol. 28, No. 3.

Stewart F. and J. Weeks (1975), "The Employment Effects of Wage Changes in Poor Countries", in F. Stewart (ed.), Employment Income Distribution and Development, Frank Cass.

Stiglitz J. E. (1969), "Rural-Urban Migration, Surplus Labour, and the Relationship between Urban and Rural Wages", East African Economic Review.

Stiglitz J. E. (1976), "The Efficiency Wage Hypothesis, Surplus Labour, and the Distribution of Income in LDCs", Oxford Economic Papers, Vol. 28.

Tokman V. E. (1975), "Income Distribution, Technology and Employment in Developing Countries", Journal of Development Economics.

Turner H. A. and D. A. S. Jackson (1970), "On the Determination of the General Wage Level - a World Analysis or "Unlimited Labour Forever" ", Economic Journal, Vol. 80.

Turnham D. (1971), The Employment Problem in Less Developed Countries, A Review of the Evidence, OECD.

Wells L. T. (1973), "Economic Man and Engineering Man: A Choice of Technology in a Low Wage Country", Public Policy, Vol. 2. 1.

# OECD SALES AGENTS
## DÉPOSITAIRES DES PUBLICATIONS DE L'OCDE

**ARGENTINA – ARGENTINE**
Carlos Hirsch S.R.L., Florida 165,
BUENOS-AIRES, Tel. 33-1787-2391 Y 30-7122

**AUSTRALIA – AUSTRALIE**
International B.C.N. Library Suppliers Pty Ltd.,
161 Sturt St., South MELBOURNE, Vic. 3205. Tel. 699-6388
P.O.Box 202, COLLAROY, NSW 2097. Tel. 982 4515

**AUSTRIA – AUTRICHE**
Gerold and Co., Graben 31, WIEN 1. Tel. 52.22.35

**BELGIUM – BELGIQUE**
Librairie des Sciences,
Coudenberg 76-78, B 1000 BRUXELLES 1. Tel. 512-05-60

**BRAZIL – BRÉSIL**
Mestre Jou S.A., Rua Guaipá 518,
Caixa Postal 24090, 05089 SAO PAULO 10. Tel. 261-1920
Rua Senador Dantas 19 s/205-6, RIO DE JANEIRO GB.
Tel. 232-07. 32

**CANADA**
Renouf Publishing Company Limited,
2182 St. Catherine Street West,
MONTREAL, Quebec H3H 1M7 Tel. (514) 937-3519

**DENMARK – DANEMARK**
Munksgaards Boghandel,
Nørregade 6, 1165 KØBENHAVN K. Tel. (01) 12 69 70

**FINLAND – FINLANDE**
Akateeminen Kirjakauppa
Keskuskatu 1, 00100 HELSINKI 10. Tel. 625.901

**FRANCE**
Bureau des Publications de l'OCDE,
2 rue André-Pascal, 75775 PARIS CEDEX 16. Tel. 524.81.67
Principal correspondant :
13602 AIX-EN-PROVENCE : Librairie de l'Université.
Tel. 26.18.08

**GERMANY – ALLEMAGNE**
Verlag Weltarchiv G.m.b.H.
D 2000 HAMBURG-36, Neuer Jungfernstieg 21.
Tel. 040-35-62-500

**GREECE – GRÈCE**
Librairie Kauffmann, 28 rue du Stade,
ATHÈNES 132. Tel. 322.21.60

**HONG-KONG**
Government Information Services,
Sales and Publications Office, Beaconsfield House, 1st floor,
Queen's Road, Central. Tel. H-233191

**ICELAND – ISLANDE**
Snaebjörn Jónsson and Co., h.f.,
Hafnarstraeti 4 and 9, P.O.B. 1131, REYKJAVIK.
Tel. 13133/14281/11936

**INDIA – INDE**
Oxford Book and Stationery Co.:
NEW DELHI, Scindia House. Tel. 45896
CALCUTTA, 17 Park Street. Tel. 240832

**IRELAND - IRLANDE**
Eason and Son, 40 Lower O'Connell Street,
P.O.B. 42, DUBLIN 1. Tel. 74 39 35

**ISRAËL**
Emanuel Brown: 35 Allenby Road, TEL AVIV. Tel. 51049/54082
also at:
9, Shlomzion Hamalka Street, JERUSALEM. Tel. 234807
48, Nahlath Benjamin Street, TEL AVIV. Tel. 53276

**ITALY – ITALIE**
Libreria Commissionaria Sansoni:
Via Lamarmora 45, 50121 FIRENZE. Tel. 579751
Via Bartolini 29, 20155 MILANO. Tel. 365083
Sub-depositari:
Editrice e Libreria Herder,
Piazza Montecitorio 120, 00 186 ROMA. Tel. 674628
Libreria Hoepli, Via Hoepli 5, 20121 MILANO. Tel. 865446
Libreria Lattes, Via Garibaldi 3, 10122 TORINO. Tel. 519274
La diffusione delle edizioni OCSE è inoltre assicurata dalle migliori librerie nelle città più importanti.

**JAPAN – JAPON**
OECD Publications Center,
Akasaka Park Building, 2-3-4 Akasaka, Minato-ku,
TOKYO 107. Tel. 586-2016

**KOREA - CORÉE**
Pan Korea Book Corporation,
P.O.Box n°101 Kwangwhamun, SÉOUL. Tel. 72-7369

**LEBANON – LIBAN**
Documenta Scientifica/Redico,
Edison Building, Bliss Street, P.O.Box 5641, BEIRUT.
Tel. 354429–344425

**MEXICO & CENTRAL AMERICA**
Centro de Publicaciones de Organismos Internacionales S.A.,
Av. Chapultepec 345, Apartado Postal 6-981
MEXICO 6, D.F. Tel. 533-45-09

**THE NETHERLANDS – PAYS-BAS**
Staatsuitgeverij
Chr. Plantijnstraat
'S-GRAVENHAGE. Tel. 070-814511
Voor bestillingen: Tel. 070-624551

**NEW ZEALAND – NOUVELLE-ZÉLANDE**
The Publications Manager,
Government Printing Office,
WELLINGTON: Mulgrave Street (Private Bag),
World Trade Centre, Cubacade, Cuba Street,
Rutherford House, Lambton Quay, Tel. 737-320
AUCKLAND: Rutland Street (P.O.Box 5344), Tel. 32.919
CHRISTCHURCH: 130 Oxford Tce (Private Bag), Tel. 50.331
HAMILTON: Barton Street (P.O.Box 857), Tel. 80.103
DUNEDIN: T & G Building, Princes Street (P.O.Box 1104),
Tel. 78.294

**NORWAY – NORVÈGE**
Johan Grundt Tanums Bokhandel,
Karl Johansgate 41/43, OSLO 1. Tel. 02-332980

**PAKISTAN**
Mirza Book Agency, 65 Shahrah Quaid-E-Azam, LAHORE 3.
Tel. 66839

**PHILIPPINES**
R.M. Garcia Publishing House, 903 Quezon Blvd. Ext.,
QUEZON CITY, P.O.Box 1860 – MANILA. Tel. 99.98.47

**PORTUGAL**
Livraria Portugal, Rua do Carmo 70-74, LISBOA 2. Tel. 360582/3

**SPAIN – ESPAGNE**
Mundi-Prensa Libros, S.A.
Castelló 37, Apartado 1223, MADRID-1. Tel. 275.46.55
Libreria Bastinos, Pelayo, 52, BARCELONA 1. Tel. 222.06.00

**SWEDEN – SUÈDE**
AB CE Fritzes Kungl Hovbokhandel,
Box 16 356, S 103 27 STH, Regeringsgatan 12,
DS STOCKHOLM. Tel. 08/23 89 00

**SWITZERLAND – SUISSE**
Librairie Payot, 6 rue Grenus, 1211 GENÈVE 11. Tel. 022-31.89.50

**TAIWAN – FORMOSE**
National Book Company,
84-5 Sing Sung Rd., Sec. 3, TAIPEI 107. Tel. 321.0698

**UNITED KINGDOM – ROYAUME-UNI**
H.M. Stationery Office, P.O.B. 569,
LONDON SEI 9 NH. Tel. 01-928-6977, Ext. 410
or
49 High Holborn, LONDON WC1V 6 HB (personal callers)
Branches at: EDINBURGH, BIRMINGHAM, BRISTOL,
MANCHESTER, CARDIFF, BELFAST.

**UNITED STATES OF AMERICA**
OECD Publications Center, Suite 1207, 1750 Pennsylvania Ave.,
N.W. WASHINGTON, D.C.20006. Tel.     (202)724-1857

**VENEZUELA**
Libreria del Este, Avda. F. Miranda 52, Edificio Galipán,
CARACAS 106. Tel. 32 23 01/33 26 04/33 24 73

**YUGOSLAVIA – YOUGOSLAVIE**
Jugoslovenska Knjiga, Terazije 27, P.O.B. 36, BEOGRAD.
Tel. 621-992

Les commandes provenant de pays où l'OCDE n'a pas encore désigné de dépositaire peuvent être adressées à :
OCDE, Bureau des Publications, 2 rue André-Pascal, 75775 PARIS CEDEX 16.
Orders and inquiries from countries where sales agents have not yet been appointed may be sent to:
OECD, Publications Office, 2 rue André-Pascal, 75775 PARIS CEDEX 16.

OECD PUBLICATIONS, 2, rue André-Pascal, 75775 Paris Cedex 16 - No. 40.027 1978
PRINTED IN FRANCE